God's Judgment through the Davidic Messiah

God's Judgment through the Davidic Messiah

The Role of the Davidic Messiah in Romans 1:18—4:25

MYONGIL KIM

WIPF & STOCK · Eugene, Oregon

GOD'S JUDGMENT THROUGH THE DAVIDIC MESSIAH
The Role of the Davidic Messiah in Romans 1:18—4:25

Copyright © 2020 Author Name. All rights reserved. Except for brief quotations in critical publications or reviews, no part of this book may be reproduced in any manner without prior written permission from the publisher. Write: Permissions, Wipf and Stock Publishers, 199 W. 8th Ave., Suite 3, Eugene, OR 97401.

Unless otherwise noted, all Scripture quotations are from the ESV® Bible (The Holy Bible, English Standard Version®), copyright © 2001 by Crossway, a publishing ministry of Good News Publishers. Used by permission. All rights reserved.

Wipf & Stock
An Imprint of Wipf and Stock Publishers
199 W. 8th Ave., Suite 3
Eugene, OR 97401

www.wipfandstock.com

PAPERBACK ISBN: 978-1-7252-8089-2
HARDCOVER ISBN: 978-1-7252-8091-5
EBOOK ISBN: 978-1-7252-8092-2

Manufactured in the U.S.A.   09/10/20

To Peace Park
for her constant love

Contents

Preface ix

List of Abbreviations xi

Chapter 1 Introduction 1

Chapter 2 The Davidic Messiah: The Agent of God's Judgment in the Old Testament 25

Chapter 3 The Davidic Messiah: The Agent of God's Judgment in the Second Temple Writings 73

Chapter 4 The Gospel of the Davidic Messiah: Romans 1:1–4 113

Chapter 5 The Judgment of God and the Davidic Messiah in Romans 1:18–4:25 145

Chapter 6 Summary and Conclusion 189

Bibliography 195

Preface

THE SINKING OF SEWOL ferry occurred six years ago. Because of the death of so many people, I have been interested in God's righteousness and his covenantal faithfulness, while many scholars have emphasized God's covenantal faithfulness as his righteousness. Since then, I attended Dr. Thomas R. Schreiner's Hebrews seminar, and I concentrated on the Davidic Messiah, who is the messianic King and Priest. Now we have a critical situation because of COVID-19, and then I continue to ask what is God's righteousness and faithfulness in his people and created world. This book is my starting point to understand his unsearchable judgments and ways.

The connection of God's righteousness and the Davidic Messiah's role in Romans is the concern of my course work and this book. Paul connects God's righteousness with the Messiah Christology in Romans 3:22: "The righteousness of God through faith in Jesus Christ for all who believe." I want to discover God's just judgment over sinners and the role of the Messiah, Jesus, in God's righteous judgment. In particular, I focus on the Messiah's covenantal faithfulness in God's judgment through the Davidic Messiah.

I appreciate Wipf & Stock for the wonderful opportunity to publish this book. The passion and diligence of Wipf & Stock's staff breathe a new life into my work. Special thanks belong to my supervisor, Dr. Brian J. Vickers, for his sincere help with my doctoral program and the labor of rough drafts for this book. I am also grateful to Dr. Jonathan T. Pennington and Dr. William F. Cook for their careful reading of this book. I would like to thank my teacher, Dr. Sungnam Kil, because I was stimulated by the study of New Testament theology at Korea Theological Seminary, as well. In addition, I want to express my appreciation to Gwangi Presbyterian Church and

Rev. Sunghyun Kim; my friends Junjae Kim, Joohyun Park, and Sungdae Kim; Zion Presbyterian Church, and Dr. Sungkoo Lee; and proofreader Rev. Richard Sytsma and editor Marilyn A. Anderson. This book is dedicated to my family—Pyeonghwa, Jiha, and Jiin—whose support has strengthened me to finish. *Soli deo gloria.*

MYONGIL KIM
Busan, South Korea
June 2020

List of Abbreviations

AB	Anchor Bible
ABD	Anchor Bible Dictionary
AGJU	Arbeiten zur Geschichte des antiken Judentums und des Urchristentums
BDAG	Walter Bauer, Frederick William Danker, William F. Arndt, and F. Wilber Gingrich, *A Greek-English Lexicon of the New Testament and Other Early Christian Literature*
BECNT	Baker Exegetical Commentary on the New Testament
BNTC	Black's New Testament Commentaries
CBQ	*Catholic Biblical Quarterly*
DJD	Discoveries in the Judaean Desert
EDNT	*Exegetical Dictionary of the New Testament*
EKKNT	Evangelisch-katholischer Kommentar zum Neuen Testament
ETL	*Ephemerides theologicae lovanienses*
EvT	*Evangelische Theologie*
ExpTim	*Expository Times*
FRLANT	Forschungen zur Religion und Literatur des Alten und Neuen Testaments
ICC	International Critical Commentary
JBL	*Journal of Biblical Literature*

JSNT	*Journal for the Study of the New Testament*
JSNTSup	Journal for the Study of the New Testament Supplement Series
JSOT	*Journal for the Study of the Old Testament*
JSOTSup	Journal for the Study of the Old Testament: Supplement Series
LHBOTS	Library of Hebrew Bible/Old Testament Studies
LXX	Septuagint
NICNT	New International Commentary on the New Testament
NICOT	New International Commentary on the Old Testament
NIDOTTE	*New International Dictionary of Old Testament Theology and Exegesis*
NIGTC	New International Greek Testament Commentary
NovT	*Novum Testamentum*
NSBT	New Studies in Biblical Theology
NTS	*New Testament Studies*
OTL	Old Testament Library
SBLDS	Society of Biblical Literature Dissertation Series
SNTSMS	Society for New Testament Studies Monograph Series
SVTP	Studia in Veteris Testamenti pseudepigraphica
TDNT	*Theological Dictionary of the New Testament*
TDOT	*Theological Dictionary of the Old Testament*
TNTC	Tyndale New Testament Commentaries
ThHK	Theologischer Handkommentar zum Neuen Testament
TynB	*Tyndale Bulletin*
WBC	Word Biblical Commentary
WMANT	Wissenschaftliche Monographien zum Alten und Neuen Testament
WUNT	Wissenschaftliche Untersuchungen zum Neuen Testament
ZAW	*Zeitschrift für die alttestamentliche Wissenschaft*

Chapter 1

Introduction

PAUL WRITES, "BUT NOW the righteousness of God has been manifested apart from the Law, although the Law and the Prophets bear witness to it— the righteousness of God through faith in Jesus Christ for all who believe" (Rom 3:21–22). In these verses, Paul highlights a key theme in Romans— the righteousness of God, which is linked to faith in Jesus, the Messiah. Paul introduces the Messiah as one born from the seed of David, and utilizes quotations about the Messiah from the Old Testament to emphasize the significance of his arguments (Rom 11:26–27; 15:12).

The relationship between the Messiah of Romans and the tradition of the Davidic Messiah is an ongoing source of controversy in New Testament scholarship. The conventional Jewish messianism identified by some[1]

---

1. The early Jewish expectations for a messianic figure or figures are not uniform because of the diversity of expectations. Villiers, "The Messiah and Messiahs in Jewish Apocalyptic," 75–100; Sanders, *Judaism: Practice and Belief*, 295–98; Horsley, *Messianism through History*, 14–29; Witherington III, *The Christology of Jesus*, 180; Wright, *The New Testament and the People of God*, 308–20.

in Paul's letters has been denied[2] or modified[3] by others. The debate about the Davidic Messiah is not merely a debate about the Messiah Christology itself in Romans because it is intertwined with the key themes in Romans. If the righteousness of God has been revealed through faith in the Messiah, Jesus, for all believers (Rom 3:22), what then is the connection between the righteousness of God and the Davidic Messiah in Romans? How does Paul's conception of the Messiah in Romans inform his understanding of the righteousness of God, a key theme in this book, as the faithfulness of God in the role of the faithful Messiah, the deliverance of God through the redeemer, or justifying righteousness through the agent of God's judgment? If Paul specifically references justification as being through the Messiah, Jesus (Rom 5:1), is justification based on union with the Messianic king, on incorporation into the messianic community, or on the forensic feature of Christ's role in Romans? With such possibilities, it is clear that Paul centers his argument on the Davidic Messiah in his gospel for the believers in Rome since the role of the Davidic Messiah influences the key themes in Romans.

THESIS

This book investigates the Davidic messianic elements of Romans. The characteristics of the Davidic Messiah in Romans provide evidence for a coherent and distinct role of the Davidic Messiah in relation to the primary themes in Romans. For Paul, the Davidic Messiah is the agent of God's judgment, demarcated by his kingly and priestly features. The Davidic Messiah features in Romans are influential for justification and the righteousness of God, both of which are closely related to the judgment of God. In Romans 1:18—4:25, Paul argues that believers can be justified through faith in the Messiah, who is the agent of God's judgment. Paul depicts Jesus as the Davidic Messiah (1:3–4; 15:12), especially referencing his enthronement as such (4:25; 8:34–35). Jesus Christ is the agent of God's judgment (2:16; 8:34; 15:1–12), and all who believe are justified through faith in the Messiah Jesus (3:22). This divine judicial activity pertains directly to the

---

2. Gager, *The Origins of Anti-Semitism*, 201; Gager, *Reinventing Paul*, 143. Lloyd Gaston asserts, "For Paul, Jesus was neither a new Moses nor the Messiah, nor the climax of the history of God's dealing with Israel, but the fulfillment of God's promises concerning the gentiles, and this is what he accused the Jews of not recognizing." Gaston, "Paul and the Torah," 33.

3. Andrew Chester understands that the term *messiah* remains, but the sense is changed. The Christology of Paul is fashioned through the death and resurrection of Jesus, not by Jewish messianic traditions. Chester, "The Christ in Paul," 109–21; Chester, *Messiah and Exaltation*, 385.

Davidic Messiah, and is accomplished in light of his tandem roles as king and high priest. Acting as God's judgment is the role of the Davidic Messiah, which is accomplished in his kingship and high priesthood. Romans quotes and alludes to other Old Testament messianic texts that are based on God's judgment through the Messiah, and propagate the messianic expectation for the Davidic Messiah. The Davidic Messiah acts to save and govern as both redeemer and ruler (11:26; 15:12), through the justification enacted by that same Messiah.

The thesis of this book is that in his arguments about justification and the righteousness of God in Romans 1:18–4:25, Paul depicts the Davidic Messiah exclusively as the agent of God's judgment without reference to the Messiah's fulfillment of the covenant. In Romans, the Davidic Messiah—Jesus—is affirmed as the agent of God's judgment, rather than as the faithful Messiah through and in whom God has fulfilled his covenant. In other words, although the Davidic Messiah has fulfilled the covenant of God, the focus on the Davidic Messiah in Romans is not the faithfulness of the Davidic Messiah, but the agency of the Davidic Messiah in executing God's judgment on sinners (Rom 2:16).

The majority of this work will be conducted through careful exegesis of selected passages concerning the Davidic Messiah in Romans, and by an investigation of relevant background material related to the Old Testament and the Second Temple Jewish writings. The exegetical approach is mainly performed following arguments regarding the Davidic messianic Christology in Romans 1:18–4:25 to examine the function of the Davidic Messiah and the Messiah's faithfulness in Paul's discourse in Romans. This study investigates Paul's understanding of the Davidic Messiah in Romans by analyzing the allusions and citations to it in other parts of Romans, as well.

This chapter introduces the thesis and a history of research within the literature related to the thesis. I will survey the major works about Messiah Christology in Paul and the faithfulness of the Messiah in Romans. In addition, I will briefly evaluate the present state of research and present my thesis as a contribution to Davidic Messiah Christology and the Messiah's faithfulness.

In chapter 2, I observe the characteristics of the Davidic Messiah in the Old Testament as the foundation for discussing the Davidic Messiah in Romans. The judgment function of the Davidic Messiah, who is the agent of the judgment of God, will be examined. I then cross-examine the judgment and atonement of the Suffering Servant in Isaiah 53, which is closely related to the faithfulness of Jesus Christ in Romans.

In chapter 3, I observe the characteristics of the Davidic Messiah, particularly the judgment function of the Davidic Messiah in the Second Temple

Literature. In the course of this observation, I evaluate whether the Messiah's faithfulness is unfamiliar in God's judgment through the Davidic Messiah.

In chapter 4, I study the evidence for the gospel concerning the Davidic Messiah, which is the context for God's judgment, asking in what sense Paul announces the gospel and the Sonship of the Davidic Messiah in Romans 1:3–4. Additionally, with an exegetical study of the messianic oracle and Romans 15:12 related to 1:3–4, I offer an analysis of the immediate context in light of the discussion about the Davidic Messiah's role as the agent of God's judgment. The relationship between the saving and ruling of the Davidic Messiah, which is based on God's judgment, is displayed in the exegesis of the Davidic Messiah in the Isaiah oracle and Romans 15:12. Paul's treatment of the Davidic Messiah in Romans 15:12 clearly shows that the role of the Davidic Messiah is the execution of God's judgment and that the Davidic Messiah's faithfulness is not a significant theme in Paul's discussion.

In chapter 5, I concentrate on the judgment function of the Davidic Messiah described in the judgment theme in Romans 1:18–4:25 to support faith in the Messiah, rather than the Messiah's faithfulness in terms of the judgment function of the Davidic Messiah. This chapter's main emphasis is the solution for God's wrath. The function of the agent of God's judgment is resolving this problem through the Davidic Messiah's the atonement. My analysis focuses on the question of the function of the Davidic Messiah's atonement in terms of God's judgment. I then identify elements of the exalted Messiah that seem to be related to the justification of believers in Romans 4:25. The present study concentrates particularly on the justification and enthronement of the Davidic Messiah, with a background in the Old Testament and Jewish tradition that demonstrates the authority of the Davidic Messiah for sinners' judgment. The atonement for God's judgment is the basis for faith in the Messiah. The exaltation of the suffering Messiah, alluded to in 4:25, is the basis of the faith (4:24). Finally, chapter 6 will include a summary of my conclusion.

HISTORY OF RESEARCH

A history of research on the Davidic Messiah in Romans must begin with the History of Religions School, with its focus on *kyrios* Christology in Paul's letters because New Testament scholarship has vacillated between Messiah Christology and *kyrios* Christology ever since then. Some scholars who have stressed *kyrios* Christology have denied the Davidic Messiahship in Paul's Christology. The vacillation originated from the division presupposed between Hellenistic Christians and Palestinian Christians according to the thought of the History of Religions School. The Jewish messiahship in Paul's ministry to Hellenistic Christians has been denied, based on the differences between the religious thoughts of the two groups—Jewish and Gentile Christians. However, it is impossible to determine the Messiah Christology in early Christianity based on a distinction between Jewish and Hellenistic Christians and to insist that there was no Jewish messianism in the Hellenistic Christians' belief concerning Jesus. Later, the *kyrios* Christology and Messiah Christology have been understood as intertwined in Paul's letter because there is no evidence of a sharp division between them in his time. Several scholars assert that Paul clearly holds to a *kyrios* Christology, which is merged with Jesus' Jewish messianism. Here I present briefly a few key figures who provide interpretations of a significant section of Paul's letter, especially concerning the *kyrios* Christology and the Messiah Christology.

Wilhelm Bousset

Wilhelm Bousset, who represents the History of Religions School, approaches early Christianity through the lens of liturgy and Christology in his book, *Kyrios Christos*. According to Bousset, the earliest Palestinian Christian movement is sharply separated from Hellenistic Christians, and he locates Paul in Hellenistic Christianity. Bousset explains that the *Kyrios* cult had been developed from Hellenistic churches, saying, "What the κύριος signified for the first Hellenistic Christian congregation thus stands before us in bright and living colors. It is the Lord who holds sway over the Christian life of fellowship, in particular as it is unfolded in the community's worship, thus in the cultus."[4] The Palestinian Christians prohibited application of the title *kyrios* to Jesus because of Jewish monotheism. The Palestinian community understood the resurrected and exalted Jesus as "the Son of Man."[5]

In Romans 1:3–4, the Son of God is synonymous with the *kyrios* idea for Paul. Bousset observes, "It is always this exalted son of God upon whom Paul focuses."[6] And, he argues,

> We have already given reason for our doubting whether the title "Son of God" at all stems from Jewish messianology and accordingly from Palestinian primitive Christianity. If the doubts are valid, then the possibility must be reckoned with that here we have to do with an independent creation of Paul.[7]

4. Bousset, *Kyrios Christos*, 134.
5. Bousset, *Kyrios Christos*, 151–52.
6. Bousset, *Kyrios Christos*, 208.
7. Bousset, *Kyrios Christos*, 206–7.

While Paul focuses on the Son of God in his writing to the Hellenistic group, he does suggest the title "Son of David," but it is less important in Paul's *kyrios* Christology. Although Paul emphasizes "Jesus' descent from David's tribe," he is simply "following the community's tradition which had come down to him."[8] In Bousset's thought, the title "Christ" was understood as a proper name in Paul's era because Paul did not hold to the Jewish messianic expectation. Instead, he followed the Hellenistic piety of the mysticism of Christ.[9]

Albert Schweitzer

Critics from among Bousset's contemporaries criticized his explanation. Albert Schweitzer contends that Paul's thought "cannot be reconstructed out of a patchwork of Hellenistic ideas but only becomes intelligible in the light of eschatology."[10] Schweitzer supports the idea that Paul's Davidic Messianism was based on Jewish eschatology, and did not represent the belief of the Hellenistic community.[11] Schweitzer maintains that the *kyrios* Christology Bousset emphasized has no evidence in the earliest church.[12] Schweitzer relates Paul's conception of Christ-mysticism to the mystical concept of "being in Christ" in the late Second Temple apocalypses, rather than to Hellenism.[13] He writes, "The problems of Pauline eschatology all go back to the two circumstances that it is, in the first place, like the Apocalypses of Baruch and Ezra, a synthesis of the eschatology of Daniel; and, in the second place, that it has to reckon with the facts, wholly unforeseen to Jewish eschatology, that the Messiah has already appeared as a man, has died, and is risen again."[14] In the Second Temple apocalypses, the Davidic Sonship was applied to the "Son-of-Man Messiah," and this concept of the Messiah of the Messianic Kingdom was applied to Jesus in Paul's writings.

---

8. Bousset, *Kyrios Christos*, 208.
9. Bousset, *Kyrios Christos*, 157–60.
10. Schweitzer, *The Mysticism of Paul the Apostle*, 138.
11. Schweitzer, *The Mysticism of Paul the Apostle*, 52–55.
12. Schweitzer, *The Mysticism of Paul the Apostle*, 29–32.
13. Schweitzer, *The Mysticism of Paul the Apostle*, 139.
14. Schweitzer, *The Mysticism of Paul the Apostle*, 76.

Rudolf Bultmann

Rudolf Bultmann, who stands in the History of Religions School, attests that the title, the Son of David, is not important to Paul.[15] The Davidic Messiah, the Son of David, did not have great significance to Paul. This term—*the Son of David* in Romans 1:3—is just a handed-down, pre-Pauline formula, and cannot reflect Pauline theology.[16] Bultmann explains, "For though the title is of no importance to him, he refers to it in Rom 1:3, a sentence which is evidently due to a handed-down formula."[17] The narrow concept of the Messiah had been changed to the apocalyptic heavenly salvation-bringer, which Paul applied to Christ.[18] He goes on to say, "The ancient title 'Messiah,' once expressing Israelitic national hope, was no longer confined to this narrower meaning but could just as well be transferred to the heavenly salvation-bringer awaited by the apocalyptists."[19] Bultmann argues with the division placed between Hellenistic thought and Palestinian Jewish thought, based on Bousset's thesis. He is skeptical of the messianic understanding in Paul because he denies the possibility of confirming an understanding about the historical Jesus.

Oscar Cullmann

Oscar Cullman criticizes Bousset's scheme in his book, *The Christology of the New Testament*, opposing the "Christ cult" in Hellenistic Christianity. He opposes Bousset's thesis that the *kyrios* for Jesus originated from the cultic setting of the Hellenistic community in Syria. The *Maranatha* passage (1 Cor 16:22) of Aramaic-speaking Palestinian Christians was used in a liturgical context, and "[in] his Greek letters Paul preserves in the Aramaic precisely the oldest characteristic prayers of the first Church."[20] He additionally mentions that the Jewish communities in Palestine also used *kyrios* to designate Christ because *kyrios* was the word the Septuagint utilized to translate the divine name *Adonai*.[21]

---

15. Bultmann, *Theology of the New Testament*, 1:49.
16. Bultmann, *Theology of the New Testament*, 1:49.
17. Bultmann, *Theology of the New Testament*, 1:49.
18. Bultmann, *Theology of the New Testament*, 1:52.
19. Bultmann, *Theology of the New Testament*, 1: 52–53.
20. Cullmann, *The Christology of the New Testament*, 200; see Rawlinson, *The New Testament Doctrine of Christ*, 235.
21. Cullmann, *The Christology of the New Testament*, 200–203.

Cullmann insists that there was no question of Jesus' Davidic descent.[22] In Cullmann's understanding, though, the early church did not accept "the terminology relative to the Messiah," and Christ will execute his Messiahship over the whole world "at the end."[23] He writes, "The kingship of the Son of David was now primarily a kingship over the church.... The early church believed that the kingship of Jesus would become visible only in the future.... Paul does expect a final event in which Christ will visibly appear, but he never allows Christ's eschatological work to take a political form."[24] Cullmann notes that "Christ" is a proper name in early Christianity,[25] which signifies the receding of Jewish messianic ideas.[26]

W. D. Davies

In *Paul and Rabbinic Judaism: Some Rabbinic Elements in Pauline Theology*, W. D. Davies suggests that there is not any difference in the Palestinian Judaism and Diaspora Judaism because of the strong Hellenizing influences in Palestine. Within this view, Paul's main ideas were derived from early rabbinic Judaism. He comments, "In the present work we shall not seek to deny all Hellenistic influence on him; we shall merely attempt to prove that Paul belonged to the main stream of first-century Judaism, and that elements in his thought, which are often labeled as Hellenistic, might well be derived from Judaism."[27] Palestinian Judaism had been influenced "with all parts of the Hellenistic world."[28]

The Jewish Messiahship of Jesus is apparent in Paul because he was plainly a Jew. According to Davies,

> Both in his life and thought, therefore, Paul's close relation to Rabbinic Judaism has become clear, and we cannot too strongly insist again that for him the acceptance of the Gospel was not so much the rejection of the old Judaism and the discovery of a new religion wholly antithetical to it, as his polemics might sometimes pardonably lead us to assume, but the recognition of the advent of the Messianic Age of Jewish expectation.... It was at this one point that Paul parted company with Judaism, at

---

22. Cullmann, *The Christology of the New Testament*, 130.
23. Cullmann, *The Christology of the New Testament*, 136.
24. Cullmann, *The Christology of the New Testament*, 135.
25. Cullmann, *The Christology of the New Testament*, 136.
26. Cullmann, *The Christology of the New Testament*, 134.
27. Davies, *Paul and Rabbinic Judaism*, 1.
28. Davies, *Paul and Rabbinic Judaism*, 6.

the valuation of Jesus of Nazareth as the Messiah with all that this implied.[29]

He points out that the suffering Messiah and the resurrection of the Messiah are connected to Rabbinic literature. Paul placed the emphasis on Jesus as the Messiah of Jewish expectation.

Ernst Käsemann

Similar to Bultmann, Ernst Käsemann focuses on *kyrios* Christology in his Romans commentary. He sides with those who understand Paul's use of *Christos* as a proper name.[30] In Romans 1:3, Paul does not concentrate on the messianic significance and "allows it to be overshadowed by the *Kyrios* title."[31] The Jewish expectation of the Messiah is denied in Romans. In Romans 11:26, the returning of the Redeemer is not a reference to "the historical Jesus, nor to the christological event as a whole, nor indeed to the *parousia* in Jerusalem, but to the return of the exalted Christ from the heavenly Jerusalem of Gal 4:26."[32] The quotation of Isaiah 11:1 in Romans 15:12 is also applied by Paul "to him who has been raised again and exalted."[33] He declares, "Christ has not just come to win the Gentiles for the community. He intends to rule over the cosmos and for this reason, as in 8:20, he is an object of hope for all creation, which is represented by the peoples."[34] Käsemann stresses the universal lordship of Christ.[35] He comprehends that Paul proclaims the eschatological fulfillment through Christ's rule (15:12). He focuses on the *kyrios* Christology, rather than on the Jewish Messiah, based on the sovereign eschatological rule of Christ in Paul.[36]

Martin Hengel

In *Judaism and Hellenism*, Martin Hengel shows that Hellenistic culture had affected Palestine. By the third century BC, the upper classes of Palestine had already been influenced by Hellenization, and the lower classes

29. Davies, *Paul and Rabbinic Judaism*, 243.
30. Käsemann, *Commentary on Romans*, 5.
31. Käsemann, *Commentary on Romans*, 5.
32. Käsemann, *Commentary on Romans*, 314.
33. Käsemann, *Commentary on Romans*, 387.
34. Käsemann, *Commentary on Romans*, 38/.
35. Käsemann, *Commentary on Romans*, 387.
36. Käsemann, *Commentary on Romans*, 387.

were affected in the next two centuries.³⁷ Therefore, Hengel challenges the History of Religions School with his historical analysis that contrasts with the thought of the History of Religions School. He states that "the putative pre-Pauline, Christologically productive 'Gentile-Christian community,' is a fiction."³⁸ The Christian communities in Syria were "at best 'mixed communities,' and the element of Jewish Christianity was predominant for years."³⁹ The missionaries of the earliest Christians were Jewish Christians.⁴⁰ Hengel, supporting the *kyrios* Christology from a Jewish background, remarks,

> The conception of the sending of the Son does not come from a pre-Christian gnostic myth—which in fact never existed—but has its roots in Jewish wisdom speculation; the confession κύριος Ἰησοῦς is not borrowed from the cult of Attis, Serapis, or Isis, but is a necessary consequence of the exaltation Christology in which Ps 110:1 in particular played a part; the Jerusalem Maranatha formula represented a preliminary stage in which the exalted Christ was called upon to return soon.⁴¹

Additionally, Hengel understands Paul to fully acknowledge the conceptions of the Χριστός within the Old Testament,⁴² and he employed this title for Jesus in Romans 1:3–4. He says,

> That Paul was perfectly acquainted with the Old Testament-Jewish conceptions bound up with the messianic name Ἰησοῦς Χριστός, can be seen from any number of texts. Thus the reference to Jesus' descent ἐκ σπέρματος Δαυὶδ κατὰ σάρκα (Rom 1:3f). The appointment to "Son of God in power . . . by his resurrection from the dead" which follows, means nothing other than the effective, powerful installation of the resurrected Jesus in the fullness of his messianic power. . . . The Davidic descent of Jesus—which Paul, in an ancient formula, presupposes to be well known as a matter of course even by the Roman Christians—probably derives from a tradition in the family of Jesus attested by Hegesippus and Julius Africanus.⁴³

---

37. Hengel, *Judaism and Hellenism*, 104.
38. Hengel, *Between Jesus and Paul*, 38.
39. Hengel, *Between Jesus and Paul*, 41.
40. Hengel, *Between Jesus and Paul*, 41.
41. Hengel, *Between Jesus and Paul*, 41.
42. Hengel, *Between Jesus and Paul*, 3.
43. Hengel, *Between Jesus and Paul*, 3.

The salvific work of Christ, who is the promised Messiah, has universal significance.[44] Hengel insists on "the 'Gentiles' access to salvation in Christ," who is the Messiah promised to Israel.[45]

Hengel and Davies contest Bousset's thought that there was a difference between the confessions concerning the Messiah in Palestinian and Hellenistic Diaspora communities. The dominance of Hellenism influenced Palestinian Judaism. The dichotomy in early Christians' Christology between Messiah Christology and *kyrios* Christology needs to be abandoned because there is no evidence of a separation between Palestinian Judaism and Diaspora Judaism. Hengel emphasizes that historical analysis, based strictly on chronological development of early Christianity, does not provide evidence for such boundaries.

Larry W. Hurtado

Larry W. Hurtado understands early Christianity to have the characteristic of "high" Christology, which stresses the divinity of Christ. He demonstrates that Jewish monotheism was applied to Jesus-devotion. The exclusive Jewish monotheism could not allow cultic worship for "revered agents of God (whether angelic or human)."[46] The devotion granted to Jesus in early Christianity has historical significance because Jesus represents a unique agent of God "the Father." In addition, it is still more important to note that the Jews resisted worshiping any figure.[47] This means that Jewish monotheism was taken over in early Christianity as "the Christian mutation."[48] He writes, "The accommodation of Jesus as recipient of cultic worship with God is unparalleled and signals a major development in monotheistic cultic practice and belief."[49] Moreover, like Bousset, Hurtado realizes that the earliest Christians had the sense and experience of the presence of the exalted Jesus and worshiped him.[50] Hurtado proposes that the divinity of Jesus as the object of worship was recognized in early Christianity. Pauline letters illustrate that early Christians "took over and perpetuated from previous circles of Christians a devotional pattern in which Jesus functioned with God as

---

44. Hengel, *Between Jesus and Paul*, 3.
45. Hengel, *Between Jesus and Paul*, 4–5.
46. Hurtado, *Lord Jesus Christ*, 31.
47. Hurtado, *Lord Jesus Christ*, 31.
48. Hurtado, *One God, One Lord*, 100.
49. Hurtado, *Lord Jesus Christ*, 53.
50. Hurtado, *Lord Jesus Christ*, 64–70.

subject matter and recipient of worship."[51] Hurtado's understanding is vital for understanding N. T. Wright's "divine identity" of Christ in relation to worship and cultic devotion of Christ.

Richard Bauckham

In Jewish monotheism, the God of Israel had been identified as YHWH in the covenant relationship.[52] God's identity is additionally characterized by the reference to "God's relationship to the whole of reality."[53] The only true God, YHWH, is "sole Creator of all things and sole Ruler of all things."[54] The exclusive worship of YHWH is a clear signal of the division "between God and all other realities."[55] Richard Bauckham shows three characteristics of the divine identity in Jewish monotheism: creational, eschatological, and cultic. These features are applied to Christ in Paul's Christology: "They include Jesus in the unique divine sovereignty over all things, they include him in the unique divine creation of all things, they identify him by the divine name which names the unique divine identity, and they portray him as accorded the worship which, for Jewish monotheists, is recognition of the unique divine identity."[56] In Bauckham's understanding, Christ has a unique divine identity because Christ is sovereign ruler over the world, and he participated in God's creation. The whole New Testament is identified as having the highest Christology—one that espouses Christ's divine identity.[57]

James D. G. Dunn

James D. G. Dunn describes his view of Christology as a "high" or moderately "high" Christology,[58] but his Christology starts from a low Christology. He proposes that Paul begins with the particular form of monotheism that he received from his Jewish upbringing. This is manifested in the idea of the subordination of Christ to God (1 Cor 15:27–28). In opposition to Hurtado's idea, the worship of Jesus, Dunn explains that the worship language

---

51. Hurtado, *Lord Jesus Christ*, 136–37.
52. Bauckham, *Jesus and the God of Israel*, 8.
53. Bauckham, *Jesus and the God of Israel*, 8.
54. Bauckham, *Jesus and the God of Israel*, 9.
55. Bauckham, *Jesus and the God of Israel*, 11.
56. Bauckham, *Jesus and the God of Israel*, 19.
57. Bauckham, *Jesus and the God of Israel*, 31.
58. Dunn, *The Theology of Paul the Apostle*, 258.

and words for praise and thanksgiving were never offered to Christ.[59] Although Christ has significance in Christian worship, worship was offered to God through Christ, as well, because "Christ is both sacrificing High Priest and sacrificial victim."[60] He writes, "Christ was never understood as the one to whom sacrifice was offered."[61] Furthermore, against the term of divine identity, Dunn warns his readers of "the danger of confusing." He emphasizes, "An identification of Jesus with and as Yahweh was an early attempt to resolve the tensions indicated above; it was labelled as 'Modalism,' a form of 'Monarchianism' (the one God operating first as Father and then as Son), and accounted a heresy."[62] In his view, Paul's interpretation is that of an interaction between his Jewish monotheism and his beliefs about Jesus within God's purpose. The influx of Gentiles influenced Paul's developing Christology, resulting in Pauline Christology being elevated higher to the "highest" moment.[63]

Dunn insinuates that to understand Davidic Messiahship, the particularity of situations within the Hellenistic communities and the Palestinian church must be considered. He notes,

> Why the identification of Jesus as Son of David was so treated in the Hellenistic church is not entirely clear—most probably because it was too peculiarly Jewish to permit its easy translation into the wider world. The Jewish hope of a messianic son of David was expressed in strongly political and so nationalistic terms: the son of David was expected to introduce a political kingdom and effect a this-worldly salvation. However amenable this was to the gospel of the Palestinian church it cannot but have been an embarrassment outside Palestine. . . . Paul does not affirm the Davidic sonship of Jesus without qualification. He does not deny it either, but he makes it clear that to describe Jesus as "born of the seed of David" is a dangerously defective and misleading half-truth.[64]

The Davidic Messiahship in Romans 1:3–4 reflects the embarrassment of the Hellenistic communities "over Jesus' Davidic sonship."[65] In Dunn's view, while Jewish messianic expectations are political and nationalistic,

59. Dunn, *Did the First Christians Worship Jesus?*, 7–28.
60. Dunn, *Did the First Christians Worship Jesus?*, 56.
61. Dunn, *Did the First Christians Worship Jesus?*, 56.
62. Dunn, *Did the First Christians Worship Jesus?*, 142.
63. Dunn, "Christology as an Aspect of Theology," 382.
64. Dunn, "Jesus—Flesh and Spirit: An Exposition of Romans 1:3–4," 136–37.
65. Dunn, "Jesus—Flesh and Spirit: An Exposition of Romans 1:3–4," 147.

Paul uses the formula in 1:3–4 to present a balanced portrayal of the Davidic Messiah for the Hellenistic Christians that does not emphasize the nationalistic kingship of the Messiah.[66] In addition, Dunn observes in terms of Romans 15:12, "The final scripture, from Paul's favorite prophet (Isa 11:10), fittingly ties together again the thought of the Jewishness of Jesus (the Davidic Messiah) and of the risen Christ, hope of the nations—an effective recall of the themes of the letter's paragraph (1:2–5)."[67] Paul elaborates on "the messianic promise" as the vindication of Israel that includes "the destruction of the Gentiles."[68] However, it "has been reversed in the outreach of the gentile mission."[69] Paul doubtlessly would not want to endanger the acceptance of his letter in Rome "by imposing a different sense" of nationalistic and political messiahship held by the Jews.[70] In Dunn's understanding, the Davidic Messiah, as such, has been enlarged to embrace a gospel message, which includes the Jewish Messiah's becoming the Son of God.[71]

New Testament scholars question the chronological schemes of the development of *kyrios* Christology in the History of Religions School, and the School's denial of the Messiah Christology. An accurate definition of the boundary between Jewish and Gentile Christianity was not given. Additionally, scholars still debate Jewish monotheists' worship of Christ.[72] Some scholars have questioned the "exclusive" Jewish monotheism in the Messiah Christology.[73] They insist that the characteristics of Jewish monotheism in Second Temple Judaism are "inclusive,"[74] although some scholars assert

---

66. Dunn, "Jesus—Flesh and Spirit: An Exposition of Romans 1:3–4," 145.

67. Dunn, *Romans 9–16*, 853.

68. Dunn, *Romans 9–16*, 850.

69. Dunn, *Romans 9–16*, 850.

70. Dunn, *Romans 1–8*, 12–13.

71. Dunn, *Romans 1–8*, 24. Concerning some scholars' denial about Paul's Jewish messianic idea, see Harvey, *Jesus and the Constraints of History*, 154, 157–58; Dunn, "How Controversial Was Paul's Christology?," 212–28; Casey, *From Jewish Prophet to Gentile God*, 116.

72. Pertaining to inclusive Jewish monotheism, see Horbury, "Jewish and Christian Monotheism in the Herodian Age," 17.

73. Regarding "inclusive" monotheism, Wright says, "The substantial and fascinating discussions that have taken place over the last couple of decades about the role of status of 'intermediary' figures in Jewish thought—angels, patriarchs, 'wisdom' and so forth—seem to me mostly beside the point in a discussion of what 'monotheism' really meant in practice." And he says, "In particular, it is simply wrong-headed to suggest that such 'monotheism' might be compromised by a recognition of the existence of non-human powers or intelligences, whether good (angels) or evil (demons); it was no part of second-temple monotheism to suggest that Israel's God was the only non-human intelligence existing in the cosmos." Wright, *Paul and the Faithfulness of God*, 626.

74. Rowland, *The Open Heaven*; Stuckenbruck, *Angel Veneration and Christology*;

that the conventional messianism of Judaism was denied by[75] or changed in[76] Pauline high Christology, and that the entrance of Gentile Christians in early Christianity resulted in outstanding christological developments.[77]

The Messiah's Faithfulness in the Messiah Christology

In his letters, especially in Romans, Paul focuses on the Messiah Christology, which is clearly presented in several verses: 1:3–4; 3:21–25; 4:25; 15:12. Several scholars maintain that these verses in Romans emphasize the Messiah's faithfulness. This is the most controversial issue in New Testament scholarship.

Richard B. Hays

Richard B. Hays opposes the claim that there was a radical division between Jewish and Gentile factions within early Christian communities. There is commonality of faith among Christians groups.[78] Some German scholars assume that Paul uses Jewish-Christian confessional traditions (e.g., Rom 3:24–26) and that he does rebut or correct them for his Gentile communities. However, Hays emphasizes that Paul quotes narrative kerygmatic traditions and argues from them to make the conclusions that he wishes to draw.[79]

Hays suggests the Messiah's faithfulness as the meaning of πίστις Χριστοῦ in the narrative structure in Paul's letter.[80] Hays contends,

> Paul's theology must be understood as the explication and defense of a story. The narrative structure of the gospel story depicts Jesus as the divinely commissioned protagonist who gives himself up to death on a cross in order to liberate humanity from bondage (Gal 1:4; 2:20; 3:13–14; 4:4–7). His death, in obedience to the will of God is simultaneously a loving act of

---

Chester, *Messiah and Exaltation*, 363–82.

75. See note 2.

76. See note 3.

77. As Bousset suggests, Maurice Casey focuses on the influence of Gentile Christians. Casey, *From Jewish Prophet to Gentile God*, 97.

78. Hays, *The Faith of Jesus Christ*, xliii.

79. Hays, *The Faith of Jesus Christ*, xliii.

80. The objective genitive of πίστις is rare, especially in Hellenistic Jewish sources. Hays, *The Faith of Jesus Christ*, xliv.

faithfulness (πίστις) to God and the decisive manifestation of God's faithfulness to his covenant promise to Abraham.[81]

Faithfulness in the messianic interpretation is applied in Romans, too.[82] The allusion of Habakkuk 2:4 in Romans 1:17 supports the Messiah's faithfulness.[83] God's righteousness is revealed through the πίστις of the Righteous One, who is the Messiah Jesus as in Habakkuk 2:4.[84] In Romans 3:22, Hays additionally attests that διὰ πίστεως Ἰησοῦ Χριστοῦ does not means "through believing in Jesus Christ." Rather, Paul's intention in this phrase is that "through the faithfulness of Jesus Christ," God's righteousness is manifested.[85] The obedience of the Messiah in the cross is Paul's point with πίστις Χριστοῦ. As some scholars support the subjective genitive with the perfect tense of "manifested (πεφανέρωται)," Hays proposes the meaning of Romans 3:22 is that the righteousness of God has been manifested "in the faith/obedience of the crucified one."[86] This corresponds with Paul's fundamental concern in Romans 3.[87] He continues,

> In the early part of the chapter, God's faithfulness (πίστις τοῦ θεοῦ, 3:3) and righteousness/justice (θεοῦ δικαιοσύνην, 3:5) are called into question, at least for rhetorical purposes. After a crushing indictment of humanity's injustice (vv. 9–20), Paul sets forth his positive affirmation of the faithfulness and righteousness of God; God, he asserts, has now revealed his righteousness in a new way, overcoming human unfaithfulness by his own power and proving himself faithful and just. We discover, furthermore, that this demonstration of God's righteousness (ἔνδειξις τῆς δικαιοσύνης αὐτοῦ, 3:25) has something to do with Jesus, that this righteousness is manifested διὰ πίστεως Ἰησοῦ Χριστοῦ (3:22).... Through the faithfulness of Jesus Christ, the one who "became a servant of circumcision for the sake of the truthfulness of God (ὑπὲρ ἀληθείας θεοῦ) in order to confirm the promises given to the fathers...." (Rom 15:8).[88]

---

81. Hays, "Πίστις and Pauline Christology: What Is at Stake?," 274–75.
82. Hays, "Πίστις and Pauline Christology: What Is at Stake?," 277–88.
83. Hays, "Πίστις and Pauline Christology: What Is at Stake?," 279–81.
84. Hays, "Πίστις and Pauline Christology: What Is at Stake?," 281.
85. Hays, *The Faith of Jesus Christ*, 158.
86. Hays, *The Faith of Jesus Christ*, 158.
87. Hays, *The Faith of Jesus Christ*, 159. In addition, he understands that the analogy of Rom 3:25 is found in 4 Maccabees, which fits smoothly into the logic of Rom 3.
88. Hays, *The Faith of Jesus Christ*, 159.

Jesus' faithful endurance and obedience to death on the cross are a "righteous act" (δικαίωμα) of "obedience" (ὑπακοή; Rom 5:18–19). The representative faithfulness of Christ overcomes the unfaithfulness of human beings.[89]

Douglas Campbell

Douglas Campbell suggests that the kingship discourse in Romans is linked to Christ in Romans in a significant interplay.[90] Because he espouses high Christology related to the messiahship of Christ, he says, "Christ's messiahship and lordship are here affirmed by his resurrection from the dead, which functions, furthermore, as a heavenly enthronement."[91] He additionally asserts, "We seem to be in touch here, then with an explanation of the resurrection—as the heavenly enthronement and glorification of Jesus, and his consequent affirmation as Messiah and the Lord, who will rule the cosmos on behalf of his divine father."[92] In Douglas Campbell's view, his messiahship is portrayed as divine kingship in the divine sonship. According to him, "He is the Son of God because, as for any divinely appointed king, God has now become his Father."[93] So he is the Davidic king not only by descent, but by royal enthronement.[94]

This kingship discourse governs Paul's arguments in Romans. He adds, "We can see in each of these other places a narrative of Jesus' heavenly enthronement informing Paul's argument—a narrative that describes Jesus as Son, Christ, 'firstborn,' and Lord, because of the enthronement by the resurrection."[95] Campbell holds that God's deliverance is one that God "has just undertaken on behalf of his messianic agent, Christ—the act of resurrection, empowerment, and heavenly enthronement."[96] Campbell thinks the ancient discourse of kingship "seems to be traditional theology that the Roman Christians share with both Paul and the Jerusalem church—an integrated, Jewish, and perhaps surprisingly 'high' christological narrative that smoothly links Jesus' messiahship, sonship, resurrection, and exalted heavenly lordship."[97] The particularity of his point regarding Jesus' messi-

---

89. Hays, *The Faith of Jesus Christ*, 160.
90. Campbell, *The Deliverance of God*, 695.
91. Campbell, *The Deliverance of God*, 696.
92. Campbell, *The Deliverance of God*, 697.
93. Campbell, *The Deliverance of God*, 696.
94. Campbell, *The Deliverance of God*, 696.
95. Campbell, *The Deliverance of God*, 698.
96. Campbell, *The Deliverance of God*, 699.
97. Campbell, *The Deliverance of God*, 700.

ahship is that God's deliverance first occurs on behalf of Christ by using 'righteousness' language from the Old Testament.

Campbell stresses God's deliverance, which is a liberating and eschatological act of God that has taken place in Christ, "in particular Christ's heavenly enthronement by God after his faithful death."[98] God "delivers" Christ and "vindicates" him. He describes, "They are merely meant to understand what he is talking about in more general terms, and they should be able to do so insofar as they inhabit this Jewish Christian discourse concerning Jesus' resurrection and kingship. Paul is merely using the words of Psalm 98:2–3 to say here what he wants to say (and presumably in a way that other Christians have already formulated and so can recognize)—that God the King has acted to save his messianic Son."[99] Paul implements a christological reading of Habakkuk 2:4 in Romans 1:17 and 3:22 to reveal God's deliverance. In Romans, Paul presents God's delivering based on the faithful Messiah, and this comes to focus in Paul's christological reading of Habakkuk 2:4 in Romans 1:17.[100] The righteous one is Christ. Because of his "faithfulness to the point of death he will live in the sense of being vindicated and resurrected."[101] Habakkuk 2:4 predicts the passion of the Messiah, to which Paul's gospel attests. He continues,

> A messianic reading of Habakkuk 2:4 directly fulfills the expectations that Paul set in motion in Romans 1:2–4. There he broke into his address—amounting to a breach of ancient epistolary etiquette—to affirm that his gospel concerned God's Son who was descended from David and declared the Son of God by his resurrection in fulfillment of God's prophets in the Scriptures. Paul's explicit indications, then, would dispose the letter's auditors to read prophetic texts from the Scriptures in Romans as witnesses to the Son of God, Christ, and in particular to either his Davidic lineage or, probably more importantly, his resurrection.[102]

Romans 3:21–22 presents God's deliverance through the faithful Christ for those who are faithful (leaving the precise nuance of this expression for discussion later), a set of claims that establishes the argument of 3:27–4:22.[103] He argues,

---

98. Campbell, *The Deliverance of God*, 702.
99. Campbell, *The Deliverance of God*, 699.
100. Campbell, *The Deliverance of God*, 613–16.
101. Campbell, *The Deliverance of God*, 613.
102. Campbell, *The Deliverance of God*, 615.
103. Campbell, *The Deliverance of God*, 603.

> So a single motif can denote the presence of the narrative—or of one of its broad trajectories—within the apostle's developing arguments: "obedience," "blood," "death," "cross/crucifixion," and so on.... So the claim that the phrase "the fidelity of Christ" could denote Jesus' entire passion more broadly is quite consistent with Paul's usual practice as that is attested elsewhere.[104]

In addition, the faithfulness of the Messiah fits a martyrological trajectory. He says,

> Indeed, the notion of fidelity fits smoothly into the downward martyrological trajectory in the story of Jesus' passion. It is largely self-evident that fidelity is an ingredient within any essentially martyrological story. Martyrs faithfully endure suffering and death (if not a horrible execution); the story of martyrdom thus encodes its heroes with the quality of fidelity, even if only implicitly in view of their endurance and steadfastness within those unfolding stories. But numerous martyrologies mention fidelity explicitly as well (see 2 Macc 7:40; 4 Macc 7:21–22; 15:24; 16:22; 17:2; see also 2 Macc 6:30; 4 Macc 17:10). So it seems entirely appropriate in terms of Paul's background to suggest that his account of Jesus' death—an essentially martyrological story—could include the element of faithfulness.[105]

Paul explicates Christ's faithfulness in a particular connection to the story of the Messiah's death, which fits the martyrology in 2 and 4 Maccabees. The faithfulness of the Messiah functions to reveal or disclose God's righteousness to vindicate his Son (3:21–22).[106] God delivers those who are faithful through the faithful Messiah, which continues in the argument of Romans 3:27–4:22.[107] Campbell delineates that *pistis* is basically identified as "fidelity," and the fidelity of Christians is closely related to Christ's own fidelity. A Christian's fidelity functions as a mark of belonging to Christ. So because *pistis* does mean fidelity, rather than faith, Christ is not the object of faith in Romans. God's deliverance is accomplished through Christ's *pistis*, which is the Messiah's faithfulness.

---

104. Campbell, *The Deliverance of God*, 611.
105. Campbell, *The Deliverance of God*, 611.
106. Campbell, *The Deliverance of God*, 603.
107. Campbell, *The Deliverance of God*, 603.

N. T. Wright

N. T. Wright applies exclusive Jewish monotheism to Jesus in his treatment of the Messianism of Jesus in the Pauline letters.[108] Paul followed the Jewish monotheism of the Second Temple period with the worldview of a zealous Pharisee.[109] The main idea implied in Jewish monotheism is that Israel's God is the Creator over all the creation; God will eventually judge all the people who worship other gods; and, finally, God will rescue his people of Israel from continued exile.[110] Wright reads Paul's Christology through the lens of Jewish monotheism because early Christians understood the divine identity of Jesus to be incontrovertible already before the New Testament (1 Cor 8:6). Jewish monotheism is revised to conceive of Jesus as God over all (Rom 9:5). Following Richard Bauckham and Larry Hurtado, Wright insists on applying the divine identity to the Messiah Jesus, who faithfully fulfilled promises in the Old Testament. Wright links the concept of Jesus' divine identity to the returning of YHWH to Zion through Jesus death and resurrection, which fulfills the Old Testament promises of YHWH's return to Zion.

The meaning of "God's gospel" is God's announcement of "the royal enthronement of the Messiah, Israel's anointed king."[111] The anointing of the Messiahship is closely connected to the resurrection of the Messiah in Lord Christology in Wright's understanding. Romans 1:3–4 echoes Psalm 2:7 and 2 Samuel 7:12–14, which manifests the Davidic "Son of God."[112] The Davidic Son is declared "through his resurrection from the dead, echoing the Septuagint, in particular 2 Samuel 7:12."[113] Additionally, he posits,

> The Gentiles will come to hope in the Davidic Messiah, the "root of Jesse" (for 'root of Jesse' as a title for the Messiah, see Rev 5:5; 22:16); he is the one who "rises to rule the nations." The echo of 1:4 should leave us in no doubt that Paul intends a reference to Jesus' resurrection. This is what constituted him as Messiah and Lord of the whole world.[114]

---

108. Wright attests, "'Monotheism' indeed: neither a philosophical speculation nor an easygoing generalized religious supposition, but the clear, sharp, bright belief that Israel's God was the creator of all, unique among claimants to divinity in possessing all those specific attributes, in the middle of which we find the politically explosive one, basileus, 'king.'" Wright, *Paul and the Faithfulness of God*, 621.

109. Wright, *Paul and the Faithfulness of God*, 625.

110. Wright, *Paul and the Faithfulness of God*, 620–21.

111. Wright, *Paul and the Faithfulness of God*, 620–21.

112. Wright, *Paul and the Faithfulness of God*, 818.

113. Wright, *Paul and the Faithfulness of God*, 818.

114. Wright, *Romans*, 748.

In other words, the Davidic Messiah in Romans incorporates the notion of monotheism. He comments,

> Paul speaks of the Davidic Messiah who "rises to rule the nations, and in [whom] the nations shall hope" (15:12). Again it is the resurrection that unveils the messianic identity, and with it the summons to worship, to "hope in him." This is deeply monotheistic language, of the second-temple creational, covenantal, cultic and especially eschatological variety.[115]

Wright's "divine identity" originates from the Davidic Messianism in Romans.[116]

In his book, *Paul and the Faithfulness of God*, Wright discusses God's righteousness and the Messiah Jesus in Romans 3:21 ff.: "In 'the gospel,' that is, the message about Jesus the Messiah and his death and resurrection as the fulfillment of God's scriptural promises, 'God's righteousness' is revealed."[117] He indicates that God's righteousness, which is closely connected with the Messiah Christology, is the faithfulness of the Messiah to God's covenant with the people of God within the "big picture" of God's covenant in the history of Israel. In this "big picture," God has been faithful to his covenant with his people through the Messiah Jesus in these significant ways.[118] One, God's righteousness is revealed through the faithfulness of the Messiah who has fulfilled the covenant and rescued his people from their "exile." Two, God has accomplished his covenantal faithfulness, which is his righteousness through the Messiah; those who are the true Israel are incorporated into Jesus the Messiah, the crucified and risen Lord, and Israel has been justified in this Messiah.[119]

Wright's Messiah Christology manifests the incorporated Christology and the faithfulness of the Messiah linked with significant arguments of Paul in Romans. God is faithful to covenant promises in terms of Jesus' faithfulness.[120] According to Wright,

---

115. Wright, *Paul and the Faithfulness of God*, 699.

116. Wright, *Paul and the Faithfulness of God*, 701.

117. Wright, *Paul and the Faithfulness of God*, 995. He also observes, "This righteousness, this world-righting covenant faithfulness, has been revealed 'through the faithfulness of Jesus the Messiah.'" Wright, *Romans*, 470.

118. Wright notes, "Paul remained a deeply Jewish theological who had rethought and reworked every aspect of his native Jewish theology in the light of the Messiah and the spirit, resulting in his own vocational self-understanding as the apostle to the pagans." Wright, *Romans*, 46.

119. About the incorporated Christology, see Cummins, "Divine Life and Corporate Christology," 190–209.

120. Wright, *Paul and the Faithfulness of God*, 844.

Working from the beginning (3.21–23) and the end (3.26) of this short paragraph into the dense statement in 3.24–25, we discover that the faithful death of Jesus (which Paul sees in 5.6–10 as an act of divine *agapē* and in 5.15–19 as the act of the Messiah's *hypakoē*, 'obedience') is more specifically an act of Exodus.[121]

The Messiah is "faithful" to God's covenant plan, which is that "Abraham's seed would bless the world."[122] The Messiah's faithfulness is presented by "obedience" in his death on the cross. Wright connects the faithful Messiah to the "righteous one" and the opening of Romans. He continues,

> And of course, for Paul, what this means in concrete terms is his death on the cross. The Messiah himself, in some versions of this narrative, is referred to as *ho dikaios*, "the righteous one." Whether or not we press that point, we see here the main thrust of Romans 1.3–4, and we understand more fully why Paul has used that opening precisely for that letter.[123]

Moreover, he relates the Messiah's death on the cross to martyrology.[124] He states, "The answer seems to lie in Paul's retrieval of certain themes available at the time in which the sacrificial overtones already there in the fourth servant song were being reused in connection with martyrs whose deaths were thought to be in some sense redemptive."[125] The redemption of the world, which is God's saving plan, was Israel's vocation. The saving was that "Israel's vocation would always involve Israel (or righteous martyrs within Israel) becoming a kind of sacrifice through which not only Israel itself but also the whole world would be rescued from its sinful, rebellious state."[126] It is fulfilled through the sacrifice offered by Israel's representative Messiah, Jesus. The Messiah is faithful to God's gracious plan, which is expressed in God's promises to Abraham.

In Romans, several scholars stress the faithfulness of Christ based on God's righteousness, which is his covenantal faithfulness, rather than faith in Christ. In God's covenantal relationship with his people, God's righteousness is fulfilled in the faithful Messiah. The suffering and death of the faithful

---

121. Wright, *Paul and the Faithfulness of God*, 845.
122. Wright, *Paul and the Faithfulness of God*, 942.
123. Wright, *Paul and the Faithfulness of God*, 942.
124. Wright, *Romans*, 474–77.
125. Wright, *Paul and the Faithfulness of God*, 845.
126. Wright, *Paul and the Faithfulness of God*, 845–46.

Christ, who is the Suffering Servant in Isaiah 53, fits a martyrological trajectory and is applied to Paul's Messiah Christology in Romans 1:18–4:25.

However, the Messiah Christology should be understood in the concept of the role of the Davidic Messiah, who is presented in the Old Testament and the Second Temple Jewish writings. The faithfulness of the Davidic Messiah does not suit his role in God's judgment. He is the agent of God's judgment, in which the covenantal faithfulness is unfamiliar. In Romans, Paul cannot emphasize the faithfulness of Christ for the faith of Christ because of discontinuity with the Old Testament and the Second Temple Jewish writings. Instead, faith in Christ, who is the Davidic Messiah and the executor of righteous judgment, is consonant with Paul's Messiah Christology in Romans 1:18–4:25. The faith of Christ does not have a meaning of the faithfulness of Christ, investigating Davidic Messiah, who is the agent of God's judgment.

CONCLUSION

The emphasis of the History of Religions School, which focused on high Christology, was the *kyrios* Christology of the Hellenistic group in early Christianity and the influence it had on Paul's Christology. New Testament scholarship has both continued and criticized the sharp division between messianic Christology and *kyrios* Christology. The Jewish and Hellenistic background in early Christianity had no strict distinction between them because Hellenism greatly influenced Palestine during Paul's era. Some have argued against the Davidic Messiahship in Paul's Christology because Paul would have known that anti-Semitic Gentile readers of his letters would have reacted against this Jewish portrayal of the Messiah. However, the recipients of Romans, with a recognizable Jewish background, clearly were able to accept the Jewish background inherent in the Davidic Messiah in Paul's letter. Rather, messianic Christology was axiomatically reconstructed in Paul's Christology, and this messianic Christology was not differentiated from the *kyrios* Christology.

In addition, some scholars have emphasized the Messiah's faithfulness in their argument for the key themes in Romans, usually when they focus on the Messiah Christology. The Messiah's faithfulness accomplishes God's covenant promises, in which God's faithfulness—which is his righteousness—is clearly presented in Paul's discourse. The faithful Messiah's endurance, obedience, and death on the cross play a key role in the deliverance of God. The Messiah's endurance, obedience, and death of the Messiah seem to correspond to the martyrology in 2 and 4 Maccabees. This is the flow of

Paul's thought in his argument in Romans, which is that God's covenantal faithfulness is revealed through the Messiah's faithfulness.

The Davidic Messiahship cannot be denied in Romans, even though some scholars support the *kyrios* Christology, instead of the Messiah Christology. The History of Religions School and some scholars have denied the Davidic Messiahship in Paul's Christology, especially in Romans. Yet, in the Old Testament and the Second Temple Jewish writings, the Davidic Messiah—an eschatological figure who executes God's judgment—clearly appears. Paul continuously employs the concept of the eschatological Davidic Messiah in the flow of his argument in Romans. The Davidic Messiah is main content of the gospel of God in Romans 1:3–4. Paul definitely maintains that, "according to my gospel, God judges the secrets of men through the Messiah Jesus" (2:16). God's judgment is accomplished in the death of the Davidic Messiah (3:25) and, through the death and resurrection of the Davidic Messiah, the sinners are justified (4:25).

Lastly, in his argument concerning the Davidic Messiah's role, the agent of God's judgment, the focus of Paul is not the Messiah's faithfulness. Paul points to faith in the Messiah, rather than to the faithfulness of the Messiah. Contrary to the interpretation of "πίστις Χριστοῦ" as "the Messiah's faith/faithfulness," Paul's statements concerning the Davidic Messiah in Romans (1:3–4; 2:16; 3:21–25; 4:25; 15:12) clearly involve the Messiah's role as the executor of God's judgment and faith in the Messiah. In this role, the Messiah's faithfulness is unfamiliar. God's salvation is accomplished through faith in the Messiah, whose role is that of executor of God's judgment. The theme of the covenantal faithfulness of the Messiah does not fit in this discourse of Paul in Romans.

Chapter 2

The Davidic Messiah

The Agent of God's Judgment in the Old Testament

INTRODUCTION

The Messiah is expected as the eschatological royal agent of God,[1] although the term *messiah* (משׁיח) corresponds to the contemporary king or the anointed high priest,[2] and משׁיח itself does not refer to an eschatological figure in the Hebrew Bible.[3] Based on an investigation of the use of משׁיח

---

1. Hess, "The Image of the Messiah in the Old Testament," 22–33; Collins, *The Scepter and Star*, 11–16; Oswalt, "משׁח," in *NIDOTTE*, 2:1123–27; Seybold, "משׁיח," in *TDOT*, 9:43–54; Laato, *A Star Is Rising*.

2. "מְשִׁיחוֹ, מְשִׁיחִי, מְשִׁיחֶךָ" (1 Sam 2:10, 35; 12:3, 5; 16:6; 2 Sam 22:51; Pss 2:2; 18:51; 20:7; 28:8; 84:10; 89:39, 52; Isa 45:1; Hab 3:13); "מָשִׁיחַ יְהוָה" (1 Sam 24:7, 11; 26:9, 11, 16, 23; 2 Sam 1:14, 16; 19:22; Lam 4:20). The term משׁיח appears thirty-eight times in the Hebrew Bible. This term refers to the king of Israel. In addition, משׁיח is used to reference the high priest. The articular adjective form refers to the anointed high priest (Lev 4:3, 5, 16; 6:22). The high priest is designated as משׁיח in Dan 9:25–26.

3. Fitzmyer, *The One Who Is to Come*, 8–25; Hanson, "Messiahs and Messianic Figures in Proto-Apocalypticism," 67–75. To characterize messianism, James Charlesworth especially takes into account those texts in which the term "messiah" is used. Charlesworth, "From Jewish Messianology to Christian Christology," 225–64; Charlesworth, "From Messianology to Christology," 3–35. Also, concerning minimalized definition,

for contemporary figures, it is difficult to provide a concrete definition for the term *Messiah*.[4] However, this perspective that views the Messiah as a contemporary figure cannot completely depict the Davidic Messiah in the messianic texts, especially in the post-exilic prophets because the eschatological messianism portrayal lies in a developed hope. In later prophetic literature, the term "*messiah*" is specifically and eschatologically used.[5] When the Davidic Messiah is expected as an eschatological figure, his main role is that of executor of God's judgment in the Old Testament. While several New Testament scholars stress the faithfulness of the Davidic Messiah in his eschatological coming to release God's people, the concept of faithfulness in God's judgment through the Messiah is not obvious. Rather, in the Old Testament, equity and righteousness are emphasized in the role of the Davidic Messiah, who is the executor of God's judgment.

THE DAVIDIC MESSIAH

The expectation of the messianic figure from the Davidic line is closely related to contemporary political and religious circumstances, so that the coming messianic figure may be immediate, instead of eschatological. The coming king is expected from the Pentateuch to the Historical Books, in which there is no eschatological meaning for this coming Davidic king. The coming king may support the idea of the Davidic Messiah. The Davidic Messiah can be expected as an ideal king in the contemporary political circumstances represented in the situation of the Davidic dynasty failure. Eschatological aspects of the Davidic Messiah in the ideal king, though, cannot be excluded in the later exilic and post-exilic period. While the contemporary nature of the term *Messiah* is still emphasized in the contemporary political situation, the figure of the eschatological Davidic Messiah emerges in the post-exilic period, in which he is understood to be the agent of divine deliverance, who is appointed by God in the eschatological age.[6]

---

see Jonge, "The Use of the Word 'Anointed' in the Time of Jesus," 132–48; Roberts, "The Old Testament's Contribution to Messianic Expectations," 39–51; Pomykala, *The Davidic Dynasty Tradition in Early Judaism*.

4. Boda, "Figuring the Future," 35–45; Oegema, *The Anointed and His People*, 21–27.

5. Chester, *Messiah and Exaltation*, 195. Concerning the broad terms of "messianic" for the eschatological messianic figure, see Klausner, *The Messianic Idea in Israel*; Mowinckel, *He That Cometh*; Horbury, *Jewish Messianism and the Cult of Christ*, 6–7; Kaiser Jr., *The Messiah in the Old Testament*.

6. Collins, *The Scepter and Star*, 12; Oegema, *The Anointed and His People*, 26–27; Chester, *Messiah and Exaltation*, 198–201; Chester, *Future Hope and Present Reality*, 208.

Pentateuch to Historical Books

The coming king—expected from the tribe of Judah—is a messianic figure, "the anointed one" (מָשִׁיחַ). This expectation for the "anointed one" is fulfilled in King David's anointing. The royal figure is expected from the tribe of Judah, from the Pentateuch to the Historical Books, but he does not have an eschatological character in himself. The Pentateuch has the roots of the royal Messiah, who would come from the tribe of Judah.[7] The coming king is predicted in Genesis 49:10, where he is expected to come from the tribe of Judah: "The scepter shall not depart from Judah."[8] The poems in Genesis 49:8–12 "are of one piece with a broader royal ideology that moves from Genesis to 1–2 Kings and centers upon God's agenda being worked out through a coming king from the line of Judah (cf. Gen 3:14–15; 4:25; 17:6–7; 38:27–29)."[9] In Balaam's oracle, the royal figure is foretold as "a star shall come out of Jacob, and a scepter shall rise out of Israel" (Num 24:17). Baruch A. Levine writes,

> As regards the nominal parallelism, שֵׁבֶט//כּוֹכָב, some commentators have taken their cue from כּוֹכָב "star," referring to a meteor or shooting star that leaves a "tail" in its wake, having the appearance of a staff or scepter, extending the usual meaning

---

7. Alexander, "Messianic Ideology in the Book of Genesis," 21. Daniel I. Block writes, "The roots of royal messianism in Israel are found in four Pentateuchal texts: (1) Yahweh's promise that 'kings would come from Abraham' (Gen 17:6, 16; 35:11); (2) Jacob's prediction that the scepter would not depart from Judah (Gen 49:10); (3) Balaam's oracular word that a star and scepter would rise from Jacob/Israel (Num 24:17); and (4) Moses' charge that in response to a desire for a king, the Israelites should put on their throne one whom Yahweh would choose (Deut 17:14–20)." Block, "My Servant David," 37.

8. Regarding the Davidic king expected in Genesis, Alexander, "Messianic Ideology in the Book of Genesis," 21, says, "Significantly, in Genesis this future king is linked to a royal dynasty descended from the tribe of Judah. Furthermore, the activity of this king is associated with the restoration of the harmonious state which initially existed between God, humanity and nature in the Garden of Eden."

9. Jipp, *Christ Is King*, 31; Alexander, "Royal Expectation in Genesis to Kings," 191–212. Adam in Genesis 1–3 has been understood to be related to the Davidic monarchy in Jerusalem. Alexander, "Messianic Ideology in the Book of Genesis," 21. See Brueggemann, "David and His Theologian," 156–81; Brueggemann, "From Dust to Kingship," 1–18; Wifall, "David-Prototype of Israel's Future?," 94–107; Wifall, "The Breath of His Nostrils," 237–40. Both Adam and David are created for kingship. Jipp says, "Adam's rise from the dust (Gen 2:7) in the ancient Near Eastern environment means to be 'enthroned' or 'exalted' as king, and 'to return to dust' (Gen 3:19) means to be deposed as king (e.g., Isa 41:2; Mic 7:16–17; Jer 49:22–24). For example, in the royal language of the OT, the exaltation of a king is frequently described in terms of a creation from dust (e.g., 1 Kgs 16:2; cf. 1 Sam 2:6–8; Ps 113:7)." Jipp, *Christ Is King*, 32.

of Hebrew שֵׁבֶט. Alternatively, one could take a cue from שֵׁבֶט in its figurative connotation of "sovereign, head," namely one who bears a scepter. Thus Genesis 49:10; "The 'scepter' (שֵׁבֶט) shall not depart from Judah, nor the magistrate (מְחֹקֵק) from the issue of his loins."[10]

The expectation of the coming king in Balaam's oracle corresponds to the glory of King David, who comes from the tribe of Judah.[11] The prediction of the victory over Moab and Edom (Num 24:17–18) is accomplished by King David, who emerges from Jacob.[12]

A shift can be detected in moving to the Historical Books. The anointing of David as king fulfills the expectation of the coming king from the tribe of Judah, who was expected in the Pentateuch. In addition, the messianic figure, "the anointed one" or "messiah" (משיח) of Yahweh, is anticipated as the King David. Hannah's song (1 Sam 2:10) announces the coming king as "his anointed one" (משיחו), who will lead God's people and be specially endowed by God for the task.[13]

Although the expectation of the royal figure of the Pentateuch is attained, the expectation of the Davidic Messiah is based on the anointing of David as king and the promise of an eternal Davidic dynasty. The expectation of the Davidic Messiah is based on God's eternal promise, which is granted to the dynasty of David in 2 Samuel 7, "the permanence of the Davidic line."[14] It is pivotal for the development of the Davidic messianic hope. 2 Samuel 7:12–16 shows "the father-son adoption formula (and the setting out of the relationship between God and David), and the absolute and unconditional promise of an eternal Davidic dynasty."[15] While the Davidic king's anointing concerns contemporary kingship, this permanent promise of God for the Davidic king is continuously appropriated for the Davidic Messiah in coming times, particularly in the Prophets. The permanence of the Davidic kingship later supports the eschatological Davidic messianic figure.

---

10. Levine, *Numbers 21–36*, 200.
11. Noth, *Numbers*, 192.
12. Noth, *Numbers*, 193.
13. Satterthwaite, "David in the Books of Samuel?," 44.
14. Condra, *Salvation for the Righteous Revealed*, 238.
15. Chester, *Future Hope and Present Reality*, 175.

Psalms

The anointed Davidic king, who is the Son of God, can be understood as an eschatological figure based on God's eternal promise for the Davidic line; however, the Psalms focus on the contemporary political situation or royal ideology in the pre-exilic context. Although, the merging of the present political reality with a future hope of an idealized kingship is an open possibility in some Psalms, which are the so-called royal Psalms,[16] the anointing of the Davidic king suggests not so much an eschatological figure because it is closely related to a description of the Davidic kingship in a pre-exilic date.

The Davidic king is his anointed one (Ps 2:2). The Davidic king is Yahweh's "anointed one" (מְשִׁיחוֹ; 2:2) and "his son" (2:6–8). David's adoption as God's son is described in Psalm 2:7, which has a particularly close intimacy: "I will tell of the decree: The Lord said to me, 'You are my Son; today I have begotten you.'"[17] This verse describes an enthronement ceremony,[18] which "denotes the adoption of the king by God as his son."[19] As anointed king, who is the Son of God, the Davidic king shares God's glory in a close relationship, which is identified as a sharing of the kingship of God (Pss 2:6–9; 89:27–29; 110:1–7).[20] The sonship of the Davidic king (89:26–27) is based on the eternal covenant (89:4, 29, 36–37; cf. 2 Sam 7:16), so the Davidic throne and line will be everlasting (89 and 132). The emphasis concerning the eternal Davidic covenant related to God's anointing of the Davidic king "is found more frequently in the Psalms than in the prophets" (18:50; 45:6–7; 72:5, 17; 89:4, 28–37; 110:4; 132:11–12).[21]

The royal Psalms include the idea of "the threat of international unrest at the time of the coronation of the Davidic king."[22] The Davidic king in Psalms 1 and 2 is the righteous one (Pss 1:5–6; 2:7–8, 12), who is identified with the deliverer of God's people, and through him the Lord saves the people.[23] The same commission is assured in Psalm 110, in which the

---

16. S. E. Gillingham writes, "In this case, of all the so-called Messianic Psalms, we see here some merging of a present political reality with an idealized future hope; in this sense, one could argue that the interpretation of this psalm is more open than others to an eschatological interpretation." Gillingham, "The Messiah in the Psalms," 222–23. Also, Wilson, "The Use of Royal Psalm at the Seams of the Hebrew Psalter," 85–94.
17. Chester, *Future Hope and Present Reality*, 179.
18. Hamilton, *The Body Royal*, 60–61.
19. Chester, *Future Hope and Present Reality*, 179.
20. Eaton, *Kingship and the Psalms*, 144, 146–49.
21. Selman, "Messianic Mysteries," 287.
22. Gillingham, "The Messiah in the Psalms," 212.
23. Jipp, *Christ Is King*, 226.

Davidic Messiah "should lead his people in battle."[24] Gillingham rightly says, "Similarly the idea of the universal dominion of the king may also explain why the psalm was used later to describe a Messianic age, but this too is a common feature in royal ideology and so again does not preclude a pre-exilic context."[25] The reference to the messianic figure from the Davidic line is initially utilized in the context of his coronation, although it is eschatologically employed for the Davidic Messiah in later times.[26] The imminent expectation of salvation is found in the all-embracing dominion of the Davidic king in Psalms, which is based on the eternal promise for the Davidic dynasty.[27] Although the royal Psalms may be based on the eschatological expectation for the Davidic messianic figure, they concentrate on the imminent expectation for the Davidic king as a ruler over the entire world.[28]

Prophets

In the Prophetic literature, the Davidic Messiah from the Davidic line is foretold (Isa 7, 9, 11; 16:5; 32:1–3; 55:3–5; Jer 23:5–6; 30:9; Ezek 34:23–24; 37:24–27; Hos 3:5; Amos 7:12–13; 9:11; Mic 5:2–5).[29] The grounds for the expectations of the new Davidic king, which are based on the eternal covenant with David (2 Sam 7), correspond with God's anointing and election of David, his servant (Ps 89:3). The Davidic Messiah is based on the idealized king, who is described as the Davidic king in 2 Samuel 7 and the Psalms. Those texts in the Prophets, including the idea of the coming Davidic king,

---

24. Longman III, "The Messiah," 26.
25. Gillingham, "The Messiah in the Psalms," 212.
26. See Craigie and Tate, *Psalms 1–50*, 66.
27. Hesse, "χριστός," in *TDNT*, 9:506.
28. Hesse, "χριστός," in *TDNT*, 9:506.
29. Antti Laato explains, "In Amos 7:12–13 Amaziah, the priest of Bethel, characterizes the temple in Bethel as 'a royal sanctuary, the temple of the kingdom.' This indicates that the cult in Bethel was closely tied to a political ideology which apparently provided the basis for belief in the well-being of the kingdom." Laato, *A Star Is Rising*, 109; Blenkinsopp, *David Remembered*, 128. According to Joseph Blenkinsopp, "Unlike Amos and Isaiah, however, Micah has little to say about David and his dynasty. At a time of deprivation and disorientation, Zion is told that the former dominion and sovereignty will return, but David is not named (Mic 4:8–10). Even more recondite is the prediction of a ruler from Bethlehem (Mic 5:2–5)." Blenkinsopp, *David Remembered*, 129. Bruce K. Waltke remarks, "Micah probably intends to note a striking coincidence between David's lowly place of birth and his social position, a coincidence that matches the Messiah's career. Only divine intervention can account for the transformation of David and the Messiah into greatness." Waltke proposes exegetical supports for the Davidic Messiah in Mic 5:1. See Waltke, *A Commentary on Micah*, 276–77.

"express a hope for the future do so by speaking of a restoration of fortunes of the Davidic line."[30] According to Williamson,

> Although 2 Sam 7:12–17 provides the closest point of comparison, the use of similar language in many other passages reminds us that this may not be so much an allusion to a specific textual authority as to a tradition which was in wider circulation and which carried its own stereotypical language.... In particular, the reference to the "rod of the oppressor" in Isa 9:3 (MT) may be an allusion to the possibility that an individual king may need to be disciplined "with a rod such as mortals use" (2 Sam 7:14) even while the promise about the dynasty as a whole is secure *ad-olam* (Isa 9:6 MT; 2 Sam 7:13).[31]

The Davidic Messiah will be characterized with the continuity of the promised Davidic king in God's promises in opposition to a fundamental discontinuity with the contemporary king of the Davidic line.[32]

In the pre-exilic period, the messianic figure is more closely related to the contemporary political situation, rather than to the last things in history.[33] Mark A. Boda writes, "Furthermore, when these texts establish the validity of 'anointed' figures in the past and note their enduring quality (especially references to *olam*), they are establishing something that has serious implications for future hope."[34] The later future in the messianic texts, though, can refer to the immediate future, instead to an eschatological time, and these texts rarely describe the eschatological coming of the Davidic Messiah. The messianic figure from the Davidic line in the Prophets may refer to a ruler who opposes contemporary kings in the present situation, although it is a figure that "encourages future hope in a later era."[35]

The birth of a new Davidic king, Immanuel (Isa 7:14), shows that "Ahaz is rejected, but the future of the dynasty is already secured."[36] Richard Schultz explains,

> Chapter 6 begins with a vision of the exalted divine king who sits to judge a sinful people, chs 7 and 8 portray Ahaz' lack of trust

---

30. Satterthwaite, "David in the Books of Samuel," 42.

31. Williamson, "The Messianic Texts in Isaiah 1–39," 256.

32. Williamson, "The Messianic Texts in Isaiah 1–39," 253.

33. John Day thinks that there is generally no eschatological interpretation of the Psalms. Day, *The Psalms*, 91, 97. See Mowinckel, *He That Cometh*, 12. Contra Hesse, "χριστός," in *TDNT* 9:505–9.

34. Boda, "Figuring the Future," 40.

35. Boda, "Figuring the Future," 40.

36. Williamson, "The Messianic Texts in Isaiah 1–39," 253.

in God and the resultant threat for Israel and Judah, while the announcements of the coming ruler in chs 9 and 11 bracket the description of the coming judgment on Assyriah (10:5-19).[37]

The point is that Isaiah is totally committed to the fact that God appoints the people's leader and guarantees the excellence of the Davidic descent, "removing the representatives of the present dynastic family."[38] The expectation for this new Davidic king draws a contrast with the contemporary kings depicted in chapter 6.[39] In chapters 9 and 11, Isaiah focuses on the justice and righteousness of the Davidic Messiah, who is completely different from the kings in chapter 6. Isaiah anticipates a better coming king, who will serve the Lord's judgment in accordance with God's will.[40]

The prophecy of the Davidic Messiah "reflects the distress of the Assyrian invasions at the end of the eighth century BC and expresses a longing for the golden days of the Davidic empire."[41] The Davidic Messiah is characterized as a futural figure, but the expectation of the idealized king looks to the immediate future in terms of the failures of contemporary kings and the threats of Israel's enemy. Isaiah's situation presses him to view a hope further in the future, but it is closely connected to the more immediate hope.

Jeremiah-Ezekiel

Additionally, the concept that the Davidic Messiah continues the hope for the king of the Davidic house is clearly contained in later prophetic literature.[42] With clear eschatological expressions (Jer 23:20; 30:24; 48:47; 49:39; Ezek 38:16; cf. 38:8) in the exilic and post-exilic periods, the eschatological concept of the Davidic Messiah can be presented with a future installation. The eschatological expectation for the Davidic king is intermingled with an expectation of the imminent restoration of the Davidic line in the contemporary political situation "after the exile when the former royal establishment has been destroyed."[43]

The future righteous ruler of Davidic descent, a righteous Branch (מצח צדיק), is expected (Jer 23:5-6). The Davidic Messiah is described as

---

37. Schultz, "The King in the Book of Isaiah," 149.

38. Williamson, "The Messianic Texts in Isaiah 1-39," 254.

39. Williamson, "The Messianic Texts in Isaiah 1-39," 254.

40. Williamson, "The Messianic Texts in Isaiah 1-39," 269.

41. Collins, *The Scepter and Star*, 28.

42. Selman, "Messianic Mysteries," 289.

43. McConville, "Messianic Interpretation of the Old Testament in Modern Context," 3.

a tending shepherd, who is the antitype of contemporary kings in Jeremiah 23:1-2.[44] Iain Provan asserts, "This sort of move from present to future is seen equally clearly in the book of Jeremiah in relation to Josiah, who becomes the model (Jer 22:15-16) for the Davidic king of the future who will rule over Israel and Judah in righteousness (Jer 23:1-8)—an antitype of the wicked Jehoiakim, who burns scrolls rather than obeying their words (Jer 36; contrast 2 Kgs 22:11 ff.)."[45] Furthermore, the Davidic Messiah who will come is described as a good shepherd in Ezekiel 34:23-24.[46] Ezekiel foretells the coming Davidic figure, whom he refers to as "one shepherd, my servant David" (Ezek 34:23-24; cf. 17:22). Ezekiel's prophecies are related to Jeremiah's condemnation of worthless shepherds (Jer 23:1-4), who are the kings of Judea (Jer 22:11-30). Paul Joyce posits,

> I now come to Ezek 21:32b (ET 27b), perhaps the most marginal of the cases to be considered in this review: "Until he comes whose right it is; to him I will give it." The context is provided by the judgment on the 'vile, wicked prince of Israel' in 21:30-31 (ET 25-26), discussed earlier. . . . The next words—those which concern us—certainly appear more positive, but they are difficult and cryptic: "Until he comes whose right it is; to him I will give it." There is no overtly royal or "messianic" language here, but in the context of judgment on the "prince," these words could imply a future, worthy royal recipient of divine favor and blessing. Such an interpretation is the more likely in view of a possible allusion here to Gen 49:10.[47]

Ezekiel 34:23 reads, "And I will set up over them one shepherd, my servant David, and he shall feed them: he shall feed them and be their shepherd." Ezekiel 34 and 37 possess overt "messianic" hope, with the scathing critique of the "shepherds," who were failed contemporary royal leaders.[48]

---

44. Allen, *Ezekiel 20-48*, 160. Allen comments, "Jer 23:1-2, in referring to shepherds, appears to relate to the last major kings of Judah, Jehoiakim and Zedekiah, as responsible for the deportation of 597 BC and Judah's ensuing ills because of their negligence. The term 'shepherd' is standard for a king throughout the ancient Near East. In this context it is combined with the use of the metaphor to portray the covenant between Yahweh and Israel (cf. Pss 74:1; 79:13; 80:2[1]; cf. the individualization in Ps 23). Accordingly, the shepherds were employees of the divine shepherd and responsible to him." Allen, *Ezekiel 20-48*, 161.

45. Provan, "The Messiah in the Books of Kings," 83.

46. Ezekiel anticipates a new Davidic ruler referred to as "one shepherd, my servant David" (34:23-24; cf. 17:22). Lucass, *The Concept of the Messiah in the Scriptures of Judaism and Christianity*, 98-99.

47. Joyce, "King and Messiah in Ezekiel," 327.

48. Joyce, "King and Messiah in Ezekiel," 328.

While the Davidic Messiah is presented as a condemnation of the contemporary shepherds and a restoration of the ruined Davidic dynasty, he is an eschatological figure on the basis of God's eternal covenant. Ezekiel reaffirms Yahweh's promise to David declared in 2 Samuel 7.[49] The coming ruler, the Davidic Messiah, is the good shepherd as in Ezekiel 34:23–24. In 2 Samuel 7:8, David's election is described as "from the pasture (נָוֶה), from following the sheep, that you should be prince (נָגִיד) over my people Israel." It is reflected as well in 2 Samuel 5:2, "And the Lord said to you, 'You shall be shepherd (תִרְעֶה) of my people Israel, and you shall be prince (נָגִיד) over Israel.'"[50] The Davidic Messiah's eschatological ruling links to the restoration of Israel and the execution of God's eschatological judgment. The restoration oracles are given in Ezekiel 34–37 and the Gog Oracle in Ezekiel 38–39.[51] In Ezekiel 37:16–28, Ezekiel relates the Davidic covenant to the promise of the Davidic Messiah, who is king over all Israel.[52] The unification of the nation is permanent as highlighted by עוֹלָם. It denotes basically "the remotest." According to Ezekiel 37:25, "David my servant shall be their prince forever (לְעוֹלָם)." Daniel Block attests,

> With his five-fold affirmation of the eternity of the restoration, Yahweh transforms this oracle into a powerful eschatological statement, envisaging an entirely new existence, where the old historical realities are considered null and void, and the new salvific work of God is perceived as final. For Ezekiel eschatological events are neither ahistorical nor super-historical; they are based upon Yahweh's past actions in history and represent a final solution to the present historical crisis. But the scope of his eschatological hope extends beyond a renewal of Yahweh's covenant with his people, incorporating all the other promises upon which the Israelites had based their security: Yahweh's covenant with David.[53]

With the eschatological term, the Davidic Messiah is shown as summoned to be a shepherd for Israel to be safe and sheltered, after executing judgment on Babylon or Gog.[54] In chapter 38 of Ezekiel, the execution of judgment on Gog and the establishment of the eschatological messianic

---

49. Block, "Bringing Back David," 171. See Jer 33:17, 20–21, 25–26.
50. Ps 78:70–72.
51. Block, "Bringing Back David," 180.
52. Ezek 34:23–25.
53. Block, "Bringing Back David," 180.
54. Eichrodt, *Ezekiel*, 523.

state of peace occur in "the last days" (בְּאַחֲרִית הַיָּמִים in 38:16).[55] Thus, while the contemporary political circumstances characterize the Davidic Messiah as an immediate coming king, the eschatological expectations for the Davidic Messiah appear in the late exilic prophets.

Haggai-Zechariah

Because the reformulation of leadership in the post-exilic period is emphasized in the context of the contemporary situation of the early Persian period, the prophecies concerning the Davidic Messiah may not be recognized as eschatological. After the exile, Israelite society was being reformulated, and leadership was being reshaped.[56] Prophecies concerning leaders are closely related to "the historical realities of the early Persian period."[57] A renewal of national independence and international rule is expected in the figure of Zerubbabel.[58] The context "in which all of this vocabulary intersects is that associated with Davidic appointment."[59] Haggai draws on traditions and literature in 2:22 connected with the coronation of Israel's kings resonating with royal Psalms, especially Psalms 2 and 110, "to place the role of Zerubbabel as Davidide within a strong political context."[60]

However, while the role of Zerubbabel can be understood in the contemporary political context, Zerubbabel, who is called a "branch," is designated as the messianic figure of the end time.[61] Boda notes, "After affirming the people for their faithfulness in laying the foundation of the temple (2:10–19), the prophet promises again a future shaking of the cosmos, but this time the speech is addressed exclusively to Zerubbabel ('governor of Judah') and the result is the catastrophic shattering of the political and military hegemony of foreign nations and the installation of Zerubbabel ('son of Shealtiel') as Davidic vice regent of YHWH on earth (2:20–23)."[62] When the

---

55. Eichrodt, *Ezekiel*, 523. "In the last days" has eschatological meaning in Jer 23:20; 30:24; 48:47; 49:39; Ezek 38:16; cf. 38:8. In these texts, Jer 23:20 eschatologically describes the messianic figure.

56. Boda, "Figuring the Future," 46.
57. Boda, "Figuring the Future," 54.
58. Boda, "Figuring the Future," 54.
59. Boda, "Figuring the Future," 53.
60. Petersen, *Haggai and Zechariah 1–8*, 100.
61. Hesse, "χριστός," in *TDNT*, 9:507.
62. Boda, "Figuring the Future," 52.

thrones of foreign nations will be destroyed in the afflictions of the last time, the salvation of the eschatological Messiah will dawn.[63]

One particular feature in the messianic figure in Zechariah is the intertwining of priestly and royal figures, which is "drawn assuredly from the description of the restoration in Jeremiah 33 (cf. 23)."[64] Zechariah prophesies to Joshua, the high priest, with the verse, "Behold, I will bring my servant the Branch" (Zech 3:8). The language of the Davidic messianic figure is applied to Joshua. Joseph Blenkinsopp states,

> In the prophecies of Haggai, Zerubbabel is linked with the high priest Joshua, and both together are charged with the essential task of rebuilding the temple and restoring its worship. In all epochs throughout the history of the ancient Near East temple-building or temple-rebuilding was a royal prerogative and task.[65]

The branch (צמח) in Zechariah "belongs to the imminent future when he will come and usher in a new day of cleansing and prosperity (3:9–10) as well as rebuilding the temple (6:12–13, 15)."[66] Mark Boda goes on to say,

> Zerubabbel symbolically affirms this by his involvement in the temple building, and Zechariah trumpets it with his declaration that the priesthood was a sign that a future Messiah would one day emerge (Zech 3:8), a hope preserved by the memorial crown in the temple (Zech 6:14).[67]

In addition, while the "sons of oil" in 4:14 has an evident messianic meaning, the joint messianic hope is specifically anticipated in texts (Zech 3:8; 4:14; 6:12–14). Boda continues,

> Often this phrase is translated as "the two anointed ones" (4:14) and linked to the two key leadership figures associated with the early Persian period: Joshua, the Zadokite high priest, and, of course, Zerubbabel, the Davidic governor of Yehud. For most interpreters this vision is expressing the political realities of Yehud in the Persian period, highlighting the elevated role of

---

63. Hesse, "χριστός," in *TDNT*, 9:507. With respect to the eschatological messianic idea in Zechariah, see Laato, *A Star Is Rising*, 208–20.

64. Boda, "Figuring the Future," 52.

65. Blenkinsopp, *David Remembered*, 75. He asserts, "In all epochs throughout the history of the ancient Near East temple-building or temple-rebuilding was a royal prerogative and task." Blenkinsopp, *David Remembered*, 120.

66. Boda, "Figuring the Future," 56.

67. Boda, "Figuring the Future," 49.

the priest in this new era and preparing the way for hierocratic hegemony in later centuries.⁶⁸

While the potential Davidic king disappears, authority is vested in the high priest described as making a crown set on the head of Joshua, and on Zerubbabel (Zech 6:11), too. Martin Selman observes, "There can be no doubt therefore that a tradition existed, apparently originating in the Jerusalem temple, that the two anointed offices of king and priest could on occasion be combined."⁶⁹ The joint ruling of priests and kings will appear as representative of the theocracy.⁷⁰ It is presupposed that the priesthood and kingship will join in the rule of the Messiah.⁷¹

The Septuagint

The Davidic Messiah in the Septuagint "will act as God's designed agent in the eschatological time."⁷² The Septuagint's rendering of certain passages has quite a different meaning, which provides evidence of eschatological messianic ideas.⁷³ M. A. Knibb comments that "in definite deviations from the Hebrew original the LXX proclaims the messianic hope in Hellenism Judaism."⁷⁴ Genesis 49:10 LXX has the interpretive rendering that "there shall not fail a ruler (οὐκ ἐκλείψει ἄρχων) from Judah," while the Masoretic text can be translated as "there shall not turn away a scepter from Judah." This interpretive rendering is "close to Nathan's promise of a never-failing Davidic line and throne, as recalled in 1 Kgs 2:4; 8:25; 9:5; 2 Chr 6:16 (LXX οὐκ ἐκλείψει); 7:18."⁷⁵ The LXX Pentateuch presents coherence of future Israelite rule, which is associated with Judah's Davidic line.⁷⁶ Horbury writes,

> The LXX version of Gen 49:10 therefore stands within a continuum of recognition of David's Judahite descent, and has a precedent in its link between this blessing and David's line. At

---

68. Boda, "Figuring the Future," 55.
69. Selman, "Messianic Mysteries," 296.
70. Mason, "Messiah in the Postexilic Old Testament Literature," 347.
71. Mason, "Messiah in the Postexilic Old Testament Literature," 347.
72. Collins, "Messianism and Exegetical Tradition," 129.
73. Mowinckel, *He That Cometh*, 282–84.
74. Knibb, "The Septuagint and Messianism: Problems and Issues," 6.
75. Horbury, "Monarchy and Messianism in the Greek Pentateuch," 109.
76. Horbury, "Monarchy and Messianism in the Greek Pentateuch," 109.

the same time it links this line of Judah and David with the last days (Gen 49,1. 10c LXX).⁷⁷

The LXX Pentateuch is appropriate to apply the expectation of the Davidic Messiah to the last days (Gen 49:1; Deut 32:35 LXX), "and a number of passages speak of the advent of a great individual Israelite ruler in the last days" (Gen 49:10; Num 24:7, 17; Deut 18:15–22; 33:5).⁷⁸

The royal figure in Genesis 49:8–12 appears again in Balaam's oracle. Numbers 24:9 reads, "He crouched, he lay down like a lion and like a lioness; who will rouse him up?" (κατακλιθεὶς ἀνεπαύσατο ὡς λέων καὶ ὡς σκύμνος, τίς ἀναστήσει αὐτόν;). Genesis 49:9 LXX states similarly to Numbers 24:9, "He lay down, he crouched as a lion and as a lioness; who does rouse him?" (ἀναπεσὼν ἐκοιμήθης ὡς λέων καὶ ὡς σκύμνος, τίς ἐγερεῖ αὐτόν;). The Septuagint of Numbers 24:17 "plainly has in view an eschatological king."⁷⁹ The man (ἄνθρωπος) in 24:7 is identified as an eschatological figure. According to Numbers 24:7, "I will show to him, and it is not now; I pronounce a blessing, and it is not near; a star shall spring up out of Jacob, and a man (ἄνθρωπος) shall stand up out of Israel, and shall crush the princes of Moab." Knibb observes,

> To return to the LXX version of Balaam's oracle, the rendering "a star shall spring up (ἀνατελεῖ) from Jacob," for Hebrew in verse 17 which can be translated "a star has marched forth from Jacob," facilitates and perhaps reflects a link with the prophets on the Davidic ἀνατολή (Jer 23:5; Zech 3:9 [8]; 6:12).⁸⁰

Balaam's third oracle in Numbers 24 has been understood as referring to the Davidic king's eschatological rule with the phrase, "in the latter days" (אַחֲרִית הַיָּמִים in MT; ἐπ' ἐσχάτου τῶν ἡμερῶν in LXX Num 24:14).⁸¹

The rendering of 2 Samuel 7:11 in the LXX shows, "God announces that David will build the temple for God." The difference is that "for David" (לְךָ) is changed to be "for God" (αὐτῷ).⁸² Second Samuel 7:16 LXX also indicates the house of David and his kingdom will exist forever "before me" (ἐνώπιον ἐμοῦ). Instead of "before David" (לְפָנֶיךָ), "before me" designates the future kingdom of David as "a transcendent one."⁸³

---

77. Horbury, "Monarchy and Messianism in the Greek Pentateuch," 109.
78. Horbury, "Monarchy and Messianism in the Greek Pentateuch," 126.
79. van Der Woude, "χριστός," in *TDNT*, 9:510.
80. Horbury, "Monarchy and Messianism in the Greek Pentateuch," 122.
81. Horbury, *Jewish Messianism and the Cult of Christ*, 50.
82. Pomykala, *The Davidic Dynasty Tradition*, 129.
83. Oegema, *The Anointed and His People*, 45.

The term "*messiah*" (χριστός) is associated with the Davidic eschatological Messiah, based on the covenant with David of 2 Samuel 7, especially in Psalms.[84] The Davidic Messiah is the hope for the restoration of the Davidic line, according to the promise to David in 2 Samuel 7. Israel looked for the promise fulfillment because there was no Davidic king in Jerusalem after the exile.[85] While differences and adaptions between the Greek version and the Hebrew texts in Psalms are not very different, the LXX offers hope for the future "not only in terms of a general eschatological outlook, but also in terms of some specific examples of Messianism."[86] Psalm 72:17 (LXX 71:17) reads, "πρὸ τοῦ ἡλίου διαμενεῖ τὸ ὄνομα αὐτοῦ" (before the sun was created, his name will remain). This emendation gives light to this figure's pre-existence.[87] LXX 109:3 reads similarly with LXX Psalm 71:17, "ἐκ γαστρὸς πρὸ ἑωσφόρου ἐξεγέννησά σε" (from the womb I have begotten you before the morning star).[88] The shift from the historical to the eschatological interpretation is demonstrated with the rendering of the messianic figure as transcendent in the LXX Psalms.[89]

In the LXX Prophets, "ἐν γαστρὶ ἕξει" in Isaiah 7:14 can be understood with the future tense as an eschatological rendering for the Davidic Messiah.[90] J. Lust holds that hopes for the eschatological royal figure, according to the Davidic line, can be envisaged in the rendering of the LXX Prophets. He remarks, "This is not to say there are no texts at all in which the LXX heightens the eschatological and transcendent dimension of messianism and of the Messiah."[91]

In sum, the Davidic Messiah is coherently described as the royal ruler upholding the Davidic kingship that has been promised, and he is shown as ruling over Israel. The oracle in the Pentateuch, which describes the coming king from Judah is taken up and continued by Psalms and the Prophets based on the Davidic covenant and hope. The royal ideology and messianic expectations are consistently and substantially echoed in the Old Testament. Before the exile, messianic texts "do not speak of a future, much less an eschatological, Messiah, but of the contemporary, earthly king of David's

---

84. The LXX Psalms have the characteristics of the eschatological provision. Schaper, *Eschatology in the Greek Psalter*; Mitchell, *The Message of the Psalter*.

85. Collins, "Messianism and Exegetical Tradition," 130.

86. Gillingham, "The Messiah in the Psalms," 230.

87. Gillingham, "The Messiah in the Psalms," 230.

88. Gillingham, "The Messiah in the Psalms," 232.

89. Gillingham, "The Messiah in the Psalms," 232.

90. Lust, *Messianism and the Septuagint*, 12.

91. Lust, *Messianism and the Septuagint*, 12. Lust provides two verses: Isa 7:14; Dan 9:25–26.

line who was just been enthroned."[92] After the exile, there are some clear clues for the eschatological understanding for the Davidic Messiah, while the expectations for the Davidic Messiah involve contemporary hopes or imminent futural hopes, as well. More clearly, the eschatological view for the Davidic Messiah is manifest in the LXX's rendering for the Davidic Messiah, in which several passages are translated as eschatological, while Hebrew texts do not have any eschatological meaning in themselves.

THE DAVIDIC MESSIAH: THE AGENT OF GOD'S JUDGMENT

When the Davidic Messiah is expected throughout the Old Testament, it is clear that the Davidic Messiah is the agent of God's judgment either as a contemporarily immediate figure or as an eschatological figure. The role as the agent of God's judgment by the Davidic Messiah is based on the administration of justice and righteousness by the Davidic king. The role of the execution of God's judgment by the Davidic king, with justice and righteousness, is particularly important to the Davidic Messiah in the Prophets.[93] While some New Testament scholars emphasize the faithfulness of the Messiah based on some texts in the Old Testament, the main role of the Messiah is that of executor of God's judgment, rather than of his faithfulness to God's covenantal promises.

Historical Books

The Davidic king functions as the executor of justice, who has the role of a judge.[94] Legal decisions are assigned and entrusted to the Davidic king because the role of serving as the highest representative of jurisdiction is transferred to the king (2 Sam 8:15; 1 Kgs 3:16 ff.). These verses are vital to understand that David himself has the supreme office of judge.[95] They show that the royal figure is involved in the court system since he has responsibility for the juridical role of manifesting God's vindication.[96]

---

92. Mowinckel, *He That Cometh*, 12.

93. Hertzberg, *I & II Samuel: A Commentary*, 293.

94. The ancient Near Eastern ideal of a king was as the supreme judge, who would establish an ideal society of God for his people. Williamson, "The Messianic Texts in Isaiah 1–39," 260.

95. Hertzberg, *I & II Samuel*, 293.

96. Malchow, *Social Justice in the Hebrew Bible*, 15; Whitelam, *The Just King*, 52. Whitelam admits, "It would appear here that the term שפט is used in contexts in

The Davidic king's administration of justice and righteousness is a reflection of God's righteous rule over the world with his impartial justice. It entails the impartial judgment of the Davidic king because God "executes justice for the fatherless and the widow, and loves the sojourner, giving him food and clothing." (Deut 10:18). The role of "execution of justice for his people often takes the form of administering equitable verdicts for the oppressed, saving and defending his people from their enemies, and securing their protection and freedom."[97] The blessing of the anointed one (מְשִׁיחוֹ), who is the expected Davidic King, in Hannah's song 1 Samuel 2:10 is closely related to Yahweh's victorious judgment. David Tsumura contends,

> Yahweh judges (דִּין) the whole world. This is a claim that assumes the kingship of Yahweh (see on 8:5). The expression the ends of the earth (אַפְסֵי־אָרֶץ), which refers to the entire world, appears almost always in the context which describes Yahweh's uniqueness, majesty, and dominion. On the kingship of the Lord and his role as judge, see Ps 96:10 (דִּין).[98]

Yahweh, who judges the entire world, grants power to the Davidic king, who is the anointed one, to judge as his human representative or vice regent.[99]

One particular characteristic of the Davidic king's judgment is that God's wisdom is granted to the Davidic king to judge justly, which is later connected to the anointing of the Spirit. God's wisdom makes the Davidic king execute God's justice. After Solomon's judgment in the case of the two prostitutes, all Israel perceived that the wisdom of God was in Solomon (1 Kgs 3:28). The concluding statement of 1 Kings 3:28 "confirms the narrative interest in demonstrating Solomon's wisdom, and it further confirms that he is indeed ready to serve as a king."[100] The people of Israel knew that wisdom from God was to implement justice.[101] The idea that wisdom proceeds from God is expressed in the Old Testament (see Prov 8:22–31),[102] and wisdom is

---

association with other terms in such a way as to suggest that it bears a more general meaning of 'ruler' or 'governor' rather than specifically 'judge.'"

97. Jipp, *Christ Is King*, 222.

98. Tsumura, *The First Book of Samuel*, 149.

99. Tsumura, *The First Book of Samuel*, 150. The divine power (עֹז) is given to the coming king from God (cf. Ps 21:1).

100. Sweeney, *I & II Kings*, 82.

101. Brueggemann, *1 & 2 Kings*, 50.

102. De Vries, *1 Kings*, 60.

understood as a special gift from Yahweh.[103] Possessing God's wisdom, the Davidic king was expected to be a righteous judge.[104]

The administration of justice and righteousness is used as the criterion for the Davidic King as the agent of God's judgment. The endowment of wisdom is mentioned in the Writings as a significant characteristic of the execution of God's judgment by the Davidic king. These features, administration of justice and righteousness for judgment and the anointing of the Spirit for wisdom, are particularly important to the Davidic king or the Davidic Messiah in Psalms and the Prophets.[105]

Psalms

The Davidic king is understood in Psalms as the viceroy of God and executor of divine justice.[106] As in the Writings, it is to the Davidic king that "the legal decisions and the legal settlements, are assigned and entrusted."[107] Psalm 72, which is "an accession or coronation psalm,"[108] is a prayer for the king with judicial authority (Ps 72:2). The Psalter reads, "May he judge your people with righteousness, and your poor with justice!" (72:2). The Davidic king is "the highest judge and responsible for the righteous function of the court system."[109]

> In the first stanza the prayer is for the king to be endowed with the justice and righteousness of God. The king's function as the agent of Yahweh (1 Sam 10:1–2) is evident in the emphasis in Ps 72:2 on his extending God's righteousness and justice to God's people, especially the poor; both the attributes and the people belong to God, and the king is the instrument that brings them together.[110]

---

103. von Rad, *Wisdom in Israel*, 55.

104. Kraus, *Psalms 60–150*, 77; Malchow, *Social Justice in the Hebrew Bible*, 15. The Davidic king, who is considered to be God's son, was thought to be imparted with God's authority and power through the Spirit to rule the people of God (Pss 2:6–9; 89:20–37; 110:1–4; cf. 2 Sam 7:12–14; 1 Chr 17).

105. Hertzberg, *I & II Samuel*, 293.

106. Kraus, *Psalms 60–150*, 77. Kraus notes, "But the king is considered the viceroy of God. To him the משפטים, the legal decisions and the legal settlements, are assigned and entrusted."

107. Kraus, *Psalms 60–150*, 77.

108. Gillingham, "The Messiah in the Psalms," 223.

109. DeClaissé, Jacobson, and Tanner, *The Book of Psalms*, 577.

110. Tate, *Psalms 51–100*, 223.

In addition, the characteristic of the Davidic Messiah as executor in Psalms is presented not just in the role of judge, but also as the victorious king over rebellious nations. He is the victorious king in God's war, which is God's judgment over his enemies. This idea is in accord with the setting of Psalm 2, which is the king's coronation: "I have set my King on Zion, my holy hill" (2:6).[111] The initiation of holy war is from the divine establishment of the Davidic king, who engages in God's war. The kings of the nations are rebellious, but their futility is underscored: "Let us burst their bonds apart and cast away their cords from us. He who sits in the heavens laughs; the Lord holds them in derision" (2:3-4). He shall destroy them "with a rod of iron" (2:9), so God gives a warning "to them to avoid destruction at the hands of his anointed by submitting to his power."[112] The battle with the kings of the nations is described as violent judgment on the nations: "He will execute judgment among the nations, filling them with corpses" (Ps 110:6). The enthronement of the Davidic Messiah (110:2, 5), as in Psalms 2 and 45, "specifically carries with it the promise of absolute victory over Israel's enemies."[113]

One specific feature of the Davidic king is God's anointing for judgment, which characterizes the Messiah. The Davidic king is capable of taking this role as the agent of God's judgment, as a result of God's anointing him. The Davidic king is his anointed one (2:2).[114] The anointing with oil that is described in Psalm 45 entails the king's righteousness (45:7). To justly judge with the wisdom or knowledge of God, the Davidic Messiah must be given the Spirit.[115]

Prophets

The role of the executor of God's judgment by the ideal Davidic king expends to the Davidic Messiah in the Prophets. Moreover, the judicial role and victorious king are the Davidic Messiah's characteristics in his administration of justice and righteousness as expected in the Davidic king. The

111. Longman, "The Messiah: Explorations in the Law and Writings," 18.
112. Longman, "The Messiah: Explorations in the Law and Writings," 18.
113. Chester, *Future Hope and Present Reality*, 183.
114. Here, God declares the special relationship with his anointed king: "You are my son" (2:7), which is reminiscent of 2 Sam 7. Longman, "The Messiah: Explorations in the Law and Writings," 18.
115. Kraus, *Psalms 60–150*, 77. An ideal king's judging should be characterized with wisdom (Prov 16:10; 20:26). Dell, "The King in the Wisdom Literature," 176. "Wisdom and understanding" are standard requirements for the Davidic king. von Rad, *Wisdom in Israel*, 36.

administration of justice and righteousness in 2 Samuel 8:15 is implemented as the criterion for the Davidic Messiah (see Isa 9:7; 11:4–5; Jer 22:3, 15; 23:5; 33:15; Ezek 45:9).[116] In Isaiah 9, the function of the Davidic Messiah is acting as an agent of God's judgment. In Isaiah 9:6–7, he is expected to establish God's ruling with justice and righteousness. Established on justice and righteousness (Isa 9:7), the throne of the Davidic Messiah will remedy injustices in the center of God's kingdom.[117] He will be an agent of Yahweh's justice, in contrast to the previous Davidic kings who failed to fulfill their function of providing justice and righteousness in their ruling.[118]

In Isaiah 11:4, the Davidic Messiah, who is the shoot from Jesse's stump (Isa 11:1), is described as judging (שפט in 11:3 and 4) with "the rod of his mouth." The term "*rod*" (שֵׁבֶט) is employed "consistently throughout Isaiah to describe an instrument of judgment and punishment."[119] The spirit-empowered Messiah will execute the function of "judging" (שפט) and "deciding" (יכח) (Isa 2:4).[120] While the verb שפט is paralleled with *hiphil* of יכח ("to decide") in Isaiah 11:4,[121] the parallel of שפט and יכח is additionally utilized in 1:17–18 and 2:4 for describing God's judgment. The judicial overtones for the Davidic Messiah in Isaiah 11 are consistent with the preceding context in Isaiah 10:1–4, in which Isaiah shows his concern about "the corruption of justice in the social realm."[122] He denounces the legislative injustice toward the needy in 10:1–2. The Davidic Messiah can fulfill just judgment, although Israelite kings cannot execute righteousness in Isaiah 11.[123] Isaiah draws a contrast between contemporary kings and the Davidic Messiah. His function is shown in Isaiah 11 as an agent of God, the supreme Judge of his people to establish God's ideal society for his people.[124]

As the Davidic king, to arrive at just judgment, the Davidic Messiah was expected to be given a share in God's capacity by the imparting of God's knowledge to him.[125] The Davidic Messiah, the righteous king, is described

---

116. Auld, *I & II Samuel*, 431.

117. Kaiser, *Isaiah 1–12*, 214.

118. Houston, *Contending for Justice*, 153. John D. W. Watts insists that the theme of Isa 11:3–4 is impartial justice and rule that belongs to Yahweh. Watts, *Isaiah 1–33*, 210.

119. Heskett, *Messianism within the Scriptural Scroll of Isaiah*, 68.

120. Leclerc, *Yahweh Is Exalted in Justice*, 68.

121. But with righteousness he shall judge (וְשָׁפַט) the poor, and decide (וְהוֹכִיחַ) with equity for the meek of the earth.

122. Leclerc, *Yahweh Is Exalted in Justice*, 66; Bovati, *Re-Establishing Justice*, 191–92.

123. Heskett, *Messianism within the Scriptural Scroll of Isaiah*, 127.

124. Williamson, "The Messianic Texts in Isaiah 1–39," 260.

125. Kaiser, *Isaiah 1–12*, 257. Just judgment is to be a characteristic of the Davidic king's judgment. See Prov 16:10; 18:5; 20:8; 24:23.

in Isaiah 11:3-4 as having concern for a just society and judging in favor of the poor and the meek according to God's knowledge imparted by the Spirit.[126] Moshe Weinfeld attests,

> Isaiah, in his description of the king from the stock stemming from Jesse, who will judge righteously (בצדק) and arbitrate with equity (במישור), begins with the traits of wisdom, knowledge, and understanding granted to this king (Isa 11:1 ff.).[127]

The empowering of the Spirit on the Davidic Messiah will provide "wisdom and understanding" (חכמה ובינה) to arrive at just judgments in judicial decisions (Isa 11:1-3).[128]

In Isaiah 42:1-4, the Davidic Messiah is bringing forth God's judgment from the heavenly courtroom. The Messiah "brings forth justice" in Isaiah 42:4 and confirms the verdict in Isaiah 11:5.[129] The Davidic Messiah will "have particular regard for those least able to defend themselves, such as the orphan and widow, and the 'bruised reed' and 'dimly burning wick' of verse 2 are admirable poetic description of such people."[130] The poor and meek suffer injustice in the judicial system.[131]

The righteous king from the Davidic line will be called "Yahweh our righteousness" (Jer 23:6). The message is clear in Jeremiah 22:1-23:6 that the Davidic Messiah's ruling stresses judicial responsibility.[132] The ruling of the Davidic Messiah entails bringing Yahweh's judgment on Israel throughout Jeremiah—especially described with righteousness language in Jeremiah 23:5-6.[133] The Davidic Messiah is described as executing justice and righteousness in the land in Jeremiah 23:5.

As in Jeremiah 23:1-4, in which the Davidic Messiah is against the shepherds who destroy and scatter their flock, Ezekiel 34 offers a devastating critique of Israel's shepherds who do not care for their flock in contrast to a comforting picture of the shepherd "who fulfills the requirement to

---

126. Houston, *Contending for Justice*, 153.

127. Weinfeld, *Social Justice in Ancient Israel and in the Ancient Near East*, 361.

128. Smith, *Isaiah 1-39*, 271; Blenkinsopp, *Isaiah 1-39*, 264-65; Roberts, *First Isaiah*, 179.

129. In the remaining Songs מִשְׁפָּט is "applied more restrictively to aspects of a legal proceeding in which the Servant is a participant." Leclerc, *Yahweh Is Exalted in Justice*, 111.

130. Roberts, *First Isaiah*, 180.

131. Roberts, *First Isaiah*, 180.

132. Craigie, Kelley, and Drinkard, *Jeremiah 1-25*, 298.

133. Chester, *Future Hope and Present Reality*, 219.

maintain justice."[134] He will feed them with justice (Ezek 34:16), which is "the reference to the justice of Yahweh's judgment against his flock (שׁפט, 'to declare the right,' vv. 17, 20, 22)."[135] The Davidic Messiah would establish the beneficent ruling of God over the people, which was expected throughout the prophets.[136] He will protect his flock with just judgment.[137] Ezekiel 34:17–22 mainly deals with the judgment of the people, over whom the Davidic Messiah is denoted as prince (נָשִׂיא).[138] Walther Zimmerli asserts,

> The key-word שׁפט dominates in v. 17, the first section of the oracle, and in v. 20, the second section, and returns once again at the end in v. 22 as a kind of signature. From the point of view of its thought, this oracle, in spite of its otherwise independent form, comes close to the oracle in 20:32ff, especially 20:35–38. There, in the context of the new exodus, reference was made also to a judgment of separation in which the godless would be weeded out.... So here also there is reference to a separation-judgment held by Yahweh as the righteous shepherd.[139]

This alludes to the promise of returning from exile, yet it is linked to future judgment as seen in Ezekiel 20:35–38, and Ezekiel 21:25–27 contains an allusion to Genesis 49:10, the context of which is the divine threat and judgment of the messianic stance.[140] In addition, as noted above, the Davidic Messiah will execute God's eschatological judgment over enemies, which is described as judgment on Gog (Ezek 38–39).

Thus, one of the significant messianic expectations for the Davidic Messiah can be supposed to be the execution of judgment through him.

---

134. Houston, *Contending for Justice*, 136. Lucass notes, "The appellation 'shepherd' is applied to the king/Yahweh and kingship is spoken of using this metaphor in other sections of the prophets: Isa 56:11; Jer 3:15; 6:3; 10:21; 12:10; 22:22; 23:4; 25:34–36; Ezek 34:2, 7–10; Mic 2:12–13; 5:4; Nah 3:18; Zech 11:7–8." Lucass, *The Concept of the Messiah in the Scriptures of Judaism and Christianity*, 99.

135. Zimmerli, *Ezekiel*, 212.

136. Jipp, *Christ Is King*, 37; Lucass, *The Concept of the Messiah in the Scriptures of Judaism and Christianity*, 94–121; Block, "My Servant David," 17–56; Schreiber, *Gesalbter und König*, 49–59.

137. Collins states, "Throughout the ancient Near East, the ideal king was envisaged as a shepherd, who would rule with wisdom and righteousness." Collins, *The Scepter and Star*, 28. Zimmerli, *Ezekiel 2*, 212. Lucass posits, "Furthermore, it is in Ezekiel that Yahweh condemns 'the shepherds of Israel' (Ezekiel 34:1–10) and she says "I myself will be the shepherd of my sheep" (Ezek 34:15)." Lucass, *The Concept of the Messiah in the Scriptures of Judaism and Christianity*, 98–99.

138. Zimmerli, *Ezekiel 2*, 212.

139. Zimmerli, *Ezekiel 2*, 217.

140. Chester, *Future Hope and Present Reality*, 224.

The role of the Davidic Messiah as executor of God's judgment corresponds to the judicial role of the ideal Davidic king, who administered justice and righteousness (2 Sam 8:15). Additionally, it is consistent from the idealized Davidic king in the Historical Books and Psalms to the Davidic Messiah in the Prophets that the execution of judgment over either his people or enemies through the Davidic Messiah, who administers justice and righteousness, is from empowered knowledge of God.

RIGHTEOUSNESS IN THE DAVIDIC MESSIAH'S JUDGMENT

A main point in God's judgment through the Davidic Messiah is that righteousness in judgment through the Messiah is not equated with covenantal faithfulness itself, while these overlap in some areas. While some scholars emphasize the Messiah's faithfulness to God's covenantal relationship with his people, the emphasis in God's judgment through the Davidic Messiah is God's impartial righteousness. The Messiah's faithfulness is unfamiliar in the judgment of the Davidic Messiah. Rather, equity and impartiality are the goals of the righteous Davidic Messiah, when he administers justice and righteousness to either his people or enemies.

The Davidic king is portrayed as the righteous king, who is characterized in his execution of judgment by his righteousness. David administers justice and righteousness to all his people as supreme judge (2 Sam 8:15), and he is a righteous king (2 Sam 22:21–25). Righteousness (צדקה) in the Davidic king's judgment denotes a concrete vindication, judgment or righteous act.[141] The feminine noun צדקה has a slightly different meaning from the masculine צדק.[142] The term צדקה is used as "speaking of a vindicating act of God (probably a nominalization of the verb), and the adjective צדיק (derived from the abstract) when signifying a retributive justice of God."[143] Because it is from the *hiphil* stem of the verb צדק, which often signifies vindication (cf. 1 Kgs 8:32),[144] צדקה denotes a judicial meaning in the Old Testament.[145]

---

141. Weinfeld, *Social Justice in Ancient Israel and in the Ancient Near East*, 34.

142. Cf. Seifrid, "Righteousness Language in the Hebrew Scripture and Early Judaism," 428; Ho, *Ṣedeq and Ṣedaqah in the Hebrew Bible*; Scullion, "Righteousness: Old Testament," 726; Weinfeld, *Social Justice in Ancient Israel and in the Ancient Near East*, 34. Scholars have a variety of definitions for righteousness. See Scullion, "Righteousness: Old Testament," 726.

143. Seifrid, "Righteousness Language," 428.

144. Seifrid, "Righteousness Language," 429.

145. Whybray, *Thanksgiving for a Liberated Prophet*, 67.

The righteousness of the Davidic king's execution of God's judgment corresponds to the righteousness of God's judgment as the righteous judge because God judges with righteousness (Pss 9:8; 35:24; 36:6; 50:6; 96:13; 98:9). The adjective צַדִּיק appears in contexts of judgment. The Psalms demonstrate God as the righteous (צַדִּיק) judge who punishes the wicked (Pss 7:9, 11; 11:7). Mark Seifrid comments, "The concentration of the adjective צדיק in these examples is highly instructive, particularly in light of the judgment that צדקה generally refers to a concrete act or thing and may often represent a nominalization of the verb."[146] God establishes the Davidic king's throne (Ps 45:7) and anoints him to kingship (45:8). This is closely linked to the Davidic king's love of righteousness (45:8). God grants justice and righteousness to the Davidic king. The Psalter reads, "Give the king your justice (מִשְׁפָּטֶיךָ), O God, and your righteousness (צִדְקָתְךָ) to the royal son!" (72:1). He will judge his people with the righteousness imparted from God (72:1–2). The Davidic king's judgment represents the Lord's justice and righteousness (89:3–14).

The Davidic king in the Psalms is the righteous judge, just as God is the righteous judge who judges the wicked with justice and righteousness. The righteousness of God is bestowed upon the Davidic king in Psalm 72, where the Davidic king is responsible for the poor. God's righteousness is sought for the righteous and oppressed. The king petitions for God's righteousness, so that he may render righteous judgment for the people.[147] This is seen in Psalm 72, "where the bestowal of God's righteousness upon the king results in justice for the poor."[148] The Davidic king's righteousness is manifest, when he does the right thing for the poor and defends his people from oppressors. The king must have "a sense of justice with which to justly judge the people and the poor."[149] Unbiased righteousness and justice are characteristics of Yahweh and of the Davidic king and "requirements of divine justice and royal rule (Ps 72)."[150] Righteousness given to the king can make him "vindicate the afflicted, save the children of the needy, and crush the oppressor" (72:1). The Psalter says that "May he judge (יָדִין) your people with righteousness (בְּצֶדֶק), and your poor with justice (בְמִשְׁפָּט)" (72:2). Righteousness and justice result in the judgment through the Davidic king over nations. The term "*equity*" in the judgment of God is utilized in the enthronement of God (98:9), who judges the nations with "equity" (בְּמֵישָׁרִים).

146. Seifrid, "Righteousness Language," 429.
147. Seifrid, "Righteousness Language," 429.
148. Jipp, *Christ Is King*, 228.
149. Weinfeld, *Social Justice in Ancient Israel and in the Ancient Near East*, 27.
150. Watts, *Isaiah 1–33*, 172.

The righteous (צַדִּיק) Davidic Messiah, who is expected to execute judgment with righteousness, is characterized as clearly impartial. As a descriptor of the Davidic king, the adjective "righteous" (צַדִּיק; Isa 53:11; Jer 23:5; 33:15) shows the Davidic Messiah as the righteous judge who follows righteous Yahweh.[151] Furthermore, the enactment of righteousness for the righteous entails the judgment of the wicked (9:22–36).[152] The righteousness of the judge would be trying the case justly. The feminine צדקה for a vindication of God's retributive characteristics is employed in significant messianic texts in the Prophets (Isa 9:7; 54:17; Jer 23:5; 33:15), in which the Davidic Messiah is described as having the role of the righteous judge. Thompson notes,

> Both terms [justice and righteousness] have a background in the covenant law, *mispat* having particular reference to the covenant laws and statutes which it was the duty of judges and kings to administer, and *sedaqa* having to do with what was right and according to the norm. In meaning they often overlap. The *sadiq* in Israel was the man who did what was right according to the norms and standards of Yahweh. The king, and indeed the whole nation, were required always to act in justice and in fairness, giving consideration to all the facts (cf. ideal king in Isa 11:3b–5).[153]

Isaiah 11:4 focuses on the poor and the oppressed because "they are the ones most likely to suffer injustice in the Israelite judicial system."[154] The theme in these messianic texts is "unbiased justice and rule, which are characteristics that belong to YHWH and should also belong to the king."[155] With knowledge from the empowering of the Spirit on the Davidic Messiah, he is able to judge with "equity" (מִישׁוֹר; Isa 11:3–4).

In addition, the Davidic Messiah's just judgment saves God's people, especially the poor and the afflicted. The term "*to judge*" (שפט) with "*equity*" (מִישׁוֹר) describes the saving of the poor and the afflicted through impartial judgment. Weinfeld explains,

---

151. The righteousness of God is identified with an attribute of God, and "as the act in which that attribute is exercised." Ropes, "'Righteousness' and 'the Righteousness of God' in the Old Testament and in St. Paul," 218–19. However, Eichrodt believes that the righteousness of God as an attribute "intrudes conceptions quite foreign to the Hebrew mind, and for which there is no basis in the naïvely realistic thinking of the Israelite." Eichrodt, *Theology of the Old Testament*, 1:240.

152. Jipp, *Christ Is King*, 225.

153. Thompson, *The Book of Jeremiah*, 473–74.

154. Roberts, *First Isaiah*, 179.

155. Watts, *Isaiah 1–33*, 210.

A similar picture of the ideal king is found in Psalm 45, which describes the king who rides upon the cause of truth and meekness and righteousness (v. 4): "Your throne, like God's, is forever and ever; a scepter of equity (מִישׁר) is the scepter of your kingdom. You love righteousness and hate evil" (vv. 7–8). Just as we read in Isaiah 11 of one who arbitrates with equity, smites the land with the scepter of his mouth, and slays the wicked with the breath of his lips, so we find in Psalm 45: "the scepter of equity" (שׁבט מישׁור) in conjunction with the love of righteousness and the hating of evil.[156]

The Davidic Messiah's just judgment is executed for the weakest in society, and they are to be delivered from oppressors. With his just judgment, the Davidic Messiah can "smite" and "slay" the wicked, who exploit and abuse the poor and meek (Isa 11:4).[157] According to Weinfeld,

> Isaiah's prophecy of a stock from the stem of Jesse who will establish an ideal government is also characterized by descriptions of "justice and righteousness." Both David, the founder of the dynasty, and his ideal descendant judge the poor with righteousness (שָׁפַט בְּצֶדֶק דַּלִּים) and arbitrate with equity for the meek of the land (Isa 11:3) and, in keeping with *misarum* typology champion the righteous and destroy the wicked upon ascending the throne.[158]

In other words, the Davidic Messiah will "smite" (נכה) and "slay" (מות) the wicked "by the judicial decision issuing like a sword from his mouth and lips."[159] The salvation of his people from their wicked enemies originates from the Davidic Messiah's just judgment.

Moreover, the unjust judgment from Israelite kings is not characterized by righteousness (Isa 59:4; Ezek 18:19–21; Mic 3:9–12), and it results in divine wrath and death due to the king's injustice (Isa 59:14–18; Ezek 18:4, 19–21; Mic 3:12; Zech 7:8–14; cf. LXX Ps 81:8). The coming Davidic Messiah will embody God's righteousness in opposition to the lack of justice on the part of Israel's kings.[160] The demand for just judgment is required for the Davidic Messiah in Jeremiah, as well. Because equity in judgment for

---

156. Weinfeld, *Social Justice in Ancient Israel and in the Ancient Near East*, 62–63.

157. Brueggemann, *Isaiah 1–39*, 101. Weinfeld suggests that a similarity of the ideal king is found in Ps 45. "Just as we read in Isaiah 11 of one who arbitrates with equity, smites the land (אֶרֶץ) with the scepter of his mouth, and slays the wicked with the breath of his lips, so we find in Psalm 45: 'the scepter of equity' in conjunction with the love of righteousness and the hating of evil." Weinfeld, *Social Justice in Ancient Israel and in the Ancient Near East*, 62–63.

158. Weinfeld, *Social Justice in Ancient Israel and in the Ancient Near East*, 62.

159. Roberts, *First Isaiah*, 180.

160. Jipp, *Christ Is King*, 223.

the needy against the oppressors should have been executed in the judgment exercised by the Israelite kings, Jeremiah prominently emphasizes righteousness and justice in his denunciation of Jehoiakim, who does not deliver the oppressed from the oppressor, in Jeremiah 21:12 and 22:3.[161] The branch in Jeremiah is called "Yahweh our righteousness" (יְהוָה צִדְקֵנוּ), which is "a play on the name of the final king of Judah, Zedekiah."[162] The branch (צמח) is "the fulfillment of the prophecy in Jeremiah, by Zechariah, and as YHWH's signet ring by Haggai."[163] The righteous branch is identified as the descendent of David who will rule over Israel.[164] Zerubbabel, who is prefigured as the Davidic Messiah, acts as the Davidic branch in Zechariah.[165] Zerubbabel is a righteous (צַדִּיק) one, who judges righteously. The coming king of Zechariah would make the nations peaceful (9:9–10).[166]

Covenantal Faithfulness or Just Righteousness in God's Judgment

A frequent objection to any such view of God's righteousness as his judging righteousness is that God's righteousness is his covenantal faithfulness. Righteousness, which implies relationship, is deeply grounded in the covenant concept. The righteousness of God can mean God's covenantal faithfulness (Isa 41:2, 10; 42:6; 45:8; 51:5; Jer 50:7).[167] The righteousness of God is executed on the basis of the covenantal faithfulness and the covenantal promises. Schrenk states, "God's righteousness as his judicial reign means that in covenant faithfulness to his people he vindicates and saves them."[168] The restoration of Israel results in the blessings of the nations, which is promised in God's covenant with Abraham. Consequently, the overcoming of exile is the final great renewal of the covenant, which is the blessing to the nations that results from the vindication of Israel.[169]

The covenant, in addition, is described as cosmic because God is the Creator of the whole world, and he is "responsible for putting that world to rights in the end."[170] The righteousness of God toward all creation—which

---

161. Thompson, *The Book of Jeremiah*, 473; Houston, *Contending for Justice*, 135.
162. Boda, *The Book of Zechariah*, 254.
163. Collins, "Messianism and Exegetical Tradition," 131.
164. See Laato, *A Star Is Rising*, 201; Rose, *Zemah and Zerubbabel*, 178.
165. Boda, "Figuring the Future," 55.
166. Blenkinsopp, *David Remembered*, 71–103.
167. Schrenk, "δικαιοσύνη," in *TDNT*, 2:195–96.
168. Schrenk, "δικαιοσύνη," in *TDNT*, 2:195–96.
169. Wright, *The Climax of the Covenant*, 250.
170. Wright, *Paul and the Faithfulness of God*, 801.

is emphasized by Ernst Käsemann, Peter Stuhlmacher, and Christian Muller—focuses on God's acts to restore the world in the saving work of the Messiah.[171] God, the Creator, is the righteous judge for the whole of creation, too.[172] God's covenantal faithfulness to all his creation is praised in the Psalms and the Prophets.[173] The righteousness of God is his power "imparted to all of creation so as to include all Gentiles and Jews as objects of salvation."[174] God's righteousness—his faithfulness that was promised to Abraham—will affect a cosmic salvation promised as a new creation, the restored Eden (Isa 46:12–13; 51:1–6).[175] Hence, the role of the Davidic Messiah is closely linked to God's covenantal faithfulness in this view. The Messiah, who is the Redeemer from the Davidic line (Isa 2:3; 59:20; Mic 4:2), will fulfill God's righteousness in the world and in his covenantal promises for his people.

However, although it is currently quite common for scholars to interpret "God's righteousness" as his "covenant-faithfulness" toward Israel, based on a relational interpretation of "righteousness," the term "righteousness" does not have the same meaning as covenantal faithfulness. "Righteousness" cannot be reduced to the concept of a "proper relation" because the usage of "righteousness" clearly involves the concept of a "norm."[176] Seifrid asserts,

> Thirdly, the claim that "righteousness" in the Hebrew Scriptures is a Verhältnisbegriff (relational concept) or involves merely Gemeinschaftstreue (fidelity to a relation) is problematic in so far as it obscures the idea of normativity associated with the word-group. If all that is intended by such designations is to underscore the concreteness or immediacy of the biblical usage

---

171. Käsemann, "'The Righteousness of God' in Paul," 168–82; Stuhlmacher, *Gerechtigkeit Gottes bei Paulus*; Muller, *Gottes Gerechtigkeit und Gottes Volk*.

172. Wright, *Paul and the Faithfulness of God*, 801.

173. Wright, *Paul and the Faithfulness of God*, 801.

174. About God's righteousness as his faithfulness to creation, see Käsemann, "'The Righteousness of God' in Paul," 178–80; Stuhlmacher, *Revisiting Paul's Doctrine of Justification*, 73; Donaldson, *Paul and the Gentiles*, 95–96.

175. Wright, *Paul and the Faithfulness of God*, 803–4.

176. The relational concept of צדק was maintained by Hermann Cremer and has had a strong influence on scholars. Cremer, *Biblisch-theologisches Wörterbuch der neutestamentlichen Gräcität*, 273–75; Cremer, *Die paulinische Rechtfertigungslehre im Zusammenhange ihrer geschichtlichen Voraussetzungen*, 34. His argument was applied in the Kittel's *TWNT*. von Rad proposes, "ancient Israel did not in fact measure a line of conduct or an act by an ideal norm, but by the specific relationship in which the partner had at the time to prove himself true." von Rad, *Old Testament Theology*, 1:371; Schrenk, "δικαιοσύνη," in *TDNT*, 2:195. See Seifrid, "Righteousness Language," 415–19.

in connection with personal relations, they are valid, even if imprecise. But the application of righteousness terminology to various inanimate objects, its association with "uprightness" and "truth," its connection with retribution in forensic settings, and its relation to parallel conceptions of "righteousness" in other cultures in the Ancient Near East all render dubious any attempt to dissociate the terminology from the concept of a norm.[177]

In addition, the righteousness of God operates in relation to the covenantal relationship, but it is not covenantal faithfulness itself. "Covenant" (ברית) and צדק-terminology rarely "appear in any proximity to one another, despite their considerable frequency in the Hebrew Scriptures."[178] Douglas Moo also rightly says,

> God's covenant commitment, these passages suggest, is a commitment to do what is "right" with reference to that covenant. When Israel's enemies are in view, or when Israel breaks the terms of the covenant, God's righteousness naturally takes on a negative, judgmental aspect (cf. Isa. 5:16; 10:22).[179]

Instead, faithfulness in covenantal relationship is denoted with the term חסד or אמונה. The covenantal relation requires love (חסד) and faithfulness (אמונה).[180] God is faithful in covenantal relationship. He is the one "who has not forsaken his steadfast love (חסדו) and his faithfulness (אמתו) toward my master" (Gen 24:27). His ways are "steadfast love (חסד) and faithfulness (אמת), for those who keep his covenant and his testimonies" (Ps 25:10). Because of his steadfast love (חסד) and faithfulness (אמונה), God's covenant will stand firm (Ps 89:28, 33, 34). Micah reads, "You will show faithfulness (אמת) to Jacob and steadfast love (חסד) to Abraham, as you have sworn to our fathers from the days of old" (Mic 7:20).

Righteousness in the Davidic Messiah's Execution of God's Judgment

The purpose of God's judgment through the Davidic Messiah is his impartial righteousness toward sinners. Righteousness (צדק) is found to be in close relation with שפט, instead of with ברית.[181] The relation interpretation

---

177. Seifrid, *Christ, Our Righteousness*, 41.
178. Seifrid, "Righteousness Language," 423.
179. Moo, *The Epistle to the Romans*, 83.
180. Seifrid, "Righteousness Language," 424.
181. Seifrid, "Righteousness Language," 425.

for righteousness cannot account for the retributive connotations of צדק. The righteousness language often expresses condemnation in judgment.[182] The righteousness in God's judgment is presented as God acts punitively and retributively.[183]

As noted above, righteousness is executed in the Davidic administration of justice and righteousness (2 Sam 8:15). Second Samuel 8:15 is located at the climax of David's reign (2 Sam 7 and 8).[184] The previous passage, which is 2 Samuel 8:11–14, sums up "the gradual expansion of the Davidic kingdom until it reached its utmost limits."[185] He defeats all the enemies of God's people (2 Sam 8:1–14), and David's reign can be recognized as the summit. It is necessary to understand the administration of justice and righteousness in a judicial meaning. Davidic administration of justice and righteousness (עשה משפט וצדקה) is continually executed in the Davidic king's judgment setting. Additionally, the righteousness language in this verse is צדקה, which is a concrete vindication judgment or righteous act, as noted above.

The administration of justice and righteousness in 2 Samuel 8:15 is a testimony that was always particularly significant to the Prophets.[186] The Davidic Messiah will establish the Davidic kingdom "with justice and with righteousness" (בְּמִשְׁפָּט וּבִצְדָקָה; Isa 9:6). He shall judge with righteousness (וְשָׁפַט בְּצֶדֶק; Isa 11:4). In Jeremiah 23:5, the Davidic Messiah will execute justice and righteousness (וְעָשָׂה מִשְׁפָּט וּצְדָקָה). Because social justice is broken down in Judah, justice and righteousness are expected as characteristics of the Davidic Messiah's reign.[187] As mentioned above, the Davidic Messiah will judge Israel and Judah in justice and righteousness (Jer 23:1–8), and he is an antitype of the wicked Jehoiakim. Jack R. Lundbom writes,

> The fact that Jehoiakim is scored by Jeremiah for not doing justice and righteousness as his father did (22:13–17) may indicate that he did not bother to sit as judge in the gate, as he should have. The present admonition to "execute justice" is doubtless spoken to Jehoiakim and his royal house.[188]

---

182. Seifrid, "Righteousness Language," 424.
183. Seifrid, "Paul's Use of Righteousness Language," 44.
184. Anderson, *2 Samuel*, 134.
185. Anderson, *2 Samuel*, 134.
186. Hertzberg, *I & II Samuel*, 293.
187. Lundbom, *Jeremiah*, 112.
188. Lundbom, *Jeremiah*, 112.

Equity in judgment will be executed in the judgment by the Davidic Messiah in opposition to Jehoiakim, in Jeremiah 21:12 and 22:3. A key activity of this restored royal figure is identified in both Jeremiah 23:6 and 33:15 as enacting justice and righteousness in the land.[189]

In the messianic texts in the LXX, the righteousness language is shown as judging righteousness in the judgment of the Davidic Messiah. David is described as "having judging righteousness in executing judgment over his people" (καὶ ἦν Δαυιδ ποιῶν κρίμα καὶ δικαιοσύνην ἐπὶ πάντα τὸν λαὸν αὐτοῦ; 2 Sam 8:15), which is "doing justice and righteousness" in MT. The idealized Davidic king is clearly characterized by his righteousness "to judge your people in righteousness and your poor people in judgment" (κρίνειν τὸν λαόν σου ἐν δικαιοσύνῃ καὶ τοὺς πτωχούς σου ἐν κρίσει; LXX Ps 71:2). Furthermore, the Davidic Messiah in the Prophets is portrayed as possessing righteousness in his execution of judgment (ποιήσει κρίμα καὶ δικαιοσύνην ἐπὶ τῆς γῆς; Jer 23:5; cf. Jer 22:3, 15).

God's salvation through righteousness

In addition, equity in the execution of God's righteous judgment through the Davidic Messiah results in salvation, especially in freedom from exile. The Davidic king in Psalms 1 and 2 is a model for the righteous one (Pss 1:5–6; 2:7–8, 12), who is identified with the deliverer of God's people, and through him God reveals his righteousness for the salvation of the people.[190] Based on holy war, described as crushing and striking down (89:23), God's righteousness (89:13–14) entails the salvation from enemies (89:38–48) through the Davidic king, the anointed one and the first-born (89:27). He is empowered by God (89:20–21, 26–27) because righteousness and justice are the foundation of his throne (89:14), and his righteousness is power to save (97:10–13; 98:1–3) and provision for just judgment (96:10–13; 98:9).

The righteousness in God's judgment through the Davidic king reflects the characteristics of God's righteousness. God's judging righteousness includes salvation for his people, but God's righteousness cannot be weakened as the concept of "salvation of God."[191] God exercises his salvation in the context of a legal dispute or contention. "God works salvation for his people, he establishes justice for them (and for himself) over against their enemies

---

189. Consequently, the employment of *saddiq/sedaqah* with *semah* ("sprout") in Jer 23:5; 33:15 is considered as the king's role in justice. See Rose, *Zemah and Zerubbabel*, 110–14.

190. Jipp, *Christ Is King*, 226.

191. Seifrid, *Christ, Our Righteousness*, 43.

and his."[192] As a result, God's righteousness is the basis of his saving activity in the covenant relationship with his people.[193]

While the Davidic Messiah is expected to deliver God's people,[194] the notion of God's doing the saving is included by the prophets (Isa 46:13; 50:5–8; Mic 7:9) in the righteousness of God because God's vindication in his righteousness results in the deliverance of his people.[195] The execution of righteousness by the Davidic Messiah means his accomplishment of salvation for God's people. The Davidic Messiah's establishing and upholding his kingdom "with justice and righteousness" (Isa 9:7) bring about the salvation of his people through judgment over violent oppressors (9:4–6). The Davidic Messiah "enacts retribution against the violent oppressors and enacts justice for the liberation of the oppressed."[196] Established on justice and righteousness (9:7), the Davidic Messiah's throne will remedy injustices in the center of God's kingdom.[197] Moreover, the Davidic Messiah was considered "a bringer of salvation," who is the righteous representative of the righteous God, so the righteousness and justice achieved by the Davidic king provide salvation for his people (9:4–7).[198]

From God's judgment through the Davidic Messiah against the oppressor and the wicked, the oppressed will have God's liberation (Isa 11:1–5). While "judging" surely includes legal decisions, it has the meaning of "delivering and saving those whose lives and well-being are threatened."[199] Joshua Jipp explains, "The king's execution of justice for his people often takes the form of administering equitable verdicts for the oppressed, saving and defending his people from their enemies, and securing their protection and freedom."[200] Therefore, because God establishes justice and brings retribution to the oppressors, the messianic hope was that God promised the Davidic Messiah, who would do justice and righteousness and deliver the poor from the power of the oppressors.[201]

---

192. Seifrid, *Christ, Our Righteousness*, 43.

193. Moo, *Romans*, 82.

194. Cummins, "Divine Life and Corporate Christology," 193.

195. Cummins, "Divine Life and Corporate Christology," 193.

196. Jipp, *Christ Is King*, 224.

197. Kaiser, *Isaiah 1–12*, 214.

198. LXX Isaiah 9:6 says, "κατορθῶσαι αὐτὴν καὶ ἀντιλαβέσθαι αὐτῆς ἐν δικαιοσύνῃ καὶ ἐν κρίματι." Jipp, *Christ Is King*, 224.

199. Leclerc, *Yahweh Is Exalted in Justice*, 69.

200. Jipp, *Christ Is King*, 222. See Weinfeld, *Social Justice in Ancient Israel and in the Ancient Near East*, 189–90.

201. Seifrid, *Christ, Our Righteousness*, 41; Seifrid, "Righteousness Language," 428.

Restoration of creation through righteousness

Moreover, God's righteousness through the Messiah is applicable to the dimension of God's creation. While God establishes what is right in terms of the covenant with his creation, the righteousness of God is a more basic concept than is covenantal relationship. The righteousness of God "clearly includes the concept of a 'norm,' an order within the world, which God graciously acts (again and again) to restore."[202] The restoration of created order is based on the righteousness of God, who does what is right.

In Psalms, the rule of the Davidic king based on judgment results in the restoration of God's created order after victory over the evil. The Davidic king's throne is the counterpart of God's throne, so that he was enthroned by God with his conquering of chaos (Ps 45:7).[203] After the conquest of the evil forces of chaos, the hatred of wickedness will contribute to the righteous rule of order.[204] Psalm 72, which is "an accession or coronation psalm,"[205] is a prayer for the king with the judicial authority (72:2) that promises the peace of fertility (72:7–17).[206] The rule of the righteous Davidic king confirms fertility and prosperity in the fields as created order (Ps 72:16; cf. v. 3; Isa 25:6–9; Joel 2:24). Lucass writes,

> Further parallels are seen in Ps 89, which deals with Yahweh's choice of David as his Anointed: just as Yahweh is first among the Gods (vv. 6–7), so David is first among the kings of the earth (v. 27); just as Yahweh ruled the sea (v. 9), so David will rule the sea (v. 25); just as Yahweh scattered his enemies (v. 10), so David's enemies will be scattered (vv. 22–23) suggesting that David now stands in Yahweh's place, administering his justice and maintaining (and re-creating) the conditions which Yahweh brought about at creation.[207]

The Davidic Messiah, who is anointed, is expected to bring justice to people and peace to all the creation of God (Isa 11:1–10).[208] He is entrusted with the responsibility of procuring righteousness, and this is derivative "from God, the divine king, who has determined to secure the good and

---

202. Seifrid, *Christ, Our Righteousness*, 41.
203. Gray, *The Legacy of Canaan*, 287; Craigie and Tate, *Psalms 1–50*, 339.
204. Craigie and Tate, *Psalms 1–50*, 339.
205. Gillingham, "The Messiah in the Psalms," 223.
206. Kraus, *Psalms 60–150*, 77.
207. Lucass, *The Concept of the Messiah in the Scriptures of Judaism and Christianity*, 86.
208. Watts, *Isaiah 1–33*, 212.

beneficial order of creation."[209] The endowment of the Spirit on the Davidic Messiah will transform the enmity among creatures, which entails the restoration of the created order in Isaiah 11:6–9.[210] Justice will dwell in the wilderness, and righteousness will abide in the fruitful field (Isa 32:16). Yahweh's work, through the Davidic Messiah, "designates simultaneously and indistinguishably the creative and the historical action of Yahweh"; so then "history is understood as the implementation of creation and the actualization of the order of creation."[211] Initiated by the anointing of God's Spirit after devastation (cf. Isa 11:1), the Davidic Messiah will make the peace produced through justice and righteousness (Isa 32:1).[212] Isaiah "takes up and reasserts the claims made in Isaiah 28:12 and 30:15 that the true way to security, peace, and well-being is maintaining justice and righteousness for others."[213] The justice and righteousness of the Davidic Messiah will reestablish the created order (e.g., Pss 85:4–13; 98:1–9; Isa 45:8, 24).[214]

Consequently, the Davidic Messiah is the righteous one who administers righteousness and justice. The Davidic Messiah's judgment in righteousness has been revealed as impartial. The impartial judgment through the Davidic Messiah, which is from an empowered knowledge of God, entails saving activity for God's people and the restoration of the created order. The faithfulness language in the covenant relationship between God and his people, or the whole creation, is closely related to the righteousness in God's judgment through the Davidic Messiah. However, it is not the same as this righteousness. Although God is faithful in his covenant relationship and in the salvation of his people, and the restoration of creation shows God's faithfulness, it is not the righteousness of God itself. In addition, the purpose of God's judgment through the Davidic Messiah is his righteousness, rather than covenantal faithfulness.

JUSTIFICATION THROUGH THE DAVIDIC MESSIAH IN ISAIAH 53

The Suffering Servant in Isaiah 53 possesses, in himself, the characteristics of the Davidic Messiah. And his role is that of the executor of God's judgment

---

209. Seifrid, "Righteousness Language," 426.

210. Smith, *Isaiah 1–39*, 273–74.

211. Schmid, "Creation, Righteousness, and Salvation," 108.

212. LXX Isaiah 32:1 says, "βασιλεὺς δίκαιος βασιλεύσει, καὶ ἄρχοντες μετὰ κρίσεως ἄρξουσιν."

213. Roberts, *First Isaiah*, 417.

214. Seifrid, "Righteousness, Justice, and Justification," 741.

in Isaiah 53. The righteous judgment of God's judgment is accomplished in the Suffering Messiah. New Testament scholars' interpretation of the Suffering Servant in Isaiah 53 as the Messiah's faithfulness for God's covenantal relationship fails to take adequate account of the execution-of-judgment aspect of righteousness. The righteousness language in the execution of God's judgment through the Davidic Messiah in Isaiah 53 is unfamiliar with covenantal faithfulness. He is the "righteous" (צַדִּיק) servant, whose role is justifying God's people. He will "make many to be accounted righteous" (Isa 53:11). This corresponds to the righteous Messiah—who executes God's judgment—instead of to the faithful Messiah—who is assumed to be faithful on the basis of translating the adjective "righteous" as "faithful."

Identity of the Suffering Servant: The Davidic Messiah

The Suffering Servant in Isaiah has characteristics that are described above as features of the Davidic Messiah. There have been debates, though, concerning the identity of the servant in Isaiah 53,[215] whether he represents Israel,[216] the prophet himself,[217] Moses,[218] or the Davidic king.[219] The Suffering Servant in Isaiah 53 can be understood as the Davidic Messiah because the Davidic Messiah can include characteristics of Moses, and the feature of the royal figure in Isaiah is more suitable to the Davidic king. The Servant is linked to the Davidic house because the royal figure is mentioned in Isaiah

---

215. See North, *The Suffering Servant in Deutero-Isaiah*, 3-4; Lindblom, *The Servant Songs in Deutero-Isaiah*, 46; Westermann, *Isaiah 40–66*, 93; Clines, *I, He, We, and They*, 25-27; Roth, "The Anonymity of the Suffering Servant," 171-79; Hugenberger, "The Servant of the Lord in the 'Servant Songs' of Isaiah: A Second Moses Figure," 105-40.

216. See Collins, *The Scepter and Star*, 28; Gray, *The Biblical Doctrine of the Reign of God*, 180; Clifford, *Fair Spoken and Persuading*, 175-81; Knight, *Servant Theology*, 171; Hägglund, *Isaiah 53 in the Light of Homecoming after Exile*; Eissfeldt, "The Promise of Grace to David in Isaiah 55:1-5," 196-207; North, *The Second Isaiah*, 256-58; Westermann, *Isaiah 40-66*.

217. See Hengstenberg, *Christology of the Old Testament and a Commentary on the Messianic Predictions*, 234.

218. See Miller, "Moses My Servant: The Deuteronomic Portrait of Moses," 251-53; Coats, *The Moses Tradition*, 133-41, 182-89; Allison Jr., *The New Moses*, 68; Hafemann, *Paul, Moses, and the History of Israel*; Phillips, "The Servant: Symbol of Divine Powerlessness," 370-74; Hugenberger, "The Servant of the Lord," 119; Baltzer, *Deutero-Isaiah*, 18-22.

219. Blenkinsopp, *Isaiah 40-55*, 349-57; Block, "My Servant David," 43-49; Schultz, "The King in the Book of Isaiah," 141-65; Goldingay, *A Critical and Exegetical Commentary on Isaiah 40-55*, 2:289.

9:7, 11:1, and 55:3. The royal figure is described as possessing the Spirit of the Lord as does the Servant (Isa 11:2; 42:1).[220] Lucass remarks,

> In Isa 11:1, the future hope of Israel will be a "shoot from the stump of Jesse and a branch out of his roots." The term "branch" also features in Isa 4:2, as well as in Jer. 23:5 and Jer. 33:14–15, where again it is expressly connected with the Davidic monarchy. In Zech. 3:8 the "Branch" is connected not only with the title "servant," but also the high priest. The term "Branch" in this passage is also understood as a messianic designation in later Rabbinic Judaism.... In Isaiah 53:2 it is said of the Servant that "he grew up before him like a young plant, and like a root out of dry ground."[221]

The Servant is compared to a young "shoot" (יוֹנֵק) and a "root" (שֹׁרֶשׁ), as is the Davidic Messiah in 11:1–10.[222] This image "should be borne in mind here that in Isaiah to talk about 'the root of Jesse' means first that the tree has been hewn down, that the Davidic dynasty has come to an end."[223] The accomplishment of the promise must start from the root. So, the plant imagery for the individual Servant is used for the Davidic Messiah, as well.[224]

Imparted knowledge for justification

The Servant in Isaiah 53 can be realized as the Davidic royal figure with these clues, and that he is the Davidic Messiah explains his anointing.[225] The Davidic Messiah is characterized by knowledge imparted by God, which is a characteristic of the agent of God's judgment, as noted above. In the fourth servant song, the Servant "shall act wisely" (יַשְׂכִּיל; Isa 52:13), so that he will be the agent of God's judgment. The wisdom of the Davidic Messiah will lead to his exaltation (52:13).[226] Jan. L. Koole asserts similarities between

---

220. He is the "Anointed Conqueror," in Isa 59:21; 61:1. Moreover, Isa 52:14 is read as in 1QIsa משחתי ('I anointed'). See Schultz, "The King in the Book of Isaiah," 155.

221. Lucass, *The Concept of the Messiah in the Scriptures of Judaism and Christianity*, 99–100.

222. Isa 4:2; Jer 23:5; Zech 3:8; 6:12. Baltzer, *Deutero-Isaiah*, 402.

223. Baltzer, *Deutero-Isaiah*, 402.

224. Stromberg, "The 'Root of Jesse' in Isaiah 11:10: Postexilic Judah or Postexilic Davidic King?," 655–69.

225. Later, in Isa 61:1–3, the Messiah is a kingly figure, who has the Spirit of God on him (cf. 11:1–2; 42:1) and will bring good news and justice to the needy (see 11:4; 42:1–4, 7; 49:9–10).

226. Goldingay, *Isaiah 40–55*, 2:289. LXX Isaiah 53:12 reads, "Ἰδοὺ συνήσει ὁ παῖς μου καὶ ὑψωθήσεται καὶ δοξασθήσεται σφόδρα."

David and the Servant, with the term *"shall succeed"* (1 Sam 18:5-14; Isa 52:13, יַשְׂכִּיל).²²⁷ The *hiphil* of שׂכל (52:13) is employed as well to denote the Davidic Messiah "in Jer 23:5 f., where שׂכל parallels the making of 'justice and righteousness' in the world."²²⁸ This verb, "act wisely," additionally can be rendered as "succeed, be successful, or have good fortune."²²⁹ Also, Goldingay says,

> Indeed, most occurrences of this verb which may be translated "succeed" appear in contexts which suggest having insight so that this is also a plausible rendering there. The verb refers to knowing what you are doing. The servant, then, will demonstrate such wisdom, and this will lead to his exaltation (v. 13b). The closing description of the servant's exaltation in 53:11-12 will speak of his knowledge and his success, again using terms which recall a king like David.²³⁰

This term שׂכל is "said to have come from God or his Spirit (cf. Neh 9:20; 1 Chr 28:19; Ps 32:8; Dan 9:22), just as 'perception' in general is in the most varied ways dependent on God, or is related to him."²³¹ Yahweh will anoint the Davidic descendant in Isaiah 40–55 as in Psalms 2 and 89, which characterize "Kingship and the role of God's anointed, comprising one of the twin pillars in the official theologumenon of Judah."²³² Concerning Isaiah 52:14, Goldingay comments, "More literally the verse reads 'just as many were appalled. . . . so his appearance [is/will be] an anointing beyond that of a human being.'"²³³ The anointing is through the endowment of the Spirit of the Lord, which is a feature of the Davidic Messiah in Psalms.²³⁴ Isaiah shows the dazzled attention of the nations and kings to the Servant as

---

227. Koole, *Isaiah III*, 2:251.

228. Koole, *Isaiah III*, 2:264. Koole says, "The Davidic king shall reign as king and deal wisely (וְהִשְׂכִּיל), and shall execute justice and righteousness in the land, which is related to the Messiah in Jeremiah 23:5." He additionally writes, "The Servant will in fact restore justice in the world, 42:4. In the way the description of the Servant's success links up with that of Israel's great leaders, Joshua (Josh 1:7 f.), David (1 Sam 18:5, 13), Solomon (1 Kgs 2:3), Hezekiah (2 Kgs 18:7), where שׂכל hiphil is used alongside צלח and explained by the fact that God was 'with' them; it is also related to the portrayal of the Messiah in Jer 23:5 f., where שׂכל hiphil is parallel with 'to execute justice and righteousness' (עָשָׂה מִשְׁפָּט וּצְדָקָה) in the world; for משפט, cf. 42:4 (and 49:4; 50:8) and for צדק, 53:11." Koole, *Isaiah III*, 2:264.

229. Baltzer, *Deutero-Isaiah*, 394.

230. Goldingay, *Isaiah 40–55*, 2:289.

231. Baltzer, *Deutero-Isaiah*, 394.

232. Hanson, "The World of the Servant of the Lord in Isaiah 40–55," 15.

233. Goldingay, *Isaiah 40–55*, 2:291.

234. Wright, *Old Testament Ethics for the People of God*, 278.

in Psalms 2 and 89 (see Isa 52:15).²³⁵ With the knowledge that is given with God's Spirit, the Davidic Messiah in Isaiah 52:13–53:12 attains the role of agent of God's judgment.

The Agent of God's Judgment

The Davidic Messiah, who is the Suffering Servant, will fulfill the judgment of God, which is expected in the heavenly courtroom scene in Isaiah 40–55. In Isaiah 40:14, Yahweh will let him know (וַיְלַמְּדֵהוּ; *piel* of למד) a way of "justice" (מִשְׁפָּט; κρίσιν) and "understanding" (דַּעַת; σύνεσις). The judgment idea is significant—corresponding to the knowledge of the Servant in Isaiah 53. The phrase, "through his knowledge," is strongly stressed in 53:11.²³⁶ With the result of this knowledge, the Messiah makes "the many" justified.²³⁷ It is the climax of the judgment scene.²³⁸

Although the covenant relationship should not be overlooked in explaining the features of the Messiah in Isaiah 40–55, the features of a lawsuit between YHWH and YHWH's people are more evident.²³⁹ This theme is an extension of YHWH's heavenly courtroom of Isaiah 6:1–5. The theme of the return from "exile" does not have any significance here.²⁴⁰ Andrew Lincoln attests,

> In the context of exile in and return from Babylon the contests with the gods of the nations dominate, Israel's God serves as both judge and prosecutor, and the purpose of the contests is to show that although Babylon appears to control history, the real ruler is Israel's God with the immediate issue being whether or not YHWH is the cause of Cyrus' advent and Babylon's downfall.²⁴¹

---

235. Hanson, "The World of the Servant of the Lord in Isaiah 40–55," 16.

236. Baltzer, *Deutero-Isaiah*, 425.

237. The people of God, who are referred to by 'we/us/our' (40:8; 42:24; 47:4), believe the Word of the Lord (Isa 53:1). Goldingay, *Isaiah 40–55*, 2:296–67. The 'many' in 53:11 are the people of God, who are the 'we' of verses 1–10. Goldingay, *Isaiah 40–55*, 2:326.

238. Goldingay, *Isaiah 40–55*, 2:325.

239. Lincoln, "A Life of Jesus as Testimony: The Divine Courtroom and the Gospel of John," 149. In the LXX, the noun κρίσις 'judgment,' occurs in 40:27; 42:1, 3, 4; 49:4, 25; 50:8, 9; 51:4, 7; 53:8; 54:17, and the verb ריב, 'to judge,' appears in 49:25; 50:8; 51:22.

240. Childs, *Isaiah: A Commentary*, 295; Watts, *Isaiah 34–66*, 75.

241. Lincoln, "A Life of Jesus as Testimony," 150. Additionally Blenkinsopp writes, "There is no mention here of preparing a route for return from exile in Babylon. It is, rather, that processional way is to be prepared for the return of Yahweh to his people." Blenkinsopp, *Isaiah 40–55*, 181.

YHWH summons nations to the courtroom for conducting a trial, in which God's sovereignty over history is manifested.[242]

The judgment of the heavenly king that is manifested in the trial of the nations is over his people, too. The Lord invites his people, who are "Judeans in exile and those remaining in Jerusalem," to the courtroom and delivers an indictment for them.[243] He is "indeed the one who has brought about their plight as an expression of justified wrath at their disobedience (cf. 42:22-25)."[244] The indictment of YHWH, though, is not the last word in this courtroom scene. The salvation of his people is assured within the salvation oracles, which "ensure that indictment is not YHWH's last word."[245] The feature of the Servant is connected to the scene of God's courtroom, in which he judges over the nations and his people. Isaiah 42:1-4, the first song for the Servant, is spoken in the heavenly court.[246] The frame of the fourth song (52:13-15; 53:11b-12) is closely related to the first song in style and in speaker.[247]

In Isaiah 52:13-15, which is paralleled with 42:1, the Servant is "introduced with the mission to bring מִשְׁפָּט ('justice') to the nations."[248] In this verse, Yahweh himself designates "the office and reward of his Servant,"[249] who in Isaiah 40–55 would establish justice, which is the first thing of God's commandment in Isaiah 42:3.[250] While the Servant will faithfully bring justice (לֶאֱמֶת יוֹצִיא מִשְׁפָּט, εἰς ἀλήθειαν ἐξοίσει κρίσιν), the term *"faithfully"* is intertwined with the judgment language in the courtroom scene, as noted above. The office of the Servant reaches its goal exactly as in Isaiah 42:4: "He will not grow faint or be discouraged till he has established justice (מִשְׁפָּט) in the earth."[251] The courtroom scene is manifested in Isaiah 53, which is in

242. Childs, *Isaiah*, 317.

243. Lincoln, "A Life of Jesus as Testimony," 150.

244. Lincoln, "A Life of Jesus as Testimony," 150.

245. Lincoln, "A Life of Jesus as Testimony," 150.

246. H. G. Reventlow writes, "The first Song (42:1-4) is a divine proclamation, spoken in the heavenly court, in which the Servant is called to his office, whereas in 49:1-6 and 50:4-9 the prophet speaks on his own behalf. An observation which recently has gained more attention, however, is that the frame of the fourth Song (52:13-15; 53:11b-12) is in style and speaker closely connected with the first Song: In both texts it is Yahweh himself who outlines the office and reward of his Servant." Reventlow, "Basic Issues in the Interpretation of Isaiah 53," 25.

247. Reventlow, "Basic Issues in the Interpretation of Isaiah 53," 25.

248. Childs, *Isaiah*, 412.

249. Reventlow, "Basic Issues in the Interpretation of Isaiah 53," 25.

250. Wright, *Old Testament Ethics for the People of God*, 277; Schultz, "The King in the Book of Isaiah," 155.

251. Hermisson, "The Fourth Servant Song in the Context of Second Isaiah," 34.

accord with God's judgment in the heavenly courtroom in Isaiah 40–55.[252] There are terms of judgment after Yahweh places the guilty verdict on the Messiah. In Isaiah 53:8, "oppression" (עֹצֶר), which can be more accurately rendered as "restrained,"[253] suggests the Messiah's arrest and imprisonment.[254] Lincoln says, "The Servant is nevertheless confident that the courtroom is ultimately that of YHWH who will provide vindication. Though justice from humans is denied him (LXX 53:8), the Servant will be lifted and glorified (LXX 52:13) and the servant will be with a glory not from humans (LXX 52:14)."[255] The last verdict in this passage (Isa 53:11) is presented on the Servant in the Judgment scene, which is "יַצְדִּיק צַדִּיק עַבְדִּי לָרַבִּים" (my servant, the righteous one, shall make many righteous).[256] As noted above, the *hiphil* of צדק means "acquit, declare innocent" (Exod 23:7; Deut 25:1; 1 Kgs 8:32; 2 Chr 6:23; Prov 17:15; Isa 5:23) in a judicial sense. In its forensic meaning, it means "declare to be in the right" (in the context of Job's debate with his friends).[257] For this reason, the Servant can acquit them in the judicial sense before the divine justice.

The role of high priest: substitution for god's judgment

While the Servant in Isaiah 53 possesses the characteristics of the agent of God's judgment, he is particularly expected to bear and atone for sins to solve the problem of sins that bring about God's wrath and judgment. The Suffering Servant presents the solution for God's imminent judgment over God's people. Moreover, it should be considered that liberation (דרור) of the wicked people from exile requires forgiveness of the sins of God's people to execute just judgment. Liberation (דרור) serves as representation for "the redemption of the individual, and particularly for the forgiveness of sins."[258] Furthermore, his role is also that of priestly messiah, who has suffered (Isa 52:14; 53:3, 7). The Lord has laid on him the iniquity of us (53:6). Through

---

252. Concerning courtroom language in Isaiah 52:13–53:12, see Baltzer, *Deutero-Isaiah*, 402.

253. Smith, *Isaiah 40–66*, 453.

254. Smith, *Isaiah 40–66*, 453.

255. Lincoln, "A Life of Jesus as Testimony," 151.

256. Baltzer, *Deutero-Isaiah*, 424; Goldingay, *Isaiah 40–55*, 2:325.

257. Chisholm, "Forgiveness and Salvation in Isaiah 53," 358, 393; Hägglund, *Isaiah 53*, 74–77; Whybray, *Thanksgiving for a Liberated Prophet*, 68–69 suggest the meaning of "leading righteous" as in Dan 12:3.

258. Weinfeld, *Social Justice in Ancient Israel and in the Ancient Near East*, 210.

this priestly role, the Davidic Messiah bears God's judgment on him.[259] The Davidic Messiah will announce liberty and release, which is "the Messiah at work, bringing in his reign of justice and righteousness (11:3-5; cf. also 1:27)."[260] Isaiah 1:27 reads, "Zion shall be redeemed by justice, and those in her who repent, by righteousness (בצדקה)." God's justice and righteousness connote his vindication and salvation.[261]

The Servant bearing the sins of the many plays a substitutionary role,[262] and he is described as atoning sins and assuaging God's wrath.[263] It echoes the scapegoat ritual (Lev 16), in which one is sacrificed as an atonement offering (חַטָּאת).[264] The other carries iniquities of all, and it is "cut-off land."[265] It recalls the Davidic Messiah, who is the Suffering Servant, being cut off from the land of the living (53:8b).[266] Indeed, the term אָשָׁם ("guilt offering") is described as an atoning sacrifice for sin in Lev 4-5, 7.[267] God accepts the Servant as "a substitute for the sacrificial guilt offering."[268] It is widely regarded as the primary expiatory offering for voluntary or involuntary sin (Lev 5:1-26 [5:1-6:7]; 7:2; 14:24).[269] It is the sacrifice for the removal of guilt and liability for punishment.[270] The "atonement" is made by the priest (5:16, 18; 6:7). The juxtaposition of atonement and forgiveness constantly appears in the atonement passages, e.g., in Leviticus 4:20, 26, 31, 35; 5:6, 10, 13, 16, 18; 6:7.[271]

---

259. Schultz, "The King in the Book of Isaiah," 159.

260. Oswalt, *The Book of Isaiah*, 565.

261. Smith, *Isaiah 1-39*, 115; Childs, *Isaiah*, 22; Blenkinsopp, *Isaiah 1-39*, 187.

262. Spieckermann, "The Conception and Prehistory of the Idea of Vicarious Suffering in the Old Testament," 1-15; Hermission, "The Fourth Servant Song in the Context of Second Isaiah," 16-47; Williams, *Christ Died for Our Sins*, 35-73. Contra Whybray, *Thanksgiving for a Liberated Prophet*, 29-97.

263. Concerning the cultic idea in Isa 53, see Williams, *Christ Died for Our Sins*, 35-73.

264. Blenkinsopp, *Isaiah 40-55*, 351.

265. Blenkinsopp, *Isaiah 40-55*, 351.

266. Blenkinsopp, *Isaiah 40-55*, 351.

267. Blenkinsopp, *Isaiah 40-55*, 118, 351; Allen, "Substitutionary Atonement in Isaiah 53," 179; Smith, *Isaiah 40-66*, 448-49; Hengel and Bailey, "The Effective History of Isaiah 53 in the Pre-Christian Period," 125.

268. Blenkinsopp, *Isaiah 40-55*, 118.

269. Averbeck, "Sacrifices and Offerings," 720; Blenkinsopp, *Isaiah 40-55*, 351; Kellermann, "אָשָׁם," in *TDOT*, 1:433.

270. Blenkinsopp, *Isaiah 40-55*, 351.

271. Allen, "Substitutionary Atonement," 179, also says, "Significant also is the fact that two additional Hebrew words in verse 10 come directly from the vocabulary of the guilt offering found in Leviticus: נֶפֶשׁ ("soul" or "life"), and the conjunction אִם."

The high priest' role in the atonement is implied with the term, יַזֶּה in Isaiah 52:15. The meaning of "sprinkling" is frequently offered for the translation of this term.[272] The sprinkling is the activity that the high priest carries out on the Day of Atonement. The Servant will expiate for the many nations. The verb נָזָה in 52:15 is the verb used for sprinkling blood on an altar in Leviticus 4:6; 5:9; 8:11, 30; 13:7; 16:14, 19.[273] According to Lucass, "An alternative suggestion for the uncertain Hebrew word often translated as 'startle' is 'sprinkle'—the act that the high priest carried out following his emergence from the Holy of Holies, having offered the blood sacrifice on the Day of Atonement."[274] In addition, this is a cultic concept, in which the Servant's atoning role is suggested.[275] The Servant is "the provision and plan of God, who himself superintends the priestly task (Lev 16:21) of transferring the guilt of guilty to the head of the Servant, giving notice that this is indeed his considered and acceptable satisfaction for sin."[276] The Davidic Messiah has "the priestly duty (Lev 16:21) of 'transferring the guilt of the guilty upon the Servant' so that he makes 'satisfaction' for sin."[277] Thus, the Suffering Servant will achieve what the Davidic kings and priests had failed to achieve.[278]

Additionally, the role of atonement is not just that of Moses because the Davidic messianic figure has the role of the high priest in the atonement. He fulfills God's judgment through his atonement as the Davidic Messiah, as noted below. Because the Messiah's sacrifice and the punishment of God, which is loaded on him. The Judge pronounces justification (Isa 53:11). While the broader theme of covenantal faithfulness might be considered in the context of the Suffering Servant, the main feature of righteousness in Isaiah 53:11 is the righteousness of God, which is mainly judging righteousness.

---

272. Contra Spieckermann, "The Conception and Prehistory of the Idea of Vicarious Suffering in the Old Testament," 1–15.

273. The ESV, NIV, NASB, HCSB render נָזָה as "sprinkle."

274. Lucass, *The Concept of the Messiah in the Scriptures of Judaism and Christianity*, 110.

275. Lucass, *The Concept of the Messiah in the Scriptures of Judaism and Christianity*, 110.

276. Motyer, *The Prophecy of Isaiah*, 42.

277. Heskett, *Messianism within the Scriptural Scroll of Isaiah*, 158.

278. Hanson, "The World of the Servant of the Lord in Isaiah 40–55," 17.

Justification for Many

Particularly, the Suffering Servant in Isaiah 53 offers a significant clue to interpret the redemption of Romans 3:21–25, as well as the justification from the resurrection of Christ in Romans 4:25.[279] Richard Hays says, "The letter to the Romans is salted with numerous quotations of and allusions to Isaiah 40–55, including several passages that seem to echo the Suffering Servant motif of Isaiah 53 (e.g., Rom 4:24–25; 5:15–19; 10:15; 15:21)."[280] The justification of God's people, the accomplishment of righteousness and atonement through his humiliation and exaltation in Isaiah 53 will be examined below. Paul's messianic "σπέρμα" can be the righteous one described in Isaiah 53 and in Habakkuk 2:4.[281] Wright understands Isaiah 40–55, which includes the Suffering Servant idea, to deal "specifically with divine faithfulness."[282] Wright describes, "Somehow the work of the 'servant,' and specially the redemptive achievement of his suffering and death, are the manifestation in action of the divine 'righteousness,' the accomplishment of the divine 'salvation,' and above all the full expression of what it means that YHWH, Israel's One God, has at last returned in glory to Zion."[283] Through the Messiah's faithfulness, the righteousness of God has been manifested while God's righteousness was questioned by the failure of Israel. The Messiah appears in the climax of Isaiah 40–55, and his obedience leads to a sacrificial death.[284] The Messiah's faithfulness is clearly presented in the Servant in Isaiah 53. Wright asserts, "His obedience leads to a shameful and shocking death, shocking partly because of his shamefulness, partly because of its vicarious character."[285] He continues, "Within the larger flow of the section, the Servant's successful mission accomplishes the renewal of the covenant (chapter 54) and of creation itself (chapter 55), with the open invitation going out to 'everyone who thirsts' to share in the covenant originally made with David."[286] Although Israel is not faithful, the Messiah has been faithful, so that "the Abraham covenant is fulfilled."[287]

---

279. Melugin, "On Reading Isaiah 53 as Christian Scripture," 67; Hays, *Echoes of Scripture in the Letter of Paul*, 29–33.
280. Hays, *Echoes of Scripture in the Letter of Paul*, 63.
281. Hays, *Echoes of Scripture in the Letter of Paul*, 135.
282. Wright, *Paul and the Faithfulness of God*, 882.
283. Wright, *Paul and the Faithfulness of God*, 682.
284. Wright, *Paul and the Faithfulness of God*, 999.
285. Wright, *Paul and the Faithfulness of God*, 999.
286. Wright, *Paul and the Faithfulness of God*, 999.
287. Wright, *Paul and the Faithfulness of God*, 999.

However, the Suffering Servant in Isaiah 53 is not just concerned with the faithfulness of the Davidic Messiah. The righteous Davidic Messiah, who will justify the many in the background of Yahweh's courtroom, is primarily manifested in terms of his agency of God's judgment. In other words, the role of the Suffering Servant in Isaiah 53 is the sufficient fulfillment of God's righteous judgment.[288] The righteous Messiah will bring justice for all the nations, "a task that is close to the king's responsibilities in Psalm 71:1–4 (cf. Isa 42:1–4)."[289] Because of God's vindication for the righteous Messiah, the Davidic Messiah can vindicate many (Isa 53:11–12). Jipp writes,

> His accomplishment of justice is shown in providing just verdicts and deliverance for the oppressed (Ps 42:2–3, 7). Like the psalmist, the Servant experiences violent oppression from his enemies and asks God to enter into judgment with him and his adversaries. The Servant expects God to deliver him from shame and appeals to divine help as the basis for his justification (Isa 50:7–9). The third Servant Song is similar to the depictions of the suffering king in the Psalter; the one whom God has commissioned to provide justice for the nations now experiences the shameful reproach of shame from his adversaries.[290]

The vindication for the righteous Davidic king in Psalms is paralleled with the righteous Davidic Messiah in Isaiah 53.[291] As noted above, God's vindication for the king arises because of the righteousness of the Davidic king. While the righteous Messiah is despised and rejected and suffers (53:1–3), he is innocent and righteous (53:8–9, 11). Since his suffering is from a failing of justice (53:8), God vindicates and exalts him (52:13; 53:11–12). God's vindication of the righteous Messiah can allow him to make many to be accounted righteous (53:11).

While the vicarious character of the Davidic Messiah's atonement is presented in his shameful and shocking death, this more aptly fits God's punishment because of the iniquity of all. The suffering of the Messiah is an articulation of God's wrath against the Messiah, rather than of the Messiah's faithfulness. It supports the sternness of God's judgment through the Davidic Messiah. The judgment of God on the Messiah because of the severe sin of all sinners leads to the shameful and shocking death to justify the many.

---

288. Heskett, *Messianism within the Scriptural Scroll of Isaiah*, 128.

289. Jipp, *Christ Is King*, 230. See Lucass *The Concept of the Messiah in the Scriptures of Judaism and Christianity*, 108–9.

290. Jipp, *Christ Is King*, 230.

291. Goldingay, *Isaiah 40–55*, 2:231.

In Isaiah 53, the speaker mainly pronounces Yahweh's power in the Servant to deliver his people. Delineating the faith of the people, instead of the Messiah's faithfulness in Isaiah 53:1, the speaker continuously talks about "the arm of Yahweh" (53:1–2).[292] Considering the context of the previous chapters (Isa 49–53), God's restoration of Israel is accomplished with his power ('his arm or hand,' 50:2; 51:5, 9; 52:10).[293] While Israel fails to recognize the "arm of Yahweh," the speaker asks Israel to believe his report, in which the "arm of Yahweh" is revealed. This request presumably "constitutes an indirect acknowledgment by the speakers that they themselves had not at first believed what they were told about the servant."[294]

What is the content of this report? The speaker focuses the report mainly on the Servant's humiliation and exaltation, which causes the deliverance of Israel.[295] The speaker's statement is an incredible report (53:1, שְׁמוּעָה).[296] This report is astonishing and shocking (52:13–14) because it has never been told (52:15). The central thought of the report is focused on the Servant's suffering and exaltation, yet the contrast is present in the people's thought.[297] The anticipation of the Messiah is totally different from the thought of the people. Blenkinsopp explains,

> But if the passage appears to break abruptly into the context at this point of the book it also has unmistakable links with previous chapters. The presentation of the servant to the nations (הִנֵּה . . . עַבְדִּי) is reminiscent of 42:1 (הֵן עַבְדִּי), the reassurance of ultimate success in the face of trials and discouragement recalls previous pronouncements about a servant (49:5–6; 50:7–9), and the transition from humiliation to exaltation, from being an object of contempt to receiving deferential treatment from kings, replicates the comment added to one of the previous servant passages ('when they see you, kings will rise to their feet, princes will pay you homage,' 49:7).[298]

The Messiah's salvation is not just through his victory over their oppressors but through his humiliation. And John Oswalt goes on to say,

> On this reading, the Gentiles will find the humiliation of the Deliverer shocking because they have never heard before that it

292. Baltzer, *Deutero-Isaiah*, 400.
293. Oswalt, *The Book of Isaiah*, 376.
294. Goldingay, *Isaiah 40–55*, 2:297.
295. Westermann, *Isaiah 40–66*, 257.
296. Blenkinsopp, *Isaiah 40–55*, 349.
297. Oswalt, *The Book of Isaiah*, 376.
298. Blenkinsopp, *Isaiah 40–55*, 349.

is through the loss of all things that the Savior will conquer all things. This seems to be the sense in which Paul uses the passage in Rom 15:21. The nations have not heard this amazing truth before, and Paul wants to be among those who tell them first.[299]

The new aspect of this report that people never dreamed comes with the Servant's bearing, and being burdened in, his suffering.[300] Westermann holds, "In this connection it should be noticed that two things are involved in what the Servant bears, what he has loaded upon him—the sins of the others and the punishment which results upon him."[301] The Servant's suffering causes the people's healing (Isa 53:5), which "includes as well the forgiveness of their sins and the removal of their punishment, that is to say, the suffering."[302] Until the "punishment" (מוּסָר, 53:5; cf. Job 5:17; Prov 22:15; 23:13), Israel's restoration never occurs.[303] The Servant must endure being subjected to this punishment, which is a legal attack, judgment (מִשְׁפָּט, 53:8).[304] The context of a court of law is assumed in speaking of others' violent action (53:8).[305] The contempt and abhorrence that the Servant experiences, smitten by God, indicates God's wrath on him.[306] The Messiah is described as suffering the condemnation of all the sins of people to declare all those who accept his offering as righteous, delivered, before God.[307] In addition, the speaker suggests an expiatory sacrifice with the term (אָשָׁם), as noted above. This means that guilt and liability for the punishment of people are removed.[308]

From this perspective, the Messiah's faithfulness is not the speaker's concern in Isaiah 53. He emphasizes the Messiah's suffering for God's judgment on the people's sins. The remarkable and new solution is that God put forth the Messiah as the sacrificial אָשָׁם bearing condemnation. While the speaker employs similar language in Isaiah 53:4–10 to describe the Servant's bearing the burden of the people's sin, "It is not said, at least not clearly and explicitly, that he volunteered to do this, or even that he accepted it

---

299. Oswalt, *The Book of Isaiah*, 380–81.
300. Westermann, *Isaiah 40–66*, 263.
301. Westermann, *Isaiah 40–66*, 263.
302. Westermann, *Isaiah 40–66*, 263.
303. Oswalt, *The Book of Isaiah*, 388.
304. Goldingay, *Isaiah 40–55*, 2:312.
305. Westermann, *Isaiah 40–66*, 262.
306. Westermann, *Isaiah 40–66*, 265.
307. Oswalt, *The Book of Isaiah*, 388.
308. Blenkinsopp, *Isaiah 40–55*, 354.

willingly."[309] Yahweh causes the suffering falling on him (53:6). The Messiah's condition is "the result of divine punishment for sin."[310] He is passively smitten by God.[311]

The people's faith in the report concerning Yahweh's arm, which is revealed in the suffering Messiah, is more focused on than is the Messiah's faithfulness. As noted above, the introduction (53:1) is linked to 52:15 with the term "*hearing*" (שְׁמוּעָה). The intention of this employment concentrates on the "believing in" of the people. Westermann notes,

> For them the event is a שְׁמוּעָה, a thing of which they have heard (1 Sam 2:24; 4:19), and, as such, tidings which they themselves have to pass on to others. To them themselves the thing was as unbelievable as it had been to the people who actually witnessed it (v. 15b). 53.1, where the tidings are passed on, continued v. 15b, stressing the element of the unheard of and the unbelievable in the event.... In order to appreciate what comes afterward it is important to remember that this introduction to the report sets the key-note for the entire passage—that of an astonishment that is still unable to comprehend what has here come about.[312]

The devout hear, believe, and confess that the Servant is smitten by God; he takes their iniquity upon himself; and he procures healing and peace.[313] It makes them righteous.

In sum, the Davidic king, who has an extremely close relationship with Yahweh, is the agent of God's judgment. It is paralleled with the righteous Messiah in Isaiah 53. The Davidic Messiah's exaltation is additionally cited for the justification of the people (Isa 52:13; 53:11–12). The righteous Messiah's significant role is described as justifying the many through his suffering. The expectations of the messianic king—which are the vindication, salvation, and restoration of his people—will start with the execution of God's judgment through the righteous Davidic Messiah.

---

309. Blenkinsopp, *Isaiah 40–55*, 350.
310. Blenkinsopp, *Isaiah 40–55*, 350.
311. Westermann, *Isaiah 40–66*, 263.
312. Westermann, *Isaiah 40–66*, 260.
313. Westermann, *Isaiah 40–66*, 263.

CONCLUSION

The features of the Davidic Messiah, who is the agent of God's judgment, have been surveyed in this chapter. The expectation of the Davidic Messiah is closely connected with the Davidic "house," which has been promised by God (2 Sam 7) and the Prophets, and it is manifested in the Psalms. The Davidic Messiah's features reveal him to be the Lord's representative. Expectations for the Davidic Messiah were based on the ideal king, who would represent the rule of the Heavenly King. Because the Davidic kings failed to be representatives of God's rule, expectations for the Davidic Messiah, which are clearly revealed in the messianic texts, were based on the promise of the permanent kingship of the Davidic line and on the Davidic king's ideal rule. While expectations of the Davidic Messiah are related to the immediate political circumstances, the Davidic Messiah develops as an eschatological Messiah based on God's eternal promise pertaining to the Davidic dynasty, especially in the post-exilic prophets and the LXX.

The agent of God's judgment is the most vital concept in the messianic texts. The Davidic Messiah is the righteous king over his people, as the heavenly king has the characteristics of a righteous king who judges the wicked and saves his people. Judging, which upholds justice, is central to the concept of the Davidic king's righteousness. It is shown through varied aspects of the executing of righteousness: vindicating the righteous, judging the wicked, saving his people, and defeating enemies. The "righteousness" functions in God's impartial judgment through the Davidic Messiah as judging righteousness.

The sprout of the judgment and atonement arises in the portrayal of the Suffering Servant in Isaiah 53. Several scholars suggest that the main theme of the Suffering Servant passage is the Messiah's faithfulness that reveals God's covenantal faithfulness. The main role of the Davidic Messiah in Isaiah 53 is that of executor of God's judgment as the Davidic king and high priest to justify the many, though, not just being faithful as the Messiah in his death. He solves the problem of sin by justifying the many with his atonement. The Davidic Messiah accomplishes God's justifying righteousness, and the Messiah's covenantal faithfulness is unfamiliar from this viewpoint.

Chapter 3

The Davidic Messiah

The Agent of God's Judgment in the Second Temple Writings

INTRODUCTION

In this chapter, the treatment by the Second Temple writings of the Davidic Messiah, who is the eschatological agent of God's judgment, is discussed within the context of the messianic texts. Terms for the messianic figure in the Second Temple writings have their foundations in Old Testament messianic passages.[1] The Davidic Messiah is manifested in these terms of Jewish writings, and Davidic messianism is "based on a dominant biblical messianic paradigm."[2] Messianic expectations for the Davidic Messiah are consistent,[3] while some texts do not contain the specific term "משיח,"[4] and

---

1. Condra, *Salvation for the Righteous Revealed*, 237. See Weinfeld, "Expectations of the Davidic Kingdom in Biblical and Post-Biblical Literature," 218–30.

2. Condra, *Salvation for the Righteous Revealed*, 224.

3. John J. Collins asserts that the consistent concept for the various titles is identified with the messianic king, based on Isa 11:1–5 and Gen 49. Collins, *The Scepter and Star*, 63.

4. Condra, *Salvation for the Righteous Revealed*, 214; Collins, *The Scepter and Star*,

the messianic figure is identified with various titles in different texts.[5] When this Davidic messianic figure eschatologically appears in the Second Temple Jewish writings, his significant role is being the agent of God's judgment. Because the focus in this chapter is the role of the eschatological Davidic Messiah, prominent portrayals of the Davidic Messiah related to God's judgment through him will be briefly surveyed.[6]

In the Second Temple writings, the Davidic Messiah, who is righteous, is described as executing God's judgment. The Davidic Messiah is portrayed as the agent of God's judgment, and righteousness language is not identified with covenantal faithfulness, although covenantal faithfulness might be a subdivision of righteousness in the God's judgment. So, it will be examined in this chapter whether righteousness language is clearly characterized as righteous righteousness in God's judgment through the Davidic Messiah. The focus in God's judgment through the Davidic Messiah is God's impartial righteousness, and the Messiah's covenantal faithfulness sparsely appears in his execution of God's judgment.

11–12; Martínez, "Two Messianic Figures in the Qumran Texts," 19–20. Andrew Chester explains that the term משיח should not be the only standard to determine whether or not a text is messianic. He called this position as a sophisticated "maximalist." Chester, *Messiah and Exaltation*, 193–98, 329–31. However, Charlesworth approaches just the texts that employ the term משיח to define messianism. He contrasts the broader use of messianism, which does not always include texts with משיח. Charlesworth, *The Messiah*; Neusner, Green, and Frerichs, eds., *Judaisms and Their Messiahs at the Turn of the Christian Era*.

5. Concerning possible titles, see Abegg Jr. and Evans, "Messianic Passages in the Dead Sea Scrolls," 191–203.

6. The materials that underwent altered conditions after the destruction of the temple are not more significant than is literature composed prior to AD 70. Non-Palestinian writings (e.g., the Jewish *Sibyllines*) do not have more value in reading Paul. Some of the Second Temple writings suggested in this chapter are pre-Pauline and important to understand the idea of the Davidic Messiah. See Seifrid, *Justification by Faith*, 78–81; Hengel, *The Pre-Christian Paul*, 18–39.

THE DAVIDIC MESSIAH

Apocrypha

Some scholars delineate that Messianic expectations seem sparse in the Apocrypha.[7] It may be due to a strong theocentrism in this era.[8] William Horbury explains, "A more clearly marked aspect of theocentrism is the readiness to portray the deity himself as a warrior king which will have been particularly influential . . . , given their incorporation into the Pentateuch."[9] Or, the absence of messianism might be "determined by the political attitudes and circumstances of the different groups within Judaism."[10] Those who hoped in their political institutions and leaders in the Maccabean period held little interest in messianism.

However, the Apocrypha characterizes the interest in messianism, the leaders in the Apocrypha have implications for the advent of a messianic figure who comes with vengeance.[11] The deliverance of Judas and his brothers results in joy among the people, and "the disgrace brought by the Gentiles was removed" (4:58), which is recognized as God's deliverance. This echoes Isaiah 25:8 and Ezekiel 36:4, in which God's deliverance is clearly shown. Similarly, God's deliverance is demonstrated in the "eulogy of Simon" (1 Macc 14:4-15). Lev 26:4, Ezek 34:27, and Zech 8:12 are alluded to in 14:8.[12] Horbury notes, "Judas Maccabaeus, 'saving Israel,' still prays to God as savior of Israel (1 Macc 4:30), and the hymns in praise of Judas and Simon still leave room for divine deliverance to come."[13] Implications exist for the Davidic messianic concept in the leaders of Maccabees who

---

7. See Horbury, "Messianism in the Old Testament Apocrypha," 406; Frost, *Old Testament Apocalyptic*, 66-67; Becker, *Messianic Expectation in the Old Testament*, 79-82; Collins, *The Scepter and Star*, 31-38, 40; Charlesworth, "Messianology in the Biblical Pseudepigrapha," 23; Klausner, *The Messianic Idea in Israel*, 9.

8. Horbury, *Messianism among Jews and Christians*, 41-45; Horbury, "Messianism in the Old Testament Apocrypha and Pseudepigrapha," 408-9. He states that a theocentric emphasis in post-exilic Israelite religion made a "missianological vacuum" in the Apocrypha.

9. Horbury, *Messianism among Jews and Christians*, 41.

10. Collins, "Messianism in the Maccabean Period," 106.

11. Horbury writes, "Thus, the prediction of divine vengeance at the end of the greater Song of Moses in Deut 32 was immediately followed by the Blessing of Moses, which was messianically interpreted by the third century, as the LXX Pentateuch shows (Deut 33:5 LXX, discussed in the previous section)." Horbury, *Jewish Messianism and the Cult of Christ*, 55.

12. Horbury, *Jewish Messianism and the Cult of Christ*, 55.

13. Horbury, *Jewish Messianism and the Cult of Christ*, 49.

carried out God's deliverance. Davidic messianism might be sparse in the Apocrypha, yet Horbury contends that expectations of the Davidic Messiah "should not be excluded from the Maccabean future hope which have just been sketched" in the last words of Mattathias (1 Macc 2:49-70).[14] In 1 Maccabees 4:30, expecting the Davidic Messiah, Judas Maccabaeus prays to God the Savior, who rescued Israel from its enemies through his servant David: "Blessed are you, O Savior of Israel, who crushed the attack of the mighty warrior by the hand of your servant David, and gave the camp of the Philistines into the hands of Jonathan son of Saul, and of the man who carried his armor." As the Davidic Messiah is expected in God's deliverance, he is the ideal figure for the leaders in the Apocrypha, and the messianic characteristics cannot be denied in these leaders. The leaders possess "the glamour of what could be called in a broad sense a fulfilled messianism."[15] Judas Maccabaeus is described as the lion of Judah (1 Macc 3:4; cf. Gen 49:9), the savior of Israel (1 Macc 3:5-12).[16] "Deliverance [of Israel is] prospered by his hand" (1 Macc 3:6). He "destroyed the ungodly out of the land" (3:8), and he "was renowned to the ends of the earth; gathered in those who were perishing" (3:9).[17] Horbury asserts,

> These admiring, almost hagiographical presentations of kings and high priests do not in themselves attest a messianic future hope, but they surround contemporary rulers with a messianic atmosphere, and show how messianic expectation would be imaginatively filled out. . . . A specifically Davidic messianic element should not therefore be excluded from the Maccabaean future hopes which have just been sketched.[18]

These verses echo Isaiah 11:12 and 12:5, which portray Judas as God's messianic king in accomplishing the prophecy of Isaian verses.

While the Davidic Messiah is not illustrated clearly, 2 Maccabees 2:17-18 relates to God's saving "all his people" (2 Macc 2:17), and restoring Israel, especially its kingship and priesthood as he promised according to the law (2 Macc 2:17-18). The temple recovery by the Maccabees corresponds to the Davidic Messiah's Old Testament rebuilding of the temple. Consequently, although the concept of messianism is weak in the Apocrypha, apocryphal

---

14. Horbury, *Jewish Messianism and the Cult of Christ*, 56-57.

15. Horbury, *Messianism among Jews and Christians*, 75.

16. "Καὶ ὡμοιώθη λέοντι ἐν τοῖς ἔργοις αὐτοῦ καὶ ὡς σκύμνος ἐρευγόμενος εἰς θήραν" (1 Macc 3:4).

17. Goldstein, "How the Authors of 1 and 2 Maccabees Treated the 'Messianic' Promises," 77.

18. Horbury, *Jewish Messianism and the Cult of Christ*, 56.

themes imply a hope for a Davidic Messiah: God's vengeance in his saving, and the kingship and priesthood of the Maccabean leaders.

Pseudepigrapha

In scholarship, regarding the Davidic Messiah expected in the Pseudepigrapha, the messianic king is understood to be indeed Davidic.[19] The Pseudepigrapha's expectations of the Davidic Messiah were based on the Davidic Covenant in 2 Samuel 7, and these expectations were shown in the employment of Genesis 49:10 and Numbers 24:17.[20] Several messianic titles are applied to the Davidic Messiah, though, a consistent idea for the Davidic Messiah—who is the eschatological savior from the Davidic line—is clearly shown in the *Similitudes* and *Psalms of Solomon*.

Similitudes (1 Enoch 37–71)[21]

Although the messianic figure is described by varied titles for the Messiah in the *Similitudes*, "Messiah, Son of Man, Righteous One, Chosen One, and the Anointed One," these terms are recognized as denoting the Davidic Messiah. The Messiah is denoted as *"the Chosen One"* (45:3–6; 48:10; 49:2; 51:3, 5; 52:6, 9), while the Righteous One (53:6) and the Anointed One (48:10; 52:4) are less frequently utilized for the Messiah in *1 Enoch*.[22] The "Chosen One" in *1 Enoch* is presented from the Davidic messianic terms "my servant" (עַבְדִי) and "my Chosen One" (בְּחִירִי) in Isaiah 42:1.[23] The "Chosen One" is also the "Righteous One" as in Isaiah 42:1 and 53:11.[24] These titles are used to cite the same eschatological figure, who is the Davidic Messiah.[25]

---

19. See Horbury, "Messianism in the Old Testament Apocrypha and Pseudepigrapha," 423–35, especially in 431–32.

20. The prophets of the Davidic restoration period from the eighth century BC continued into the Hellenistic and Romans periods. Laato, *A Star Is Rising*, 33; Condra, *Salvation for the Righteous Revealed*, 219.

21. This is understood to be written in 105–64 BC. The English translation in this book is of Isaac, trans., *1 (Ethiopic Apocalypse of) Enoch*, in *The Old Testament Pseudepigrapha*, 639–70. Regarding discussion about the date of the *Similitudes*, see Boccaccini, ed., *Enoch and the Messiah Son of Man*, 415–98.

22. VanderKam, "Righteous One, Messiah, Chosen One, and Son of Man in 1 Enoch 37–71," 169–76.

23. Kvanvig, "The Son of Man in the Parables of Enoch," 188.

24. VanderKam, "Righteous One, Messiah, Chosen One, and Son of Man in 1 Enoch 37–71," 187–90.

25. VanderKam, "Righteous One, Messiah, Chosen One, and Son of Man in 1

There is another term for the messianic figure in the *Similitudes*. "The Son of Man" is clearly related to Isaian passages with strongly messianic overtones.[26] 1 Enoch 71:14 reads, "You, Son of Man, who art born in righteousness and upon whom righteousness has dwelt, the righteousness of the Antecedent of Time will not forsake you." Similarly, 1 Enoch 62:2 reads, concerning the righteousness and wisdom of the Davidic Messiah, that "the righteousness has been poured out upon him. The word of his mouth will do the sinners in; and all the oppressors shall be eliminated from before his face." This wisdom motif recalls Isaiah 11:2, 4.[27]

Psalms of Solomon

Chapter 17 of the *Psalms of Solomon* chapter 17 includes prominent instances of the Davidic Messiah, with "an extended messianic hymn describing the reign of this king, the anointed son of David."[28] The Davidic Messiah is the messianic king in the *Psalms of Solomon*, who is a Davidic descendant (*Ps. Sol.* 17:21). The Psalmist proclaims in 17:4, "Lord, you chose David to be king over Israel, and swore to him about his descendants forever, that his kingdom should not fail before you," which is based on 2 Samuel 7 and royal psalms (Pss 89 and 132).[29] While the Davidic Messiah is God's vicegerent, accomplishing God's purpose on earth, his function in the *Psalms of Solomon* 17–18 echoes the eleventh chapter of Isaiah.[30] These chapters are filled with allusions to Isaiah 11:2-4 and Psalm 2. The messianic figure is called the "son of David" (*Ps. Sol.* 17:21); "king" (17:21, 32); "Messiah" (18:5, 7);

Enoch 37–71," 185–91; Nickelsburg, "Son of Man" and "The Parables of Enoch," *ABD*; Nickelsburg, *Ancient Judaism and Christian Origins: Diversity, Continuity, and Transformation*, 104–6.

26. Chialà, "The Son of Man: The Evolution of an Expression," 161.

27. Chialà, "The Son of Man: The Evolution of an Expression," 161.

28. Wright, trans., *Psalms of Solomon*, in Charlesworth, *The Old Testament Pseudepigrapha*, 639. This is recognized to be written in the mid-first century BC. The English translation in this book is of Wright, *Psalms of Solomon*, 639–70.

29. Gillingham, "The Messiah in the Psalms," 234.

30. Collins, *The Scepter and Star*, 58; Evans, "The Messiah in the Dead Sea Scrolls," 98. Isaiah influenced these texts. Davenport, "The 'Anointed of the Lord' in Psalms and Solomon 17," 67–92.

and "Lord Messiah" (17; 32).³¹ He possesses the "beauty" (εὐπρέπεια, 17:42) of the Davidic king as in Isaiah.³²

Certainly, the messianic idea in the *Psalms of Solomon* is innately eschatological.³³ The Psalmist implores God, "See, Lord, and raise up (ἀνάστησον) for them their king, the son of David, to rule over your servant Israel in the time known to you, O God" (17:21; cf. Jer 23:5; 37:9; Amos 9:11). The Davidic Messiah, with glory and beauty, shall be raised up by God (18:6) in the appointed time.³⁴ According to S. E. Gillingham,

> The plea to "raise up a king" demonstrates that the belief in the historical David has been increasingly transformed into an eschatological hope. This coming deliverer will purge Jerusalem—not so much with military might, as in Qumran, but with justice and righteousness. As the royal king in Ps 2:9 was promised success in his reign by breaking the nations with an iron rod, so the coming 'Son of David' (the first time this title has been used in Jewish writings) will smash with an iron rod his opponents—not only the Gentiles, this time, but the sinners of his own people as well (17:24).³⁵

The messianic figure in the *Psalms of Solomon* is "a divinely appointed king, but unlike the Davidic dynastic rulers, who were dependent upon successive leaders, the figure here is a once-for-all-time Deliverer."³⁶ The Davidic Messiah's main role is eschatologically restoring the kingdom of Israel and preparing the devout for the coming of the Day of Yahweh with his purifying activity—all of which means the Last Judgment.³⁷ The wrong-

---

31. Hahn, "Christos kyrios in PsSol 17:32: 'The Lord's Anointed' Reconsidered," 620–27; Wright, *Psalms of Solomon*, 48–49, insists that Χριστὸς κύριος is original. Several scholars support the messianic figure with Χριστὸς κυρίου. Davenport, "The 'Anointed of the Lord' in Psalms and Solomon 17," 77–79; de Jonge, "The Expectation of the Future in the Psalms of Solomon," 111n25; Atkinson, *I Cried to the Lord*, 131n2.

32. William Horbury writes, "In any case, however, the occurrence of εὐπρέπεια in Greek versions of these royal psalms is a pointer to contexts likely to be important for interpretation of the psalmodic portrait of a coming king in *Psalms of Solomon* 17. Both the passages concerned in the Psalms of David are exalted in style. . . . It seems likely, then, that in *Ps. Sol.* 17.47 (42) the king's beauty is considered to be known to God." Horbury, *Messianism among Jews and Christians*, 61.

33. Ábel, *The Psalms of Solomon and the Messianic Ethics of Paul*, 54. The historical background is Pompey's encroachment in Palestine and conquest of Jerusalem, which is the basis of the eschatological perspective.

34. Horbury, "Messianism in the Old Testament Apocrypha," 432.

35. Gillingham, "The Messiah in the Psalms," 235.

36. Gillingham, "The Messiah in the Psalms," 235.

37. Ábel, *The Psalms of Solomon and the Messianic Ethics of Paul*, 57.

doings of sinners, whether from the Hasmonean dynasty or the Roman invasion, are the basis of eschatological events.[38] The Davidic Messiah's central role presents the ultimate solution for these difficulties in the last days (*Pss. Sol.* 7:10, 11; 15:12, 17; 18:6–10).[39] The last chapter of the *Psalms of Solomon* concludes with a hopeful message, which is the Messiah's coming. The climax of the eschatological events is presented "preceding the end of this age and its replacement by the age to come."[40] God appointed the Davidic Messiah to install the his new world order in the *Psalms of Solomon*.[41]

Testaments of the Twelve Patriarchs[42]

Certain citations of the Davidic Messiah are shown in the *Testaments of the Twelve Patriarchs*, which recall 2 Samuel 7. While it is unclear whether the Testaments originated from the Jewish community and were redacted by Christians, or were thoroughly Christian,[43] a certain parallelism to *T. Levi* 18 and *T. Jud.* 24:5 announces an eschatological messianic king as the root (ῥίζα) of Israel, employing the images of a "scepter of kingship" (σκῆπτρον βασιλείας) and a "sprout" (πυθμήν).[44] The "sprout" sounds like an allusion to the royal promises of Isaiah 11:1; Jeremiah 23:5; 33:15, and the "scepter" recalls Genesis 49:9, and Numbers 24:17 (LXX).[45] *T. Levi* 18:3, 4 read that "his star (ἄστρον) will arise in heaven, as a king. . . . He will shine as the sun on the earth." *T. Jud.* 24:1 reads, "And after these things a star (ἄστρον) will arise to you from Jacob in peace and a man will arise from my seed like the sun of righteousness," which echoes Numbers 24:17. The "salvation of Israel" (τὸ σωτήριον Ἰσραήλ) occurs after the fall of the kingship (*T. Jud.* 22:2b, 3). This recalls Genesis 49:10 and 2 Samuel 7:16, which discuss the divine promise of the eternal existence of the kingship of Judah.[46]

---

38. Abel, *The Psalms of Solomon and the Messianic Ethics of Paul*, 58.

39. Abel, *The Psalms of Solomon and the Messianic Ethics of Paul*, 58.

40. Abel, *The Psalms of Solomon and the Messianic Ethics of Paul*, 57, 187.

41. Gillingham, "The Messiah in the Psalms," 235.

42. This is recognized as being written in the second century BC. The English translation in this book is of Kee, trans., *Testaments of the Twelve Patriarchs*, in Charlesworth, *The Old Testament Pseudepigrapha*, 775–828.

43. Pertaining to the difficult determination of the Christian or Jewish elements, see de Jonge, "Christian Influence in the Testaments of the Twelve Patriarchs," 182–235; Higgins, "Priestly Messiah," 221–39; Kraft, "Setting the Stage and Framing Some Central Questions," 371–95.

44. Schreiber, *Gesalbter und König*, 251.

45. Schreiber, *Gesalbter und König*, 251.

46. Schreiber, *Gesalbter und König*, 253.

Dead Sea Scrolls[47]

The term משיח in Qumran writings frequently cites an eschatological figure—a priest, a prophet, or Moses, who is not Davidic.[48] However, the Dead Sea Scrolls additionally contain the expectation of a royal figure from the Davidic line, who is given several titles based on the Old Testament messianic passages.[49] These scrolls describe the eschatological messianic figure as one who is Davidic. While there are various titles for the Davidic Messiah in Qumran literature, the Davidic Messiah concept in Qumran is cohesive because a close association for the Davidic Messiah terms can be demonstrated.[50] Genesis 49:10, Numbers 24:17, Isaiah 10:34–11:5, and the royal psalms are mainly alluded to in these passages in the Qumran writings.[51] The quotation of 2 Samuel 7:11–14 is understood in Qumran writings as a promise of the Davidic kingship, a succession, the sovereignty of the kingdom, and a particular divine relationship that is presented in the image of father and son, too.

The Branch of David

The "*Branch of David*" (צמח דויד) represents the eschatological destination of the promise for David's descendants and is expected on the basis of 2 Samuel 7:11–14. The image of father and son, which carries within it a legitimating and empowering moment, characterizes the unique closeness of his relationship to God.[52] The Branch of David is equated with the Davidic Messiah by the citation of 2 Samuel 7:11–14 (4Q174 [4QFlor] 1 1:21, 2 lines

---

47. The English translation in this book is of Martínez and Tigchelaar, eds., *The Dead Sea Scrolls Study Edition*.

48. See Fuller, "The Davidic Messiah in Early Jewish Literature," 65–86; Xeravits, "The Early History of Qumran's Messianic Expectations," 113–21; Abegg and Evans, "Messianic Passages," 191–203.

49. Oegema, "Messianic Expectations in the Qumran Writings," 52–82. Some texts (1QS, 1QSa, 1QSb, 4Q175, and CD) are dated from the Maccabean period, about 150–75 BC and earlier (4QpIsa^a). During the Herodian/Roman period (75 BC–AD 68), some texts are believed to be written (1QpHab, 1QM, 4Q252. 4Q174, 4Q246, 1QH, and 4Q171). Oegema understands that there is change in royal messianic expectation in terms of political situations. See Stegeman, "Some Remarks to 1QSa, to 1QSb, and to Qumran Messianism," 479–505; Knibb, "Eschatology and Messianism in the Dead Sea Scrolls," 389–400.

50. Collins, *The Scepter and Star*, 63.

51. Chester, *Messiah and Exaltation*, 273; Evans, "The Messiah in the Dead Sea Scrolls," 91.

52. Schreiber, *Gesalbter und König*, 225.

10–13), and he is the anointed one (lines 19, משיה) in the "last days" as in Psalm 2:1.[53]

> (10) [And] YHWH [de]clares to you that "he will build you a house. I will raise up your seed after you and establish the throne of his kingdom (11) [for ev]er. I will be a father to him and he will be a son to me" (2 Sam 7:12–14). This (refers to) "branch of David." Who will arise with the Interpreter of the law who (12) [will rise up] in Zi[on in] the [l]ast days, as it is written, "I will raise up the hut of David which has fallen" (Amos 9:11). This (refers to) "the hut of (13) David which has fall[en," w]hich he will raise up to save Israel.

The messianic title in 4Q174 is connected with Amos 9:11.[54] The raising up of the hut of David is fulfilled with the salvation of Israel (4Q161). This is described quite broadly by the quotation of Amos 9:11 as the reestablishment of the overthrown house of David.[55] The Davidic dynasty rule is evidently broken off in the author's eyes, and thus requires eschatological reestablishment by the appearance of the Branch of David and implies a new salvation time for Israel.[56]

In addition, the Branch of David is identified with the Davidic Messiah in 4Q252 5:1–7. The identity of the two titles, "the Messiah of righteousness" (משיה הצדק) and "Branch of David" (צמח דויד), predicates the same figure ('until the messiah of righteousness comes, the branch of David,' in 5:3–4).[57] In the fourth line, the writer presents "God's eternal covenant with David's descendants based on 2 Samuel 7:11–16 and Psalm 89:4–5."[58] The writer's employment of "these scriptural passages is undoubtedly intended to emphasize the Messiah's Davidic association."[59] The term "*Branch*" (צמח) is related to the messianic texts of Zechariah and Jeremiah, as well.[60] It is the same with the plant imagery in Isaiah 11:1 (חֹטֶר מִגֵּזַע יִשָׁי and נֵצֶר מִשָּׁרָשָׁיו).[61]

---

53. Condra, *Salvation for the Righteous Revealed*, 246; Collins, *The Scepter and Star*, 63–68.

54. See Brooke, *Exegesis at Qumran*, 197–205; Zimmermann, *Messianische Texte aus Qumran*, 99–113; Xeravits, *King, Priest, Prophet*, 55–57; Pomykala, *The Davidic Dynasty Tradition in Early Judaism*, 191–97.

55. Schreiber, *Gesalbter und König*, 226.

56. Schreiber, *Gesalbter und König*, 226.

57. עד בוא משיה הצדק צמח דויד

58. Atkinson, *I Cried to the Lord*, 161.

59. Atkinson, *I Cried to the Lord*, 161.

60. Xeravits, *King, Priest, Prophet*, 158.

61. Xeravits, *King, Priest, Prophet*, 158. Also see VanderKam, "Messianism in the Scrolls," 216.

The Prince of the Congregation

The Davidic Messiah in Isaiah 11 is alluded to in 4Q161(4QpIsa^a) 2–6 and 8–10, and is echoed in 1Q28b (1QSb 5:21–26), in which the blessing is to be pronounced upon the *"Prince of the Congregation."*[62] This is obviously a description of military engagement in the end time. The background of Old Testament terminology can be seen in the usage of the term נָשִׂיא: "Prince" (נָשִׂיא) is utilized for political leaders (e.g., Exod 16:22; Num 4:34; 2 Sam 7:8), along with for a future expected Davidic ruler (Ezek 34:24; 37:25).[63] 4Q285(4QMg) connects the Prince (נְשִׂיא) of the Congregation to the Branch of David (4QMg 5:2), who is the Davidic Messiah.[64]

The Prince of the Congregation must be recognized as the anointed Davidic King of the end time, who kills his opponents in the eschatological battle.[65] The "Prince of the Congregation" is—on the basis of the text combination of 1QSb 5:20 and 4Q161 2:15; 3:12–25—proof of the denotation of the title as a single anointed end-time king, and therefore corresponds to the "Messiah of Israel" of other texts. Moreover, this is indicated by the correlation of the image of the "scepter" (cf. 1QSb 5:27; 4Q252 5:2) and the customary interpretation of Numbers 24:17, with an expected anointed bringer of salvation.[66]

The Prince of the Congregation is identified as the "Branch of David," which is the Davidic messianic title in the Prophets. According to John J. Collins,

> Thus far we have traced allusions to the titles "Branch of David" and "Prince of the Congregation," which are juxtaposed in 4Q285 and in the *pesher* on Isaiah. What we have found is a network of interlocking references, in which messianic titles and biblical allusions are combined in various ways. This network includes two major rule books, the Damascus Document and the War Rule, several exegetical texts (*pesherîm* on Isaiah and Genesis 49, the Florilegium) and a liturgical collection of benedictions (1QSb). The references are tied to a few biblical texts, sometimes linked together, sometimes in separate passages. Chief of these passages are Isaiah 11 and Numbers 24, and the expression צמח דויד from Jeremiah 23 and 33 (where

---

62. Evans, "The Messiah in the Dead Sea Scrolls," 92; Schreiber, *Gesalbter und König*, 215.
63. Schreiber, *Gesalbter und König*, 215.
64. Chester, *Messiah and Exaltation*, 235.
65. Schreiber, *Gesalbter und König*, 219.
66. Schreiber, *Gesalbter und König*, 222.

it appears as לדוד צמח). Each of these passages occurs several times. Genesis 49, 2 Samuel 7 and Amos 9 are also interested with reference to a Davidic messiah at least once. These passages by no means exhaust the references to the Davidic messiah in the Scrolls.[67]

Furthermore, the Prince of the Congregation is identified as the Messiah of Balaam's oracles (Num 24:17) in the Damascus Document (CD 7:20).[68] The Damascus Document 7:18–20 reads,

> (18) And the star is the interpreter of the law, (19) will come to Damascus, as it is written, "A star moves out of Jacob, and a scepter arises (20) out of Israel" (Num 24:17). The scepter is the prince of the whole congregation and when he rises "he will destroy (21) all the sons of Seth."

The "*star*" is the interpreter of the law (דורש התורה), who came to Damascus and who is the scepter. The interpreter of the law is an eschatological messianic figure, who is probably the eschatological priest in 4Q541. The preceding context provides an explanation of Amos 5:26–27 and 9:11. This interpretation takes its origin from the correlation of Amos 5:26f and Amos 9:11—by means of a wordplay—whereby the king's "*Sikkuth*" (idols) from Amos 5:26 and "*Suk-koh*" (סֻכָּה) of David overlap, and are connected by a conceptual association with Amos 9:11 (CD 7:14–16).[69] In line 18, the "star," which is omitted from the MT in the quotation of Amos 5:26, is introduced and aligned with the "*interpreter of the law*," which in turn becomes the quotation from Numbers 24:17. The interpretation of Numbers 24:17 positions the interpreter of the law in parallel with the Prince of the Congregation, hence demonstrating that he possesses a messianic character, too. This is due to the assignment of the interpreter of the law to the Branch of David, terminologically compared to the Prince of the Congregation. This is confirmed in 4Q174 3:11.[70]

---

67. Collins, *The Scepter and Star*, 64.

68. According to Collins, "This *pesher* on Gen 49 was distinctive in one respect. The word for staff (מחקק) also occurs in the Damascus Document, CD 4:3–9, where it is cited, not from Genesis 49, but from Num 21:8 ('the well which the princes dug, which the nobles of the people delved with the staff')." Collins, *The Scepter and Star*, 71.

69. Schreiber, *Gesalbter und König*, 221.

70. Schreiber, *Gesalbter und König*, 221.

The Son of God

The Davidic Messiah is portrayed as "*Son of God*" in the Aramaic "Son of God" text (4Q246), as well. The Messiah shall be called "Son of God" and "Son of the Most High" in 4Q246. Because "a future successor to the Davidic throne in an apocalyptic or eschatological context is by definition a messiah," the Son of God who accedes to the throne is the Messiah.[71] This figure is surely a Davidic redeemer spoken of with exalted language.[72] In 4Q369, the messianic figure is denoted as the "firstborn." He is "the 'first-born' son of God at Psalm 89:28, who (as similarly at Ps 2:7-8) is made ruler over the whole earth."[73]

Melchizedek.

11QMelchizedek text is related to numerous interwoven texts (Lev 25:13; Deut 15:2; Ps 82:1-2; Isa 52:7; and Dan 9:25). "*Melchizedek*" is a priestly figure mentioned in Genesis 14:18 and Psalm 110:4.[74] He can be the messianic king, though, "as it is written concerning him in the Songs of David (Ps 82:1)."[75] Isaiah 61:1-2 is based on the 11QMelchizedek text, in which the eschatological context presents favor and vengeance developed from the figure of Melchizedek.[76] Melchizedek is the ancient king of Salem and priestly forebear of David (Ps 110:3).[77] He is "to bring about the conviction of Belial and his cohorts as well as the granting of forgiveness for the Sons of Light."[78] In addition, he is the anointed one, although this "is not taken from the biblical text, but is most likely construed under the influence of Isa 61:1."[79] Lidija Novakovic observes, "It serves as a link between Isa 52:7 and Dan

---

71. Fitzmyer, *The One Who Is to Come*, 107.

72. Lucass, *The Concept of the Messiah in the Scriptures of Judaism and Christianity*, 128.

73. Chester, *Messiah and Exaltation*, 237.

74. John Collins insists that Melchizedek can be identified as the eschatological priest in 4Q541 frag. 9. Collins, *The Scepter and Star*, 148.

75. Dunn, *The New Perspective on Paul: Collected Essays*, 392.

76. Miller, "Function of Isa 61:1-2 in 11QMelchizedek," 469.

77. Horbury, "Messianism in the Old Testament Apocrypha and Pseudepigrapha," 428.

78. Baumgarten, "Messianic Forgiveness of Sin in CD XIV, 19 (4Q266 10 I, 12–13)," 539.

79. Novakovic, "4Q521: The Works of the Messiah or the Signs of the Messianic Time?," 218.

9:25b. Since the latter contains the reference to the 'anointed one,' it is very likely that this verse was quoted after כאשר אמר דניאל."[80] She comments,

> In 2:18, the text identifies "the messenger" (המבשר) from the scriptural text as "the anointed of the spir[it]" ([ח]משיח הרו) about whom Daniel spoke. The designation משיח הרוח is not taken from the biblical text, but is most likely construed under the influence of Isa 61:1. It serves as a link between Isa 52:7 and Dan 9:25b. Since the latter contains the reference to the "anointed one," it is very likely that this verse was quoted after the introductory clause [אשר אמר דנ[יאל]. If so, then, as most scholars assume, "the anointed of the spirit" should be identified with "the anointed prince" of Dan 9:25. The fragmentary state of the text, however, prevents any certainty regarding the identity of משיח הרוח in 11Q13, so that other interpretations remain possible.[81]

Some scholars have connected the "Anointed One" in 11Q13 to the messianic figure, who holds the role of judge, in *1 Enoch* 55:4.[82] As noted above, the Anointed One is enthroned on the throne of glory and possesses the royal title of Messiah (*1 En*. 48:10; 52:4). The Anointed One in the *Similitudes* is located in the heavenly council (40:5; 61:10), and metes out the judgment meted out on God's behalf (46:1–6). It is similar to the function of Melchizedek in 11Q13.[83]

Two Messiahs?

It seems that two Messiahs are expected in Qumran (1QS 9:11; CD 7:18 f.; 19:10 f.; 20:1; cf. 4Q175 9–13, 14–20), "one royal and one priestly,"[84] while the high priest Messiah has the function of the eschatological High Priest.[85] The "Two Messiahs" idea has "its biblical precedent in Zechariah's 'two sons

---

80. Novakovic, "4Q521: The Works of the Messiah or the Signs of the Messianic Time?," 218.

81. Novakovic, "4Q521: The Works of the Messiah or the Signs of the Messianic Time?," 219.

82. Zimmermann, *Messianische Texte aus Qumran*, 404.

83. Kvanvig, "The Son of Man in the Parables of Enoch," 190.

84. See Cross, "Notes on the Doctrine of the Two Messiahs at Qumran and the Extra-Canonical Daniel Apocalypse (4Q246)," 1–13; Collins, *The Scepter and Star*, 75; Schniedewind, "Structural Aspects of Qumran Messianism in the *Damascus Document*," 523–36.

85. Collins, *The Scepter and Star*, 81.

of oil.'"⁸⁶ The high priest Messiah wields equal or greater authority to that of the royal messiah (1QSa 2:11–16). In the eschatological war, which is conducted as a holy war, the high priest again plays a far more dominant role than does the prince of the community, for it is he who draws up the ranks.⁸⁷ Collins notes,

> These several other texts indicate that the royal messiah must defer to priestly authority. In 4QpIsaᵃ, the biblical phrase, "He shall not judge by what his eyes see" (Isa 11:3), is taken to mean that the messiah will defer to the teachings of "the priests of renown." 4Q285 (the "dying messiah" text), line 5, after the reference to the Prince of Congregation, reads "and a priest will command. . . ." The High Priest in the War Scroll enjoys greater prominence than the Prince of the Congregation in any case. In the Scroll of Blessings (1QS) the blessing of the High Priest precedes that of the Prince of Congregation. Further, in Florilegium 1:11, the Branch of David is accompanied by the Interpreter of the Law, and likewise in CD 7:18 the Prince of the Congregation is linked with the Interpreter, who can plausibly, though not certainly, be identified as a priestly messiah. In fact, all the major rule and law books, the *Community Rule*, the *Messianic Rule*, the *Damascus Document*, and the War Rule, support the bifurcation of authority in the messianic era. We might add that the Temple Scroll, which some scholars regard as the Torah for the end of days, clearly subjects the king to the authority of the High Priest: "on the instructions he shall go out and on his instructions he shall return home."⁸⁸

Additionally, Atkinson states,

> Because the writers of the Dead Sea Scrolls also oppose the illegitimate combination of the priesthood and kingship by the Hasmoneans, they insist that the messiah cannot be both a priest and a king. Consequently, the authors of these two Dead Sea Scrolls, namely 1QSa and 1QSb, have a special interest in explaining the bifurcation of authority between the Davidic messiah and the high priest. There must be both a priestly

---

86. Collins, *The Scepter and Star*, 77; Evans, "'The Two Sons of Oil': Early Evidence of Messianic Interpretation of Zechariah 4:14 in 4Q254 4 2," 72. Collins comments that Qumran's diarchic messianism is based on Zechariah 3–4 (cf. Zech 6:12–13). Collins, *The Scepter and Star*, 77.

87. Collins, *The Scepter and Star*, 77.

88. Collins, *The Scepter and Star*, 82–83.

messiah and a royal messiah because the two offices can never be combined.[89]

However, the overlapping of these messianic figures is coherent and is based on biblical references, while the dating of Qumran material and the theories of the development of messianic ideas are difficult to determine.[90] The royal messianic figure in some Jewish texts is described as having priestly authority in the religious area (4Q161 8–10 3:21–24; 4Q285 5 4–5; 4Q174 1:11–12; cf. *Jub.* 31:11–17; *T. Levi* 8:2–17; 18:3; *T. Jud.* 21:1–5; 25:1; *T. Iss.* 5:7; *T. Naph.* 5:3–5; *T. Jos.* 19:11).[91] Because the allusion to the LXX Pentateuch and Chronicles is applied in these two messianic figures, Horbury insists,

> Thus, the Rule of the Community in its Cave 1 copy includes the clause "until the coming of the prophet and the messiahs of Aaron and Israel (9.11)." In its duality this clause seems to be consistent with reference to "the messiah of Israel" and "the priest" in the Rule of the Congregation, and with blessings for the prince of the congregation and for a figure likely to be the high priest in the collections of Blessings. On the other hand, the Damascus Document presents the singular form "Messiah of Aaron and Israel." This also can be interpreted as a reference to two figures, but it need not be. Moreover, the particularly elaborate development of the Davidic figure is evident in the Rule literature already cited, and in Qumran biblical interpretation.[92]

In addition, while the two messiahs should be considered in the messianism of the Second Temple literature, it is necessary to realize that a certain messianic figure is inclined to take on the role of the other messianic figures.[93] In other words, the Davidic Messiah assumes a greater role as he takes on the roles of priestly, prophetic, or transcendent figures.[94] As mentioned above, the priest messiah is combined with the eschatological teacher in Qumran, and the heavenly figure is identified with the messianic king—who is a militant king. The Davidic Messiah is evidently portrayed as

---

89. Atkinson, *I Cried to the Lord*, 147; Lichtenberger, "Messianic Expectations and Messianic Figures," 9–20; Oegema, "Messianic Expectations in the Qumran Writings," 65–66.
90. Collins, *The Scepter and Star*, 77–80.
91. Collins, *The Scepter and Star*, 71–101.
92. Horbury, *Jewish Messianism and the Cult of Christ*, 60.
93. Condra, *Salvation for the Righteous Revealed*, 230.
94. Condra, *Salvation for the Righteous Revealed*, 230.

a prophet in Targums.⁹⁵ These verses are allusions to Numbers 24:17, and linked with Isaiah 11:1. Moreover Collins attests,

> There follows a passage on the failure of the kingship of Judah, "until the salvation of Israel comes, until the appearing of the God of righteousness" (22:2), which is quite probably Christian. The initial distinction between the kingship and the priesthood, however, addresses no situation in Christianity, whereas it has an obvious *Sitz-im-Leben* in Judaism. The warning that the priesthood falls away from the Lord when it lets itself be dominated by the kingship is surely a criticism of the Hasmoneans. The one leadership is emphasized concerning one figure, who is identified as Messiah.⁹⁶

The point is that the Damascus Document anticipates a single office of kingship and priesthood,⁹⁷ while scholars can explain the hint of a prominent priesthood and the concept of two messiahs in some Qumran writings as reflecting the political and historical situation of the Maccabean and Hasmonaean era.

In sum, the messianic figures in the Pseudepigrapha and Qumran writings possess cohesive characters of the Davidic Messiah from the Davidic line—which corresponds to such messianic texts as Genesis 49:10, Numbers 24:17, and other texts in the Prophets—while the messianic emphasis is sparse in the Apocrypha. In other words, several messianic titles for the eschatological messianic figure are presented in these texts. In the Second Temple writings, though, is the constant description for the Davidic Messiah, who will be from the Davidic line based on 2 Samuel 7. These titles do not present different messianic figures.

THE DAVIDIC MESSIAH: THE AGENT OF GOD'S JUDGMENT

The consistent Davidic Messiah description includes the concept that he mainly executes God's eschatological judgment. The Old Testament terms employed in describing the Davidic Messiah's judgment are applied to the messianic figure in the Second Temple writings. The Davidic Messiah is the eschatological judge, who is empowered by God's Spirit and granted with

---

95. With respect to the Davidic Messiah having features of other messianic figures, specifically the prophetic messiah, see Evans, *Jesus and His Contemporaries*, 447–51.

96. Collins, *The Scepter and Star*, 101. See especially de Jonge, "Two Messiahs in the Testaments of the Twelve Patriarchs," 191–203.

97. Collins, "The Nature of Messianism in the Light of the Dead Sea Scrolls," 209.

righteousness, and he is described as judging the wicked in the heavenly court, conquering the oppressors, and carrying out the vengeance of God's judgments.

Similitudes (1 Enoch 37–71)

In the *Similitudes*, the Son of Man is described as the eschatological judge.[98] His main function is additionally judgment as is the case of the Davidic Messiah in Isaiah.[99] His glorious throne is like that of a judge (62:5; 69:29).[100] The Spirit seated him on the heavenly throne, which is in the heavenly courtroom (61:8).[101] This concept is related to the Messiah Christology of early Christianity. Horbury writes,

> But the *Parables of Enoch* on messianic enthronement (45:3), viewed in combination with rabbinic interpretation of both Dan 7 and this psalm [110] and the implications of Mark 12:35–37, have been held to suggest that the beginning of the psalm could indeed be understood messianically at the end of the Second Temple period. Similarly the exaltation of Christ over heaven and earth and in the general resurrection and judgment is comparable with the messianic exaltation at the last judgment depicted in the *Parables of Enoch* (46–53, 62–64).[102]

The Davidic Messiah's exaltation at the eschatological heavenly court is depicted in the *Parables of Enoch*. He shall sit down on the heavenly throne and judge "the secret things" and the disobedient angels (49:2-4; 55:4; 61:8-9). The throne of glory designates the executor of God's judgment (45:3; 51:3; 55:4; 61:8; 62:2, 3, 5; 69:27, 29).[103]

The Messiah as the agent of God's judgment is characterized by wisdom that is imparted from God as in the Old Testament. The wisdom endowed to

---

98. Chialà, "The Son of Man," 196.

99. Chialà, "The Son of Man," 161.

100. "And, pain shall seize them when they see that Son of Man sitting on the throne of his glory" (62:5). "The Son of Man has appeared and has seated himself upon the throne of his glory" (69:29).

101. The "Lord of the Spirits" will seat the "Elect One on the throne of his glory; and he [the Elect One] shall judge all the works of the holy ones in heaven above, weighing in the balance their deeds" (61:8).

102. Horbury, *Messianism among Jews and Christians*, 14–15.

103. Kvanvig, "The Son of Man in the Parables of Enoch," 189. Enthronement and judgment are from Ps 110, in which the Son of Man and the Chosen One are combined. See Theisohn, *Der auserwählte Richter*, 92–98; Black, "The Messianism of the Parables of Enoch," 150–55.

the Davidic Messiah entails righteous judgment (49:3–4).[104] In these verses, 49:3–4, the Messiah shall judge the secret things because the spirit of wisdom dwells in him. The spirit of wisdom is the spirit of righteousness, which was poured upon him, so that he may judge all oppressors as noted above (62:2). This righteousness is closely connected with wisdom as in Isaiah 11, and the righteous judgment of the Davidic Messiah.

Psalms of Solomon

In the *Psalms of Solomon*, the Davidic Messiah is the agent of God's judgment, accomplishing God's judgment on sinful Israel. This king's role is violent because he is "to destroy the unrighteous rulers, to purge Jerusalem from Gentiles" (17:22). He will "smash the arrogance of sinners like a potter's jar" (17:23), "shatter all their substance with an iron rod," and "destroy the unlawful nations with the word of his mouth" (17:24).[105] Loren T. Stuckenbruck remarks,

> This retribution against the enemies of God's people might leave the impression that the Messiah is essentially a warrior figure—that is, one who will deliver Israel through military conflict. Indeed, it is at least true in principle that the author claims he "will crush all their substance with an iron rod" (v. 24), which borrows language from Ps 2:9. However, this may in fact be a description of the effect rather than the means, since it is "by the word of his mouth" that this will be accomplished (v. 24; cf. v. 35: "he will strike the earth with the word of his mouth forever").[106]

The judgment will be violent overthrow and destruction, which is described as occurring "with an iron rod."[107] He "ushers in a rule of righteousness over a holy people he gathers together."[108]

---

104. "In him dwells the spirit of wisdom, the spirit which gives thoughtfulness, the spirit of knowledge and strength, and the spirit of those who have fallen asleep in righteousness. He shall judge the secret things. And no one will be able to utter vain words in his presence. For he is the Elect One before the Lord of Spirits according to his good pleasure" (*1 En.* 49:3–4).

105. With regard to similarity with Ps 2, see Schaper, *Eschatology in the Greek Psalter*, 75.

106. Stuckenbruck, "Messianic Ideas in the Apocalyptic and Related Literature of Early Judaism," 95.

107. Reiser, *Jesus and Judgment*, 49.

108. Condra, *Salvation for the Righteous Revealed*, 240.

The Davidic Messiah will judge God's people (17:26) and nations "in the wisdom of his righteousness" (17:29).[109] According to 17:23 (cf. 29), his wisdom of righteousness forms the image of the hoped-for king in the *Psalms of Solomon* 17 (righteousness: 17:26, 29, 32, 37, 40; wisdom: 17:29, 35, 37).[110] The wisdom of righteousness "justifies the Davidic nuances."[111] God raises up the anointed one (18:6), and the spiritual endowment on the king is stressed.[112] Horbury attests, "It is consistent with this interpretation that the spiritual endowment of the king is emphasized; in a passage noted above with regard to investiture by bestowal of the spirit, he is pure from sin, and God has made him 'mighty in holy spirit' (*Ps. Sol.* 17:41–42 [36–37]; cf. Isa 11:2; 61:1)."[113] Consequently, through "wisdom of righteousness," he judges God's people (17:26) and peoples and nations (17:29).

Testaments of the Twelve Patriarchs

The Davidic Messiah is described as the executor of judgment (ποιήσει κρίσιν in *T. Levi* 18:2), and judge as the messianic king, who judges (κρῖναι in *T. Jud.* 24:5–6) the nations. His judgment is described as coming with "a rod of righteousness" (ῥάβδος δικαιοσύνης in *T. Jud.* 24:5). This ideal king will be endowed with God's spirit. (*T. Levi* 18:6–7). As the Davidic Messiah, "the glory of the Most High shall burst forth upon him, and the spirit of understanding (πνεῦμα συνέσεως) and sanctification shall rest upon him" (*T. Levi* 18:6–7).

Dead Sea Scrolls

The various names for the Davidic Messianic figure mainly describe his role as the agent of God's judgment. The judgment image of the Davidic Messiah is based on Isaiah 10:34–11:5, in which the agent of God's judgment is associated with the eschatological war in the Qumran writings.[114] The Branch of David (4Q161 8–10 11, 18) clearly has the role of eschatological judge over the nations in the final days, in which the context is martial. James C. VanderKam describes,

---

109. "Κρίνει λαοὺς καὶ ἔθνη ἐν σοφίᾳ δικαιοσύνης αὐτοῦ."
110. Schreiber, *Gesalbter und König*, 170.
111. Mack, "Wisdom Makes a Difference," 40.
112. Horbury, "Messianism in the Old Testament Apocrypha," 432.
113. Horbury, "Messianism in the Old Testament Apocrypha," 431–32.
114. Collins, *The Scepter and Star*, 64.

In addition to his standing in the latter days, he does something to his foes, God will sustain him with a spirit of strength, he will have a glorious throne, a holy crown, splendid clothes, and he will rule over the nations, whom his sword will judge.[115]

Another term for the Davidic Messiah, the Prince of the Congregation, who is identified with the Branch of David, is "one of the protagonists of the eschatological battle (1QM, 4Q161, 4Q285) or a simple warrior (1QSb, CD 7, non-eschatologically 4Q376),"[116] and he shall slay the enemy (4Q285, 1QSb 5:24–25, and 4Q161).[117] According to Géza G. Xeravits,

> The נָשִׂיא appears in the Midrash Amos-Numbers of the Damascus Document, where a short, yet important exegetical hint is connected to him (CD vii 20–21). Noteworthy in the present instance is that the Midrash identifies the eschatological warrior prophesized by the Balaam oracle (Num 24:17) with the נשיא כל העדה. His task is to "destroy all the sons of Seth," that is, to liberate his people. This image is very close to the eschatological battle; moreover, the basic biblical text of the passage appears also in 1QM xi 6. The blessing that 1QSb v 20ff contains over the נשיא העדה again emphasizes the militant character of this figure.[118]

God establishes the Prince of the Congregation with the scepter: "For God has raised you to a scepter" (כיא אל הקימכה לשבת; 1Q28b 5:27). The scepter in 1Q28b (1QSb), which also shows characteristics of judgment, recalls Isaiah 11:4, Genesis 49:10, and Numbers 24:17.[119] It bears royal messianic symbolism as a sign of sovereignty over kings and peoples. The influence of Psalm 2:9 on the motive needs to be considered where the "iron rod" serves to destroy the enemies like pottery in 1Q28b col. 5.[120] The power of his mouth and the breath of his lips (1Q28b 5:24), based on Isaiah 11:4 and the parallel construction in Psalm 17:24, echo the idea of the effective word of the anointed.[121]

While the messianic figure has the role of military warrior, it is paralleled with the judicial judgment role. The role of the Prince of the

---

115. VanderKam, "Messianism in the Scrolls," 216.

116. Xeravits, *King, Priest, Prophet*, 147.

117. These texts allude to the Davidic Messiah in chapters 11 and 12 of Isaiah. See Collins, *The Scepter and Star*, 64.

118. Xeravits, *King, Priest, Prophet*, 147.

119. The mention of the Spirit in 1QSb 5:25 recalls Isa 11:2 f. (cf. Pss 17:32; 18:7).

120. Schreiber, *Gesalbter und König*, 216.

121. Schreiber, *Gesalbter und König*, 216.

Congregation in 1Q28b has judicial aspects: "And he will renew the covenant of the [Com]munity for him, to establish the kingdom of his people forever, to judge the poor with righteousness" (1Q28b 5:21). These verses are blessings that are heavily indebted to Isaiah 11.[122] The Damascus Document 8:1 ff. announces the judgment on rebels, in which the Prince of the Congregation is evidently described as fulfilling a juridical function.[123] The judgment "will be that of all who reject God's precepts and forsake them and move aside in the stubbornness of their heart" (CD 8:18–19). Because in the Damascus Document 7:16–21, the congregation itself is identified with the "king" of the quotation from Amos 5:26 ff., which is defined as David in Amos 9:11, one may presume—with some justification—the community participation in the judgment of the "prince."[124]

The Davidic Messiah, Son of God in 4Q246, has the role of performing God's judgment. This Davidic Messiah's kingdom will be an eternal kingdom, and all of his paths lead to truth (4Q246 2:5). He will judge the earth in truth, and all will make peace (lines 5–6).[125] The result of the Davidic Messiah' judgment is that all of the provinces will pay him homage (line 7).

In 11QMelchizedek, Melchizedek is described as the eschatological agent of God's judgment.[126] Melchizedek is identified as אליהים from Psalm 82:1 and placed as a judge among the angels (11Q13 2:10).[127] Although the identity of Melchizedek is still controversial, he is described as high priest, but as judge, too. Helge S. Kvanvig insists that "he is presented in a heavenly environment, portrayed as a high priest, acting as judge for the wicked and eschatological savior for the righteous."[128] This function of the judge is given to Melchizedek:

> For it is time for the year of grace of Melchizedek, and of [his] arm[ies, the na]tion of the holy ones of God, of the rule of judgment, as it is written about him in the songs of David, who said: "Elohim (אליהים) will [s]tand in the assem[bly of God], in the midst of gods (אליהים) he judges." And about him he sai[d: "And] above [it] to the heights return: God will judge the peoples" (11Q13 2:9–11).

---

122. Collins, *Apocalypticism in the Dead Sea Scrolls*, 82.

123. Schreiber, *Gesalbter und König*, 221.

124. Schreiber, *Gesalbter und König*, 222.

125. The term דין is employed rather than שפת, in 4Q246. ידי[ן] ארעא בקשט וכלא יעבד שלם.

126. Xeravits, *King, Priest, Prophet*, 195.

127. The date of 11Q13 is estimated as the end of the second century BC.

128. Kvanvig, "The Son of Man in the Parables of Enoch," 190.

His revenge is expected to be accomplished as the messianic king (1 *En.* 48:7; cf. Ps 2:9; Isa 11:4; 61:2; *Ps. Sol.* 17:23-27; 2 Esd. 12:32-33; 13:37-38; 2 Baruch 72:2-6).[129] He "will execute the vengeance of the judgments of God" (11Q13 2:13). God's revenge through Melchizedek will be executed on the wicked who followed Belial and his evil spirits. Bringing the vengeance of God's judgment is referred to in the phrase וְיוֹם נָקָם לֵאלֹהֵינוּ in Isaiah 61:2. According to Andrew Chester,

> The prophetic role of proclamation is defined in terms of Isa 52:7, interpreted to show this figure to be the prophet of the final age, and Isa 61:1-2, where the anointing with the Spirit legitimates his message and gives it divine authority. His role as messenger would appear to be that of a forerunner of Melchizedek, but that does not in itself preclude a specifically messianic status for him: by his proclamation he plays a decisive part in helping bring in the final judgment and deliverance, which will have its fulfillment in the coming of Melchizedek.[130]

The phrase "in the year of the Lord's favor" is an allusion to Isaiah 61:2, "the day of vengeance for our God." While God himself is executor of the judgment in Isaiah 61:2, "Melchizedek will execute the vengeance of the judgment of G[od]" (11Q13 2:13).

11QMelchizedek applies Psalm 82:1 to Melchizedek: "Elohim [God] takes his stand in the assembly of El, in the midst of Elohim [gods] he judges." Melchizedek is described as mighty among gods in Psalm 82, and simultaneously he is "the ancient king of Salem and priestly forbear of David" (Ps 110:3).[131] This shows Melchizedek is not just compared with the angelic figures, yet with the great messianic king to make the Lord's judgment.[132] He is "treated as a spirit who answers to what is envisaged in Isa 61:1-2, when God's day is announced by one who is anointed and upon whom is the spirit of the Lord."[133] Melchizedek's name is replaced with that of "the Lord" in the phrase "in the year of the Lord's favor" (Isa 61:2).[134] Horbury argues, "Although the fragmentary state of the text makes judgment tentative, it seems on balance likely that he is indeed a messianic figure, a king of old who has gained angelic status and will return as deliverer and judge."[135] He

---

129. Horbury, *Messianism among Jews and Christians*, 85.
130. Chester, *Messiah and Exaltation*, 261.
131. Horbury, *Messianism among Jews and Christians*, 85.
132. Horbury, *Messianism among Jews and Christians*, 85.
133. Horbury, *Messianism among Jews and Christians*, 85.
134. VanderKam and Flint, eds., *The Meaning of the Dead Sea Scrolls*, 225.
135. VanderKam and Flint, eds., *The Meaning of the Dead Sea Scrolls*, 225. See

represents the kingship of the Lord, and he is the deliverer from the burden of the sins of God's people in the year of jubilee. The Psalter requests just and impartial judgment on the wicked in the next verse (Ps 82:2). James D. G. Dunn posits,

> As for that which he s[aid, "How long will you] judge unjustly and show partiality to the wicked? Selah" (Ps 82.2), its interpretation concerns Belial and the spirits of his lot [who] rebelled by turning away from the precepts of God.... And Melchizedek will avenge the vengeance of the judgments of God... (11QMelch 9–13).[136]

In 11Q13, Melchizedek's execution of God's judgment additionally is universal and extending to the transcendent sphere, while Psalm 82:1 is applied to Melchizedek.[137]

As a result, the Davidic Messiah implements God's judgment role. The Davidic Messiah is expected as the eschatological judge and redeemer, who fulfills the role of the priestly messianic figure in the Second Temple literature, as well. He is empowered by God's spirit, and righteousness is endowed to him to execute righteous judgment. With "an iron rod," he ushers in a rule of righteousness. The Davidic Messiah, who is the agent of God's judgment, carries out bringing God's vengeance over the wicked.

THE DAVIDIC MESSIAH'S RIGHTEOUS JUDGMENT

The righteousness language describes the judgment of the messianic figure as righteous judgment in the messianic texts. Rather, the impartiality in just judgment, through the Davidic Messiah, is focused on in the righteousness language in eschatological-judgment scenes. The Davidic Messiah executes righteous judgment beyond covenantal relationship, which is identified as God's relationship with his people. The righteousness in the God's judgment through the Davidic Messiah demonstrates that the righteousness in the Messiah's judgment is not same with faithfulness language, and the Messiah's faithfulness is sparse in the Second Temple Jewish writings.

Vermès, *The Complete Dead Sea Scrolls*, 500–502; Collins, *The Scepter and Star*, 176; Puech, *La croyance des esséniens en la vie future*, 516–62.

136. Dunn, "Jesus the Judge: Further Thoughts of Paul's Christology and Soteriology," 392.

137. Xeravits, *King, Priest, Prophet*, 196.

The Righteous Messiah

The messianic figure is portrayed as the righteous judge, who executes just judgment. As the adjective "*righteous*" signifies a retributive justice in judgment as noted in the previous chapter, the Davidic Messiah condemns the wicked in his righteous judgment in the Second Temple literature. Desta Heliso affirms, "'The righteous one' and 'messiah' are epithets for a continuing royal-messianic and forensic-eschatological ideology within Judaism."[138] The righteous Messiah's judgment represents God's justice and righteousness. When the adjective "righteous" is employed in the Messiah's judging, it does not describe his covenantal commitment or faithfulness.

In the *Similitudes*, the "Righteous One," who is the Davidic Messiah, executes just judgment. The Davidic Messiah, who is the Chosen One, sits "on the throne of glory" (*1 En.* 45:3) in the heavenly courtroom (61:6–13). Those who have committed sin and crime shall be destroyed by judgment before the glorious throne (45:5–6). The Chosen One shall judge their secret ways by "righteous judgment" in heaven above (61:8–9). The judgment of the Chosen One, who is the Righteous One (38:2–3; 47:1), will be righteous judgment (50:4; 61:9), which corresponds to the Lord's impartial judgment in righteousness (63:8–9).

The righteous Messiah concept can be identified with the role of judge, and it corresponds to the righteous God in the *Psalms of Solomon* (2:10, 15, 18, 32; 3:3; 4:8, 24; 5:1; 8:7, 24–26; 9:2, 5; 10:5). In the *Psalms of Solomon* 17:32, God will teach the righteous Messiah will be taught by God, and "there will be no unrighteousness among them during his reign."[139] The dominion and judicial function of the Davidic Messiah, χριστός κυρίου, is symbolized by "under the rod of discipline" (ὑπὸ ῥάβδον παιδείας) in 18:7, which corresponds to the Davidic Messiah's judgment in Psalm 2, Isaiah 9, and 11, and it is from his fear of God, spiritual wisdom, righteousness, and strength (18:7).[140] The king is the righteous ruler over a sanctified Israel, out of which the unjust, sinners, and strangers are removed (17:26–28).[141]

The *pesher* of Isaiah, 4Q161 frag 8–10 13, which follows the statement in Isaiah 11, says the Davidic messianic figure "will not judge by appearance, he will judge in righteousness." This messianic figure is the Branch of David (צמח דויד; 4Q161 frag 8–18) as in 4Q252, and the Branch of David

---

138. Heliso, *Pistis and the Righteous One*, 51n51. Cf. Isa 11:1–5; 53:11; Jer 23:5; *1 En.* 38:2–3; 52:4; 53:6; *Ps. Sol.* 17:32; 4Q161; 4Q252; 4Q285.

139. "Καὶ οὐκ ἔστιν ἀδικία ἐν ταῖς ἡμέραις αὐτοῦ ἐν μέσῳ αὐτῶν, ὅτι πάντες ἅγιοι, καὶ βασιλεὺς αὐτῶν χριστὸς κυρίου" (17:32).

140. Schreiber, *Gesalbter und König*, 173.

141. Schreiber, *Gesalbter und König*, 173.

is identified as "the righteous messiah" in Qumran *pesher*, 4Q252. He is "the messiah of righteousness, the branch of David" (משיח הצדק צמח דויד; 4Q252 col. 5. 3–4). These titles reflect "the 'Righteous Branch' of Jeremiah 23:5 and 33:15, and show beyond doubt that Jeremiah's 'Branch' could also be called 'messiah' at Qumran."[142]

Judgment through the Davidic Messiah in Righteousness

The Messiah judges "in righteousness," by which the term "righteousness" cannot refer to the covenantal faithfulness itself in messianic texts. This righteousness describes distributive justice, by which the Messiah justifies his people and condemns the wicked. This feature of righteousness is shown as related to God's judgment through the Davidic Messiah in the *Similitudes*. The Davidic Messiah—the Son of Man—is described as the one to whom righteousness belongs and in whom righteousness dwells (*1 En*. 46:3). As the result of righteousness, he will judge the kings, the mighty ones, and the strong ones (46:4), and he will crush the sinners (46:4). In him dwells the spirit of righteousness, so that he shall judge the secret things (49:3). George W. E. Nickelsburg explains,

> The Chosen One has taken his stand before the Lord of Spirits. His qualifications are divine wisdom and righteousness (*1 Enoch* 49:2–4). This passage draws its motifs from Isaiah 11:2–5, which stresses the judicial functions of the Davidic king, primarily the divinely given wisdom that enables him to penetrate facade and judge human deeds righteously and with equity. Into this allusion is added reference to the persecuted righteous, whose vindicator the Chosen One is.[143]

After sitting on his glorious throne and pouring out the spirit of righteousness upon himself (62:2), he will eliminate all the sinners and oppressors (62:2). The judgment of the Messiah will be executed in righteousness (62:2–3). Charles Lee Irons says that "thus, 'the righteousness of the Head of Days' that will not depart from the Son of Man is a judicial righteousness that involves his role as God's vice-regent who executes judgment on the world."[144] His throne is the place of heavenly judgment, and the Messiah carries out judgment in righteousness (62:3).

---

142. Collins, *The Scepter and Star*, 79; Zimmermann, *Messianische Texte aus Qumran*, 126; Schreiber, *Gesalbter und König*, 212.

143. Nickelsburg, "Salvation without and with a Messiah," 60–61.

144. Irons, *The Righteousness of God*, 196.

The Davidic Messiah is the impartial executor of God's judgment for the wicked who have oppressed the righteous (46:1–8). *1 Enoch* 38:3 reads, "When the secrets of the Righteous One are revealed, he shall judge the sinners, and the wicked one will be driven from the presence of the righteous and the elect." In the Messiah's judgment in righteousness, sinners and all oppressors shall be destroyed from before the face of the Davidic Messiah (62:2). Hence, "oppression cannot survive his judgment and the unrepentant in his judgment shall perish" (50:4).

In the *Psalms of Solomon*, the theme of righteousness in the seventeenth chapter is reminiscent of Isaiah 11:3–5, Psalm 72:2. Retributive judgment against the wicked characterizes his judgment. He will judge peoples and nations in righteousness (17:23, 29), destroy the unlawful nations (17:24), and condemn sinners (17:25).

The purpose of righteousness is perceived as just judgment (17:23–24). In 17:26, the Davidic Messiah will lead in righteousness. His leading corresponds with his judgment over the tribes of the people.[145] The judging with righteousness is manifested in his intolerance of unrighteousness, which is described as evil: "He will not tolerate unrighteousness (ἀδικίαν) to dwell among them again, and no person who knows evil will live with them" (17:27). With his judicial function, he participates in the righteousness of God (*Ps. Sol.* 2:30–36).[146] He is an expected and idealized king, with the characteristics of David's righteousness. His just judgment reflects God's impartial judgment (*Pss. Sol.* 2:18; 9:5), and God's righteousness over sinners is demonstrated in his judgment, which is according to people's behavior (*Ps. Sol.* 2:16).[147] František Ábel maintains,

> God's righteousness is therefore the basis of God's passing judgment on all human beings' actions, whereby God is judging the whole world in the wisdom of God's own righteousness. Therefore, the judging activity of the Messiah himself is in accordance with the justness and righteousness of God and applies to all nations on the earth.[148]

Israel's salvation highlights the exercise of judgment by the new king, with God's power (17:3–4).[149] The salvation can begin after the Davidic Messiah imposes judgment on the oppressors of Israel (17:21–25). The judgment

---

145. "Καὶ συνάξει λαὸν ἅγιον, οὗ ἀφηγήσεται ἐν δικαιοσύνῃ, καὶ κρινεῖ φυλὰς λαοῦ ἡγιασμένου ὑπὸ κυρίου θεοῦ αὐτοῦ" (17:26).

146. Schreiber, *Gesalbter und König*, 432.

147. Ábel, *The Psalms of Solomon and the Messianic Ethics of Paul*, 61.

148. Ábel, *The Psalms of Solomon and the Messianic Ethics of Paul*, 186.

149. Schreiber, *Gesalbter und König*, 175.

in righteousness effects the vindication of the pious, but condemnation or destruction for the wicked. The Davidic Messiah is described in 17:40 as one who faithfully and righteously shepherds his people.[150] The Davidic Messiah's righteous shepherding is impartial, and it is an aspect of his agency of God's judgment as in Jeremiah and Ezekiel. According to the *Psalms of Solomon* 17:41, "He will lead them all in equity and there will be no arrogance among them, that any should be oppressed."[151] The judgment through the Davidic Messiah has features embodied in the phrase, "with equity" (ἐν ἰσότητι) to justly judge his people and nations.[152] The next verse 42 demonstrates that the Davidic Messiah has knowledge from God, which is the required condition for the just judgment, as an allusion to Isaiah 11, as mentioned above ("This is the beauty of the king of Israel which God knew").[153] So then, the Davidic Messiah shall judge the peoples in the assemblies and the tribes of the sanctified (17:43).

1Q28b characterizes God's judgment through the Davidic Messiah as impartial judgment. The Davidic Messiah, the Prince of the Congregation, "will judge the poor with righteousness" (ולשפוט בצדק אביונים; 1Q28b 5:21). His judgment for the afflicted (לענוי) is impartial because he will judge them with equity (במישור; 1Q28b 5:22), which recalls Isaiah 11:4. The wicked are the main object of his impartial judgment (1Q28b 5:25), or the impartiality in the Davidic Messiah's judgment characterizes the meaning of righteousness. The interpretation of Isaiah 11 in this *pesher* has interpreted the idea to be one of judgment with righteousness through the Davidic Messiah. Righteous judgment means dealing with the poor in righteousness in 4Q161. The Davidic Messiah "will not judge by appearance or give verdicts on hearsay alone; he will judge the poor with righteousness (בצדק) and decide with honesty for the humble of the earth" (4Q161 frag 8–10 13–15), and "will kill the wicked" (4Q161 frag 8–10 16).

The righteousness in judgment through the Davidic Messiah entails judgment over all the peoples, who are the wicked, including the enemy. The Messiah's "sword will judge all the peoples" (4Q161 3:22). His judgment is impartial for the poor and the humble of the earth, so that the enemy, who is characterized as *Kittim*, will be killed by "the rod of his mouth and the breath of his lips" (4Q161 3:14–15, 19). In 11Q13, the messianic figure,

---

150. "Faithfully and righteously shepherding the Lord's flock" (ποιμαίνων τὸ ποίμνιον κυρίου ἐν πίστει καὶ δικαιοσύνῃ).

151. "Ἐν ἰσότητι πάντας αὐτοὺς ἄξει, καὶ οὐκ ἔσται ἐν αὐτοῖς ὑπερηφανία τοῦ καταδυναστευθῆναι ἐν αὐτοῖς."

152. The term "ἰσότης" means state of being fair, fairness. With δικαιοσύνης it means justice and fairness. BDAG, 481.

153. "Αὕτη ἡ εὐπρέπεια τοῦ βασιλέως Ισραηλ, ἣν ἔγνω ὁ θεός."

Melchizedek, executes God's judgment as noted above. His execution of God's judgment, which is impartial, is expected. The Davidic Psalm, Psalm 82, is referred to in Melchizedek's judgment, "How long will you judge unjustly and show partiality to the wicked?"

Covenantal Faithfulness?

Although righteousness might be said to be within the covenantal relation with God's people, righteousness in God's judgment cannot be covenantal faithfulness itself. The broader notion of covenantal faithfulness may overlap with the language of righteousness because righteousness can fulfill God's covenant promises in his covenantal relationship with his people. However, covenantal faithfulness is not righteousness itself, but a subset of righteousness.[154]

Sanders provides some consideration pertaining to righteousness in covenantal relationship. In the Qumran writings, "being righteous" has meaning in relation to "covenant."[155] While the consideration of Sanders is associated with early Judaism, instead of with the Old Testament, it should be thought that "righteousness" frequently appears with "covenant."[156] In addition, Wright believes that righteousness should be rendered "covenantal membership," and a feature of covenantal faithfulness is that it reveals God's judgment based on covenantal curse.[157] It is "evident in Deuteronomy itself."[158] He holds that

> the covenant involves (a) God's judgment on Israel because of unfaithfulness and then (b) renewal at the time when God will "circumcise the heart." ... What Paul has done, in parallel with other second-Temple retrievals of this great narrative such as we find in 4QMMT or Baruch, is to say: now at last we see what it means to "fulfil Torah" in the sense Deuteronomy 30 had in mind. . . . This is the real "return from exile," the lifting of the covenantal curse, the giving of the 'life' which Torah itself had promised but by itself could not give.[159]

---

154. Irons, *The Righteousness of God*, 196.
155. Sanders, *Paul and Palestinian Judaism*, 204–5, 312.
156. See 1QM 17:7–8; 18:8; 1QS 1:1–2:24; 10:1–11:22; 1QSb 3:23–24; CD 1:19–20; 3:15; 8:14; 19:27–31; 20:11; 20:29.
157. Wright, *Paul and the Faithfulness of God*, 514.
158. Wright, *Paul and the Faithfulness of God*, 514.
159. Wright, *Paul and the Faithfulness of God*, 514–15.

In his understanding, "the exile" status is God's judgment, which is his righteousness in the covenantal curse based on Deuteronomy 30. While God's righteousness is his faithfulness in the covenantal relationship with his people, the faithfulness of God includes God's judgment within the covenantal curse.

Yet, Wright is mistaken in categorizing righteousness in God's judgment as noted above. Righteousness may be associated with covenant and, in some degree, it cannot be separated from covenantal faithfulness. But, as Irons asserts, covenantal faithfulness is a subcategory of righteousness.[160] Consequently, the concept of faithfulness in covenantal relationship cannot be identified with righteousness in judgment of the Davidic Messiah in the messianic texts, when the term "covenant" infrequently appears in messianic texts. The righteousness in the execution of God's judgment through the Davidic Messiah can be identified with judging righteousness, which is impartial in just judgment.

Righteousness effects God's judgment over all peoples, who do not have a covenantal relationship with God. Righteousness itself means doing what is right and good before him, and this illustrates that righteousness has the meaning of action according to norm, as noted in the previous chapter. 4QMMT C line 31, reads, "And it shall be reckoned to you as righteousness when you do what is right and good before him."[161] In this verse, the meaning of צדקה is certainly doing what needs to be done.[162] Moreover, God's righteousness is "a commitment to do what is 'right' with reference to that covenant."[163] God's righteousness assumes a judgmental aspect when Israel breaks the covenantal relationship, but the righteousness of God, which is doing what is "right," is not limited just to the covenantal relationship with his people.

---

160. Irons, in *The Righteousness of God*, 196, argues the righteousness in the Second Temple Jewish writings is based on the Old Testament. He says, "We also saw that the relational interpretation—in which 'righteousness' is conformity to the terms of a relationship rather than to an external norm—is incorrect. We also saw that 'the righteousness of God' in the OT is not a cipher for God's covenantal faithfulness." It is especially evident in the DSS, as he writes, "The following table seeks to summarize the data for all occurrences of 'righteousness' (masculine and feminine) in the DSS, using nearly the same categories that were used in our analysis of OT usage in Chapter 4." Irons, in *The Righteousness of God*, 200.

161. ונחשבה לך לצדקה בעשותך הישר והטוב לפנו

162. Contra Sanders, for examples of the righteousness with covenant in Second Temple writings, see Seifrid, "Righteousness Language in the Hebrew Scripture and Early Judaism," 433–38.

163. Moo, *The Epistle to the Romans*, 83.

In the *Pseudepigrapha*, covenant is barely presented in the messianic texts, especially in the Messiah's judgment scene. This corresponds to God's righteousness in his righteous judgment. According to Irons,

> In all of these cases, God's righteousness as judge is manifested in his punishment of the sinners among the nation of Israel. Indeed, the dispersion of Israel among the nations was God's righteous punishment upon the nation for its "acts of lawlessness" (ἀνομίαι). The language of the "justification" of God, that is, the acknowledgment that God is right and just in his judgments, occurs seven times in the *Pss. Sol.* (2:15; 3:5; 4:8; 8:7, 23, 26; 9:2).[164]

In the Davidic Messiah's judgment scene, mercy, love, and truth (ἔλεος, ἀγάπη, and ἀλήθεια) are employed for faithfulness in the covenantal relationship in the *Psalms of Solomon* (*Pss. Sol.* 17:15-17, 45; 18:3). Furthermore, in Qumran literature, faithfulness (CD 7:5; אמנות) and mercy (4Q491 1:2; חסד) are used for God's covenantal faithfulness in the Messianic texts. While God or the Davidic Messiah can be faithful to the covenantal relationship, the term for faithfulness should be recognized as differentiated from righteousness.

In addition, while righteousness overlaps with the covenantal concept, the covenantal relationship cannot support righteousness in God's judgment through the Davidic Messiah over all Gentiles in the earth. The Gentiles' relationship with God is totally different from Israel's covenant; it possesses "no explicit assertion of covenantal identity."[165] It is difficult to include Gentiles in the covenantal categorization, as Ellen Juhl Christiansen contends that "the boundaries (covenantal boundaries) are drawn not to mark off the people from the outside world of the Gentiles, but are demarcation lines within Israel."[166] God's righteousness in his judgment through the Davidic Messiah, however, is effective over all nations, including Gentiles. *1 Enoch* 45:6 states, "But sinners have come before me so that by judgment I shall destroy them from before the face of the earth." God's judgment through the Davidic Messiah is based on their works and deeds, instead of on a failure in covenantal relationship (61:8). Of course, when it is applied to the covenantal people, God's judgment can be supported with the covenantal curse. Yet, it is not possible to apply the covenantal curse to all Gentiles. In *1 Enoch*, the sinners include the kings, the mighty ones, and the strong ones (46:4; 62:3, 6), and they are sinners (46:4), who are described as fulfilling the criminal deeds of their hands and eating all of the produce of crime

---

164. Irons, *The Righteousness of God*, 223.
165. Christiansen, *The Covenant in Judaism and Paul*, 214.
166. Christiansen, *The Covenant in Judaism and Paul*, 143.

(53:2). It is their way of life (48:7). Peoples in the earth will be judged on the basis of their own deeds. The Davidic Messiah will judge them (46:4) in his righteousness (46:3). Righteousness corresponds to judging righteousness over all nations in this description, rather than to Messiah's faithfulness itself, based on the covenantal curse. Additionally, righteousness can be described as doing what is right to the peoples in the earth, rather than as their faithfulness in the covenantal relationship because the covenantal explication of righteousness can be effective only in the case of God's people in the covenantal relationship.

A similar case can be made concerning the judgment of the Davidic Messiah in the *Psalms of Solomon* (*Ps. Sol.* 17:23, 24, 25, 29). The Davidic Messiah "will not tolerate unrighteousness (ἀδικίαν) to dwell among them again, and no person who knows evil will live with them" (17:27). While unrighteousness (ἀδικία) is "an act that violates standards of right conduct,"[167] unrighteousness of the Gentiles on the earth is not couched in covenantal language. The Davidic Messiah will judge their unrighteousness by his righteousness—not in a covenantal curse. In the *Psalms of Solomon*, the author presents the crimes of a Gentile sinner, who is a man that is foreign to our race (*Ps. Sol.* 17:11). What this Gentile man "did in Jerusalem was just as the nations do in their cities for their gods" (*Ps. Sol.* 17:15). In these verses about the Gentile sinner, the treatment of Jerusalem is different from that of Gentiles.[168] Atkinson declares,

> Because this man is "foreign to our race" he is clearly a Gentile. The psalmist condemns the Gentiles throughout this poem as the "nations" (*Ps. Sol.* 17:14, 22, 24, 25, 29, 31, 34). In addition to denouncing the Gentiles as "lawless" (*Ps. Sol.* 17:24), the writer views them as "people of mixed origin" (*Ps. Sol.* 17:15) who are not part of the covenant community.[169]

The condemnation of the Gentile sinners shows that the category of covenantal relationship cannot be indiscriminately applied in God's judgment through the Davidic Messiah with his righteousness.

In Qumran writings, similar to other writings, the Davidic Messiah shall judge the nations in righteousness. They not only may be oppressors of Israel; they are unrighteous peoples, who do not do what is right. 1Q28b 5:24–27 reads,

---

167. BDAG, 20.
168. Atkinson, *I Cried to the Lord*, 134.
169. Atkinson, *I Cried to the Lord*, 134–35.

> With the breath of your lips may you kill the wicked. . . . May righteousness be the belt of [your loins, and loyalt]y the belt of your hips . . . and may you trample the nation]s like mud of the streets. For God raised you to a scepter for the rulers be[fore you . . . all na]tions will serve you.

In these verses, all the nations are not simply the oppressors of God's people. They are the peoples of the earth, who are to be judged in the presence of the Davidic Messiah's exaltation and enthronement (5:23). The Davidic Messiah "will give verdicts, judge the poor with righteousness, and decide with equity the humble of the earth" (5:14–15). And, he "will rule over all the pe[oples] and Magog [. . .] his sword will judge [al]l the peoples" (5:21–22). In 11Q13, Melchizedek's judgment is "over [the]m . . . [. . .] accor[ding to] a[ll] their [wor]ks" (2:8). While it is understood as in covenantal relationship, the object of judgment through Melchizedek is not limited to God's people. Instead, it is applied to all the peoples (2:11). In addition, while God's judgment in 11Q13 is focused on spiritual enemies as in 11Q5, categorization of faithfulness for righteousness cannot include this aspect. Charles Irons writes, "The judicial aspect is most clearly seen in his judgment on the various spiritual forces of oppression, together with his vindication of his servants and placing them within the community where they may learn God's righteousness."[170] The judging righteousness should include implicit judgment over the spiritual foes in the Second Temple Jewish writings because the righteousness in God's judgment can be described as developed cosmic and spiritual judgment. The term *righteousness* in God's judgment, through the Davidic Messiah, must include this concept, which is different from a limited categorization of faithfulness for righteousness in judgment.

Consequently, although the faithfulness of God or the Messiah in covenantal relationship with his people and God's faithfulness in general can be related to the term *"righteousness,"* the righteousness in God's judgment through the Messiah is not the same as covenantal faithfulness. Righteousness has a broader meaning, which is based on doing what is right, including God's judgment over all peoples, who do not have a covenantal relationship with God.

---

170. Irons, *The Righteousness of God*, 206.

THE DAVIDIC MESSIAH OF ISAIAH 53 IN THE SECOND TEMPLE JEWISH WRITINGS

While whether the suffering Messiah of Isaiah 53 is anticipated in the Second Temple Jewish literature is a difficult question, the Davidic messianic figure in Isaiah 53 is undeniably characterized as the Davidic Messiah in the Second Temple Jewish literature. His main role is that of the agent of God's judgment like the Davidic Messiah in the Second Temple Jewish literature. As in the Old Testament, the Messiah's faithfulness as an impossible consideration of the suffering Messiah will be examined from this perspective in this section.

1 Enoch

The Davidic messianic figure, the "son of man" in the *Similitudes* of *1 Enoch*, can be identified with features of the Servant of Isaiah.[171] As noted above, the messianic figure in *1 Enoch* 53:6 refers to "the Righteous and the Chosen One" in Isaiah 42:1 and 53:11.[172] Isaiah 42:1 and 49:1–7 are understood as connected to the messianic figure in the *Similitudes*; qualities are picked up from Isaiah's figure (*1 En.* 39:7; 62:7, and Isa 49:2), and his role is introduced as light for the nations (*1 En.* 48:3, and Isa 42:6).[173] The designation, "the Chosen One," could return to "the Righteous One" in Isaiah 53:11 ("the righteous . . . my servant").[174] There is a probable allusion to Isaiah 53:12 in 1 Enoch 62:5.[175] This verse reads, "One half portion of them shall glance at the other half; they shall be terrified and dejected. . . . they see that Son of Man sitting on the throne of his glory." Peter Stuhlmacher explains, "When people look at each another in alarm and lower their gaze in shame, they also tend to fall silent."[176] The Son of Man in 1 *Enoch* shares characteristic traits of the Suffering Servant in Isaiah 35 (1 *En.* 62:1–16 and 63:1–11),

---

171. See Black, "The Messianism of the Parables of Enoch," 160, 167–68.

172. Hengel and Bailey, "The Effective History of Isaiah 53 in the Pre-Christian Period," 271.

173. Hengel and Bailey, "The Effective History of Isaiah 53," 99; Zimmermann, *Messianische Texte aus Qumran*, 271; Black, *The Book of Enoch or 1 Enoch*, 195.

174. Zimmermann, *Messianische Texte aus Qumran*, 271. Concerning the correspondences between *1 Enoch* 62, 63 and Isa 53, see Nickelsburg, *Resurrection, Immortality, and Eternal Life in Intertestamental Judaism*, 71 ff.

175. Hengel and Bailey, "The Effective History of Isaiah 53," 100.

176. Hengel and Bailey, "The Effective History of Isaiah 53," 100.

but the role of the Son of Man is that of the righteous judge, instead of rather than the faithful Messiah.[177]

Dead Sea Scrolls

In Qumran writings, while some scholars have denied a direct connection of these trials with the Suffering Servant in Isaiah 53,[178] the messianic figure in this line can be identified with the Servant of Yahweh in Isaian texts.[179] Some scholars maintain that the messianic figure in Isaiah 53 and in 1QIsa^a is a priestly messiah.[180] It is considered as in agreement with the priestly messiah in Qumran writings. 1QIsa^a presents Isaiah 52:14 as "משחתי." This form consists of MT's *hapax legomena* "marring" or "disfiguration" as מִשְׁחַת with suffix, a *yod*. 1QIsa^a reads this *hapax legomena* as *qal* perfect singular, "I have anointed." This messianic figure, whom God anoints, corresponds to the priest in Leviticus 21:10 and Exodus 30:31-32.[181] The priestly messiah is recognized as sprinkling numerous nations as in LXX 52:15.

Yet, the anointing in 1QIsa^a also can present the enthronement of a Davidic king in Psalm 45.[182] The introductory על. . .כן with anointing (משח) and מן in 1QIsa^a appears in MT Psalm 45:8 (עַל־כֵּן מְשָׁחֲךָ אֱלֹהִים אֱלֹהֶיךָ).[183] Moreover, this corresponds to the anointing of the Davidic Messiah in Isaiah 61:1. In addition, the character of the Davidic royal Messiah in Isaiah, whose role is that of judge, is clarified in the *pesher* of Isaiah 53. In MT, Isaiah 53:11 includes the "knowledge" of the Messiah as a means of the Suffering Servant's satisfaction: "Out of the anguish of his soul he shall see and be satisfied by his knowledge."[184] Isaiah 53:11 in 1QIsa^a begins with a new sentence: "And through his knowledge his servant, the righteous one, will

---

177. Hengel and Bailey, "The Effective History of Isaiah 53," 100.

178. Collins, "Pre-Christian Jewish Messianism: An Overview," 25, opposes the reading of the Suffering Servant in Isa 53 from 4Q541.

179. Puech, "Fragments d'un apocryphe de Lévi et le personnage eschatologique. 4QTestLévic-d(?) et 4QAJa," 449–501; Starcky, "Les quatre étapes du messianisme à Qumran," 492.

180. Barthelemy, "Le grand rouleau d'Isaïe," 546–49; Grelot, "Sur Isaïe LXI: La première consécration d'un grand-prêtre," 414–31; Puech, "Fragments," 449–501.

181. Barthelemy, "Le grand rouleau d'Isaïe," 546–49; Barthelemy, *Etudes d'Histoire du Texte de l'Ancien Testament*, 17 ff.

182. Hengel and Bailey, "The Effective History of Isaiah 53," 104.

183. עליכה רבים כן משחתי מאיש מראחו ותואר ו מבני האדם.

184. Hengel and Bailey, "The Effective History of Isaiah 53," 103, in Isa 53:1 מֵעֲמַל נַפְשׁוֹ יִרְאֶה יִשְׂבָּע בְּדַעְתּוֹ.

make many righteous."[185] The Servant of Yahweh justifies the many through knowledge.

A significant role of the suffering Messiah in Qumran writings is atonement. Isaiah had assigned to the servant of the Lord the role of atonement (Isa 42:6; 49:6; 53:12; cf. Heb 8:8; 9:15; 12:24 and 4Q541[TestLevi(?)] frag. 9 1:2-7, frag. 24 2:25). This is clearly echoed in Qumran writings.[186] His wisdom will be known by all the earth—a characteristic of the Messiah in Isaiah 53, as mentioned above, and he will atone for the people (4Q541 frag. 9). The messianic figure, who possesses characteristics of the Suffering Servant, is described as "despised and rejected" in 4Q541 as in Isaiah 53.[187] The term *"smitten"* (מכאבין) in 4Q541 frag. 9 1:5-6 can be considered to come from "אִישׁ מַכְאֹבוֹת" (man of sorrows) in Isaiah 53:3-4.[188] Surely, the atonement of this messianic figure is associated with יכפר (frag. 9 line 2) and אָשָׁם (Isa 53:10). While 4Q541 frag. 9 is similar to the *T. Levi* 18, the messianic figure in 4Q541 is "portraying his potentially atoning death as well."[189] It is plain that the messianic figure in 4Q541 "will atone for all the children of his generation" (4Q541 frag 9 1:1; ויכפר על כול בני דרה).

This must be realized in light of the nature of the messianic atonement referred to in the Damascus Document 14:18-19.[190] The term "כפר" is not always utilized to refer to divine forgiveness without ritual sacrifice (Jer 18:23; CD 4:9-10; 4Q221 4:4). It can be related to "the sense of expiation; the allusion to the hostile disparagement suffered by the priest suggests that like the Suffering Servant (Isa 53:10) his humiliation was itself considered to constitute an אָשָׁם, a guilt offering for the sins of his generation."[191]

The overlap of these roles, atonement and judgment, is undeniable in Qumran writings. The eschatological messianic figures in Qumran writings, the priestly messiah and Melchizedek, illustrate well the tendency in Second

---

185. ובדעתו יצדיק צדיק עבדי.

186. Second Samuel 21:1, 3 suggest David as the subject of כפר in the meaning of sacrifice. See Janowski, *Sühne als Heilsgeschehen*, 111-14.

187. Collins, "The Suffering Servant at Qumran," 25; Hengel and Bailey, "The Effective History of Isaiah 53," 116-17.

188. Puech, "Fragments," 498; Hengel and Bailey, "The Effective History of Isaiah 53," 116-17.

189. Chester, *Messiah and Exaltation*, 257. See Starcky, "Les quatre étapes du messianisme à Qumran," 481-505; Puech, "Fragments," 493-96; Brooke, "4QTestament of Levid and the Messianic Servant High Priest," 83-100; Stuhlmacher, "Isaiah 53 in the Gospels and Acts," 161; Zimmermann, *Messianische Texte aus Qumran*, 268-77; Hengel and Bailey, "The Effective History of Isaiah 53," 106-18.

190. Baumgarten, "Messianic Forgiveness of Sin," 539.

191. Baumgarten, "Messianic Forgiveness of Sin," 540. The atonement of the Messiah with term "כפר" should be considered with the priestly Messiah in CD 19:18-19.

Temple apocalyptic literature to assign divine functions, such as judgment and atonement, to heavenly or earthly intermediaries. The role of the agent of God's eschatological judgment was demonstrated in the previous section.

Qumran writings refer to the Suffering Servant's exaltation. "Seeing light" (Isa 53:11; 1QIsa$^{a\text{-}b}$) is alluded to in 4Q541 frag. 24 2:6, as well.[192] The Suffering Messiah has the role of atonement and judgment, and it can be inferred in his suffering and exaltation as in Isaiah 53. Richard Hess writes,

> This hymn has been identified in at least four fragments and variants.... This collection of prophetic references (4Q491c. frag. 1, lines 7–11) includes allusions to the unique text of Isa 53, the passage of the suffering servant. The psalmist of this Qumran text therefore identified with the suffering of that servant and, in the same breath, with the exaltation to the highest places of heaven, in the presence of God.[193]

The Davidic Messiah of Isaiah 53 appears in Qumran writings, which is vital in the suffering passage and its close connection to an exalted figure.[194] When the "glory" (כבוד) of the messianic figure in lines 15, 24, and 36 recalls the LXX Isaiah 53, line 16—as in Isaiah 53:13—emphasizes the Suffering Servant's exaltation.[195] Hengel and Bailey argue regarding the Suffering Servant in 4Q491c, "The justification or vindication by God of Isaiah 50:8 ('he who vindicates me is near') and Isaiah 53:11 LXX (δικαιῶσαι δίκαιον) occurs here through the exaltation to the heavenly 'mighty throne' in the congregation of the angels, which can also be understood as the judgment seat in the heavenly court of judges."[196] The Messiah's role is not expected just as suffering, but the exaltation of the Suffering Servant is concerned in his judgment role in the heavenly court. The suffering and exaltation are connected to present his role as the executor of God's judgment.

The role of atonement and judgment is primarily related to eschatological judgment by Melchizedek in 11Q13. 11QMelchizedek col. 2 begins with a quotation of Leviticus 25:13 and Deuteronomy 15:2. Melchizedek "will make them return" (2:5–6) in the last days. Those who return are "the captives" (1:5–6). To them, "liberty will be proclaimed." This freedom is from the debt of their sin (1:6). On the day of atonement at the end of the tenth day, atonement will be executed by Melchizedek (2:7–9).[197] For this

---

192. Puech, "Fragments," 497.
193. Hess, "Messiahs Here and There," 108.
194. Hess, "Messiahs Here and There," 108.
195. Hengel and Bailey, "The Effective History of Isaiah 53," 145.
196. Hengel and Bailey, "The Effective History of Isaiah 53," 145.
197. David assumes the role of atonement with the verb "כפר" in 2 Samuel 21:3,

reason, the roles of judgment and forgiveness are attributed to him.[198] He will liberate sinners from the burden of their sins. The role of atonement is clearly suggested with "כפר" in lines 7–8. God's forgiveness is essential to understand the atonement of the Davidic Messiah in the judgment of God. God relieves his people from his judgment through the Davidic Messiah's atonement.

The Messiah's Faithfulness?

While the suffering Messiah in his atonement is described as the Messiah who has the role of executing God's judgment, the suffering Messiah's atonement in Qumran writings does not support his covenantal faithfulness. The terms covenant and faithfulness never appear in terms of his suffering. Rather, God's judgment is closely related to the Messiah's suffering or atonement. Focusing on iniquity, the atonement is articulated in the role of the Messiah in the Damascus Document 14:18–19: "And this is the exact interpretation of the regulations by which they shall be ruled until there arises the messiah of Aaron and Israel. And their iniquity will be atoned." In the Damascus Document, the arising of the Davidic Messiah, who is additionally the priestly Messiah, has the purpose of atoning the iniquity of people in relation to just ruling with an exact interpretation of regulations. The Messiah's rule is presupposed as just ruling and atonement of iniquity in these lines.

This is similar to 11Q13, which connects God's judgment through the Davidic Messiah and the Messiah's atonement. There is no mention of the Messiah's faithfulness. Instead, the role of God's judgment is emphasized. Correspondingly, the messianic figure in *1 Enoch* possesses the characteristics of the Suffering Servant, but the role of the Davidic Messiah is mainly God's judgment in righteousness, rather than faithfulness in suffering, as noted above. In the context of *1 Enoch*, the Messiah's faithfulness is unfamiliar in the role of God's judgment.

In the Messiah's atonement, he is described as smitten as in Isaiah 53. God's judgment for being guilty results in the suffering of the Messiah in 4Q541 frag. 4 line 4. This line reads that "here [. . .] your [ju]dgment and you will not be gui[lty . . .]." The term "*smitten*," which alludes to "*man of sorrow*" in Isaiah 53:3–4, more aptly fits God's judgment than the Messiah's faithfulness. The Messiah is "smitten" and "afflicted" by God for the

---

addressing the Gibeonites concerning Saul. "What shall I do for you? And how shall I make atonement (וּבַמָּה אֲכַפֵּר)?"

198. Baumgarten, "Messianic Forgiveness of Sin," 539.

iniquities of God's people as in Isaiah 53:4-6. The Messiah is the object of God's judgment.

Furthermore, that the wisdom of the Suffering Servant leads to God's judgment, rather than to the Messiah's faithfulness as in Isaiah 53, is alluded to in 4Q541 frag. 9 1:3-7. The wicked do not receive the word of the Messiah, who atones for God's people. They instead "will utter many words against him, and an abundance of [lie]s; they will fabricate fables against him, and utter every kind of disparagement against him" (4Q541 frag. 9 1:5-7). The wicked are in opposition to the Messiah's words and wisdom (1:1-3). The Messiah's wisdom is a significant characteristic that leads to his just judgment, in the LXX Isaiah 52:13. Considering the faith in the reports about the wisdom of the Messiah and the Suffering Servant in Isaiah 53:1, the writer assumes the wicked's denial of the suffering Messiah in these. The Suffering Servant's role is shown as the executor of God's judgment in his suffering and exaltation.

The language of covenantal faithfulness does not appear in the Davidic Messiah's atonement. This is due to the fact that the focus in the Messiah's atonement is forgiveness, which brings about salvation from God's judgment. The priestly Messiah's principal role is resolving sinners' severe problem in the presence of God's judgment.

CONCLUSION

The Messiah mainly assumes the role of the agent of God's judgment in the Second Temple literature. While the specific term משיח is usually not employed, several terms for the messianic figure have a close relation to the Davidic Messiah as mentioned in the previous chapter. The messianic figure has the same characteristics as does the Old Testament Davidic Messiah, who is endowed with God's wisdom to prepare or execute God's judgment. In addition, impartial judgment is another Davidic Messiah's feature. The righteousness in God's judgment through the Davidic Messiah is righteous righteousness in the messianic texts, so the concept of impartiality may be closely related to judging with righteousness. The identification of God's faithfulness as righteousness is a mistake in categorizing. While these two terms can overlap, *the righteousness of God* is not *God's faithfulness* itself. Also, the concept that God's faithfulness and righteousness cannot be identified supports that the judgment through the Suffering Servant concentrates on God's judgment in righteousness, rather than on the Messiah's faithfulness in covenantal relationship. The purpose of the Messiah's suffering is God's righteous judgment, instead of his covenantal faithfulness.

While the two messiahs appear in some writings in the Second Temple literature, it is undeniable that the roles of the priest Messiah and royal Messiah overlap. The priest Messiah's role is not merely to atone for God's people; he has resolved the problem of sinners in the presence of God's judgment. In other words, the priest Messiah, whose function is mainly atonement, is closely related to God's judgment. For executing God's judgment, the presupposed requirement is not faithfulness to the covenantal relationship between God and his people. Rather, just judgment in righteousness is stressed in the characteristics of the righteous Messiah, with the role of the agent of God's judgment.

Chapter 4

The Gospel of the Davidic Messiah

Romans 1:1–4

INTRODUCTION

The previous chapters examined the Davidic Messiah and his execution of God's judgment in the Old Testament and the Second Temple Jewish writings. I concluded that there is significant continuity with respect to the Davidic Messiah and his main function as the agent of God's judgment. In terms of God's judgment through the Davidic Messiah, the term *"righteousness"* cannot be equated with covenantal faithfulness itself, and the covenantal faithfulness of the Davidic Messiah is mentioned infrequently in the Old Testament and the Second Temple Jewish writings. Rather, impartial righteousness is emphasized in God's judgment through the Davidic Messiah in messianic passages.

With this background in place, this issue in the case of Romans remains for consideration. Some scholars do not think Paul employs Jewish messianism for Jesus at all, and some contend that Paul defuses and neutralizes messianic hope in the term *Messiah*, as noted above. However, in the introduction of his letter to believers in Rome, Paul utilizes messianic language, referring to the gospel concerning Jesus, who was descended from

David. Stanley K. Stowers argues strongly that Paul uses Davidic messianic terms in Romans: "My hypothesis is as follows: Paul believed that God commissioned the man Jesus, chosen descendant of Davidic lineage, to be his messiah."[1] Paul's wording for the Davidic Messiah is inseparably related to the Davidic Messiah described in the Old Testament and the Second Temple literature because echoes of the Davidic Messiah in Romans draw connections to the Old Testament and the Second Temple literature.[2]

This chapter has two main sections. The first section treats Paul's emphasis on the Davidic Messiah. In the introduction to Paul's letter that emphasizes the entire content of his letter, his introduction to the gospel presents the accomplishment of the Davidic Messiah, Jesus. The second section explains God's judgment through the Davidic Messiah in God's gospel as related in Paul's discourse in Romans 1 and 15. Some scholars stress the Messiah's faithfulness in fulfilling God's covenantal faithfulness in Romans 1:3–4 related to Romans 15. Of course, God is faithful in his covenantal faithfulness, which is clearly demonstrated in God's gospel. In his judgment through the Messiah, though, the concept of the Messiah's faithfulness does not play a significant role in Paul's discourse.

THE GOSPEL CONCERNING THE DAVIDIC MESSIAH

Opening his letter by proclaiming God's gospel, Paul refers to the Davidic Messiah especially characterized in the Old Testament and the Second Temple Jewish writings. Paul employs messianic language in the Scriptures to support Christ's Davidic Messiahship.[3] Matthew Novenson maintains,

> Paul's prose does all that we normally expect any ancient Jewish or Christian text to do to count as a messiah text. He writes at length and in detail about a character whom he designates with the Septuagintal word χριστός, and he clarifies what he means by this polysemous term in the customary way—by citing and alluding to certain scriptural source texts rather than others. Paul's letters meet all of the pertinent criteria for early Jewish messiah language.[4]

---

1. Stowers, *A Rereading of Romans*, 213–14.
2. See Das, *Paul and the Stories of Israel*, 4.
3. Novenson, *Christ among the Messiahs*, 137–73; Whitsett, "Son of God, Seed of David," 661–81; Jipp, "Ancient, Modern, and Future Interpretations of Romans 1:3–4," 241–59.
4. Novenson, *Christ among the Messiahs*, 138.

The usage of Χριστός as a titular name is clearly drawn in 1:2-4, which illustrates the idea of the Davidic Messiahship of Jesus as the fulfillment of Israel's messianic hope.[5] Paul clearly suggests the titular meaning of Χριστός in the double formula Χριστός Ἰησοῦς.[6] The royal connotations are included in Χριστός, which implied the messianic king.[7]

The Gospel of God

The gospel content regarding Jesus, the Messiah (Χριστός), is elaborated in verses 2-4.[8] The Messiah, Jesus, who is the fulfillment of Davidic messianic hope, is the risen one from the dead, the exalted one at God's right hand. This can be clearly recognized in Romans 1:2-4.[9] Paul uses the phrase "εὐαγγέλιον θεοῦ... περὶ τοῦ υἱοῦ αὐτοῦ" (Rom 1:1-3), connecting the gospel with God's visitation, salvation, and ruling for his people through the messianic figure.

The gospel in Paul's mind is influenced by Isaian texts (Isa 40:9; 52:7; 60:6; 61:1) and the Second Temple writings (Ps. Sol. 11:1; 1QH 18:14; 11Q13).[10] These texts, which include the term "*the gospel*," are clearly related to the Davidic Messiah. Martin Hengel and Anna Maria Schwemer hold that εὐαγγέλιον in early Christianity was from the Aramaic *besoretha* and its renderings in the LXX.[11] The verb form of εὐαγγέλιον, εὐαγγελίζεσθαι, and its participle form εὐαγγελιζόμενος, which are renderings of the verb

---

5. Dunn, *Romans 1-8*, 8.

6. Cullmann, *The Christology of the New Testament*, 112. Dunn argues, "It is just possible that the distinctly Pauline use of the double name 'Christ Jesus' (as against 'Jesus Christ') is a direct translation equivalent of 'Messiah Jesus,' with *Christos* still bearing its titular force." Dunn, *The Theology of Paul the Apostle*, 199. The interchange of these two words "counts against the axiom χριστός that is a proper name for Paul." Novenson, *Christ among the Messiahs*, 101.

7. Wright, *Paul and the Faithfulness of God*, 815-36; Collins and Collins, *King and Messiah as the Son of God*, 101-22.

8. Schreiner, *Romans*, 33.

9. Concerning the messianic emphasis on Rom 1:1, see in particular Nils A. Dahl, *Jesus the Christ*, 37-47; Kramer, *Christ, Lord, Son of God*, 203-14.

10. Dunn, *Romans 1-8*, 1:10.

11. Hengel and Schwemer note, "Sie verbietet sich für diese Frühzeit schon aus chronologischen Gründen und verkennt völlig das profetisch-palästinischen Ursprung und darüber hinaus die Besonderheit der paulinischen Predigt, die von ersten Anfängen an ihr eigenes, von der Sprache der Psalmen und Profeten her bestimmtes Gepräge gehabt haben muß." Hengel and Schwemer, *Paulus zwischen Damaskus und Antiochien*, 154. Hengel is following Stuhlmacher's arguments for εὐαγγέλιον. See Stuhlmacher, *Das paulinische Evangelium*, 122-53.

בָּשַׂר and participle מְבַשֵּׂר, are utilized for the announcement and herald of good news (Pss 40:10; 68:12; Isa 40:9; 41:27; 52:7; 61:1).[12] In the context of the return of God's people from Babylon in Isaiah (Isa 40:9; 52:7; 60:6; 61:1), this verb form is used in the proclamation, which is "the announcement of a coming salvation and liberation connected with the exercise of the sovereignty and rule of God."[13] The heralding of the good news is additionally the proclamation of Yahweh's victory (Isa 52:7) because these terms describe God's eschatological victory (Isa 40:9; 60:6; 61:1; Joel 2:32; Nah 1:15).[14] The herald of Isaiah 52:7 is identified with the anointed one, the Davidic Messiah, of Isaiah 61:1.

The *Psalms of Solomon* 11:1, also linked to the herald of Isaiah 52:7 and the anointed one in Isaiah 61:1, reads that "sound in Zion the signal trumpet of the sanctuary; announce in Jerusalem the voice of one bringing good news, for God has been merciful to Israel in watching over them."[15] The anointed one, the Davidic Messiah, is the herald of the jubilee of Leviticus 25:9–10, with an Isaianic voice (*Ps. Sol.* 11:1).[16] This Isaian voice is particularly the bringer of new tidings to Zion as in Isaiah 40:6, 9; 52:7 in the day of divine deliverance or visitation (cf. 1QS 4:6, 19, 26), which is viewed as the supreme liberating jubilee (Lev 25:9–10) and echoed in Isaiah 61:1.[17]

The message of good news is the announcement of God's deliverance through the Davidic Messiah for his people who are described as the afflicted, and it proclaims God's ruling over Zion. These terms, the verb בָּשַׂר and participle מְבַשֵּׂר, in Qumran writings, are used to herald good tidings. The "servant" of God is "to be the herald (מבשר) of ... your goodness, to proclaim (לבשר) to the poor" (1QHa 23:11–14, formerly 18:14).[18] The Davidic Messiah, who is the "servant" of God, follows the pattern of Isaian texts, the

---

12. Horbury, *Herodian Judaism and New Testament Study*, 80.

13. Byrne, *Romans*, 42.

14. Moo, *The Epistle to the Romans*, 43; Käsemann, *Commentary on Romans*, 9; Stuhlmacher, *Das paulinische Evangelium*, 152–53, 177–79, 204–6; Horbury says, "Possible instances of its nominative plural euangélia in the sense 'good news' do indeed occur in the account of the bringing of the double news of victory over the rebels and the death of Absalom in II kingdoms = II Sam 18:22; 25." Horbury, *Herodian Judaism and New Testament Study*, 88. The term בְּשׂרָה, which corresponds to εὐαγγέλιον, means "compensation for a message of victory" (2 Sam 4:10; 18:22) or "message of victory" (1 Sam 31:9; 2 Sam 18:20, 25, 27; 2 Kgs 7:9). In the Septuagint, εὐαγγέλιον has the same meaning with the plural form (2 Kgs 4:10). The feminine form, ἡ εὐαγγελία has the meaning of "good tidings" (2 Kgs 18:20–27; 4 Kgs 7:19). Strecker, "εὐαγγέλιον," 71.

15. Horbury, *Herodian Judaism and New Testament Study*, 97.

16. Horbury, *Herodian Judaism and New Testament Study*, 99.

17. Horbury, *Herodian Judaism and New Testament Study*, 97

18. See Martínez, *The Dead Sea Scrolls Translated*, 359.

herald in Isaiah 52:7 (מבשׂר) and the anointed one in Isaiah 61:1 to proclaim (לבשׂר) good news to the afflicted.[19] In 11Q13, the verb "to preach good news" (בשׂר) is taken from Isaiah 52:7: "How beautiful upon the mountains are the feet [of] the messen[ger who] announces peace" (11Q13 2:15-16). The allusion to Isaiah 61:1-2 in 11Q13 is apparent.[20] The herald's function of the herald in 11Q13 is proclaiming deliverance and good news to the poor of Zion as in Isaiah 61.[21] Melchizedek is "presented in terms of Isa 61:1-2 and the jubilee of Lev 25:9-10 (11Q13 2:4-7, 9, 13)."[22] In 11Q13 are the themes of the jubilee-like proclamation of liberty, the year of grace, and the Day of Atonement. "The year of the Lord's favor" (Isa 61:2) is connected with "Melchizedek's year of favor" (11Q13 2:9).[23]

In consideration of the phrase, "through God's prophets in the holy scriptures" (προεπηγγείλατο διὰ τῶν προφητῶν αὐτοῦ ἐν γραφαῖς ἁγίαις in Rom 1:2), there is a strong influence of these Isaian texts and the Second Jewish Temple writings on the gospel (as shown as well in Rom 10:15-16).[24] The Isaian texts (40:9; 52:7; 60:6; 61:1) clearly influence the Jewish Second Temple writings that relate the Davidic Messiah to God's gospel (*Ps. Sol.* 11:1; 1QH 18:14; 11Q13). Paul's employment of Isaian texts for the Davidic Messiah has coherence with the description of the coming of the Davidic Messiah, who is promised through the Old Testament prophets.

The Son of God

In Romans 1:3, Paul articulates the gospel of God as a message concerning God's Son. The "Son of God" is known with reference to the Davidic Messiah, who was expected as being "in David" or "in the son of Jesse" (1 Sam 19:43–20:2; cf. 1 Kgs 12:16; 2 Chr 10:16).[25] The "Son of God" should be recognized as a royal title, which includes the idea of the Davidic Messiah (2 Sam 7:14; Pss 2:7; 89:26-27; 1QSa 2:11-12; 4QFlor 1:10 ff.; 4Q246 2:1). The relationship between God and the Davidic king is expressed in terms of sonship (2 Sam 7:12-14).[26] In this passage (7:12-14), the king is understood to be God's son. Psalm 2 shows the enthronement of the Davidic

---

19. Horbury, *Herodian Judaism and New Testament Study*, 96–97.
20. Kobelski, *Melchizedek and Melchireša'*, 3–23.
21. Collins, *The Scepter and Star*, 134.
22. Horbury, *Herodian Judaism and New Testament Study*, 99.
23. Collins, *The Scepter and Star*, 133.
24. Dunn, *Romans 1–8*, 10.
25. Wright, *Romans*, 416.
26. Eskola, *Messiah and the Throne*, 59.

king, in which the Davidic king is appointed as the Son of God (Ps 2:7),[27] exclusively as the firstborn Son of God (89:27).[28] Psalm 2 emphasizes God's begetting of the Davidic king, who is the ideal king and ruler.[29]

In addition, this theme appears in Psalm 110, in which divine sonship is attributed to the king from the Davidic line as in Psalm 2.[30] In Psalm 110, the begetting of God is introduced because God "begets" a new king (110:3).[31] Timo Eskola observes, "In Psalm 110 this is expressed by a statement (110:1) that has become a standard for later Jewish theology and New Testament Christology."[32] In the Second Temple Jewish writings, the Davidic Messiah, who is a royal figure and the enthroned one, can be represented as God's Son. Richard N. Longenecker writes as follows:

> 4QFlorilegium, which is a collection of selected OT passages and interpretive comments dateable to the end of the first century BC or the beginning of the first AD, the words of 2 Sam 7:14, "I will be to him a father, and he will be to me a son," are given explicit messianic import in the comment. "The 'he' in question is 'the Branch of David' who will appear in Zion in the Last Days, alongside 'the Expounder of the Law.'" 4QFlor 1:12–13. For "the Branch of David" as a messianic title, see Jer 23:5; 33:15; Zech 3:8; 6:12. Likewise in *4 Ezra* 7:28–29; 13:32, 37, 52; and 14:9—which are passages written by a pious Jewish author only a few years after the apostolic period of early Christianity, probably about 100–120 AD—God is represented as speaking repeatedly of the Messiah as "my Son." So also *1 En.* 105:2 in portraying God as speaking in a messianic context of "I and my Son" (though this verse has often for this very reason been viewed as a Jewish Christian interpolation into earlier Enochian material).[33]

---

27. Cooke, "The Israelite King as Son of God," 202–25; Mowinckel, *He That Cometh*, 96–98; Eaton, *Kingship and the Psalms*, 111–13; Eskola, *Messiah and the Throne*, 60.

28. The relationship of "sonship" between God and king is an "adoptional relationship" in Nathan's prophecy. Eskola, *Messiah and the Throne*, 59.

29. On the royal shape and editing of the Psalter, see Wilson, *The Editing of the Hebrew Psalter*, 85–94.

30. Eskola, *Messiah and the Throne*, 59. Regarding the argument that 2 Sam 7:12 is the background for the "seed" of David in Rom 1:3, see Becker, *Auferstehung der Toten im Urchristentum*, 25; Duling, "Promises to David and Their Entrance into Christianity," 73; Dahl, *Studies in Paul*, 128; Betz, *What Do We Know about Jesus?*, 96; Kim, *The Origin of Paul's Gospel*, 109; Barrett, *The Epistle to the Romans*, 19–20.

31. Eskola, *Messiah and the Throne*, 60.

32. Eskola, *Messiah and the Throne*, 61.

33. Longenecker, *The Epistle to the Romans*, 67–68.

As mentioned above, the idea that the Messiah is God's Son is rooted in Jewish tradition.[34]

The divine sonship, which has quite a close relationship to the messianic king idea, is a feature of the Davidic Messiah. Moreover, while this term serves to stress the intimacy of the relationship between the Davidic Messiah and God, Paul points out the unique relationship between Jesus and the Father with this term "υἱός."[35] The "Son of God" is implemented as a key term to focus on Christ's uniquely intimate relationship with God, and the description of the Davidic king with messianic significance is applied to Jesus.[36]

Calling Jesus God's Son, Paul makes Jesus as God's Son the destination for God's people, Israel (Exod 4:22-23; Jer 31:9; Hos 11:1; Wis 18:13; *Jub.* 1.24-25; *Ps. Sol.* 18:4; *T. Moses* 10:3; *Sib. Or.* 3:702).[37] The people of God, as God's "sons," have a relationship with Jesus. Paul describes believers as God's "sons" in Christ (Rom 1:9; 8:29; 1 Cor 1:9; Eph 4:13; Col 1:13).[38] Abraham's blessing can be offered to God's "sons" in Christ as in Galatians 3:14-16.[39] Thomas Schreiner concludes as follows:

> Paul contends that Jesus is the true Son of God. He is the true Israel. The OT promises regarding the vindication of Israel have been fulfilled through him. The promise of a Davidic king and a Messiah also apply to Jesus. Thus the expectation that God would vindicate his people through a Davidic ruler has also become a reality (Pss 2:7-12; 89; Isa 11; Jer 23:5-6; 33:14-18; Ezek 34:23-31; 37:24-28; *Ps. Sol.* 17.21-46). Jesus reigns from heaven as the messianic king. God's promise to bring in a new

---

34. Collins, *The Scepter and Star*, 169. See also Hurtado, *Lord Jesus Christ*, 101-8.

35. See Cullmann, *The Christology of the New Testament*, 270-305; Marshall, *The Origins of New Testament Christology*, 111-29; Ridderbos, *Paul*, 68-78; Wright, *Paul and the Faithfulness of God*, 692; E. Schweizer, "υἱός," in *TDNT*, 8:360-62; F. Hahn, "υἱός," in *EDNT*, 3:383.

36. Moo, *Romans*, 44.

37. Schreiner, *Romans*, 39, cites these texts for support. Against a collective interpretation, see Collins, "The Son of God Text from Qumran," 74, 181. According to Collins, "A collective interpretation is not impossible in the text from Qumran, but nonetheless it seems unlikely. Although Israel is often said to be God's son, 'Son of God' is scarcely used as a title with reference to the people. The eschatological kingdom of Israel, which is well attested, is usually associated with an eschatological ruler under God, whether an angel, such as Michael in Daniel and the War Scroll, or a messianic figure. While certainty is not possible because of the fragmentary state of column 1, an interpretation that allows for such an individual ruler here should be preferred." Collins, "The Son of God," 74.

38. Schreiner, *Romans*, 38-39; Moo, *Romans*, 44.

39. Schreiner, *Romans*, 39.

world order through the resurrection of Israel has dawned as well (Ezek 37). Jesus as the Son of God is the true Israel who has been resurrected from the dead. God has fulfilled his promises made to Israel through and in the Messiah Jesus.[40]

The phrase, "God's Son," demonstrates Paul's understanding of God's salvation history, which is accomplished through Jesus Christ, who is the Davidic Messiah.[41] The promise of God, the blessing of the whole world through Abraham, is fulfilled through God's Son.[42] It is not strange that the seed of David and the Son of God are juxtaposed in the messianic designation.[43] The Son of God is recognized as the Messiah, including the office of Savior in the messianic sense.[44]

The Seed of David

The emphasis of Romans 1:3 with κατὰ σάρκα is that Jesus is the messianic king, who is the son of David in terms of physical descent.[45] This corresponds to the expectations of Jewish traditions and God's Old Testament promises (Rom 1:2).[46] It is clearly shown with the phrase of "the seed (σπέρμα) of David." Based on the Old Testament and the Second Temple Jewish writings, the messianic figure, who stems from the Davidic line based on 2 Samuel 7:12, is expected to come from the "seed" (σπέρμα, זרע) of David. James Scott writes, "Furthermore, Paul is able to argue in Galatians 3:16 that Christ is the 'seed' (σπέρμα) of Abraham promised in Genesis 15:18 precisely because he is also the 'seed' (σπέρμα) of David promised in 2 Samuel 7:12; for, according to Old Testament and Jewish tradition, the Abrahamic promise would be fulfilled in the Davidic Messiah."[47] Moreover, James Dunn comments,

---

40. Schreiner, *Romans*, 45.

41. Stuhlmacher, "Theologische Probleme des Römerbriefpräskripts," 378–86; Moo, *Romans*, 50; Schreiner, *Romans*, 43. Contra Schweizer, "πνεῦμα," in *TDNT*, 6:416–17.

42. Schreiner, *Romans*, 45.

43. Longenecker, *Romans*, 67. The Messiah and the Son of God appear together to designate Jesus as the Coming One in the New Testament (Matt 16:16; 26:63; Luke 4:41; John 11:27; 20:31; Acts 9:20–22).

44. Schweizer, "υἱός," in *TDNT*, 8:360–62; Hahn, "υἱός," in *EDNT*, 3:383.

45. "Περὶ τοῦ υἱοῦ αὐτοῦ τοῦ γενομένου ἐκ σπέρματος Δαυὶδ κατὰ σάρκα" (Rom 1:2).

46. The phrase "through prophets" (διὰ τῶν προφητῶν) denotes all of the Old Testament. Schreiner, *Romans*, 38; Moo, *Romans*, 44.

47. Scott, *Adoption as Sons of God*, 233.

["From the seed of David" is] a clear assertion that Jesus was the anointed Son of David, the royal Messiah, the fulfillment of prophetic hopes long cherished among the people of Israel for the age to come (Isa 11; Jer 23:5-6; 33:14-18; Ezek 34:23-31; 37:24-28; *Ps. Sol.* 17:23-51; 4QFlor 1.10-13; 4QpGen 49; 4QpIsa^a 2.21-28; *Shemoneh Esreh* 14-15). That Jesus was descended from David's line is a common assertion in the NT, including the tradition lying behind the different birth narratives of Matthew and Luke (Matt 1:1-16, 20; Luke 1:27, 32, 69; 2:4; 3:23-31) and the older formulations quoted here and in 2 Tim 2:8 (see also Acts 2:30; Rev 5:5; 22:16 and regularly in Matt—1:1; 9:27; 12:23; 15:22; 20:30-31; 21:9, 15).[48]

The Davidic descent of Jesus has a significant role in Romans because Paul claims in Romans 15:12 that Jesus fulfills the messianic promise in Isaiah 11:10.[49] In this verse, "the root of Jesse" implies Jesus as the son of David.[50] Wright states,

> Others have seen "according to the flesh" as Paul's way of hinting that, while Jesus was indeed of the seed of David, this was not the most significant thing about him. In other words, this was Paul's way of distancing himself from Jewish messianic beliefs in order to hurry on to the more important point about Jesus' divine sonship. This, too, is misleading for the reasons already given. The whole point of Paul's gospel is that Jesus, precisely as Israel's Messiah, is now Lord of the world. That belief informs and undergirds much of this letter.[51]

The messianic king based on the Jewish expectations is related to the covenant of God, which is accomplished in God's salvation history.

According to Paul, the gospel that had been promised in the Scriptures is fulfilled in the event of Jesus Christ. In Paul's understanding of the gospel, the messianic expectations for the Davidic Messiah are a significant part of the Old Testament promises. Based on this understanding, "κατὰ σάρκα" illustrates Paul's emphasis on Christ's Davidic line, rather than inferiority. The "flesh" never means "human nature" for Paul; nor is it a specific mention of physical humanness.[52] The phrase κατὰ σάρκα refers to Christ's

---

48. Dunn, *Romans 1-8*, 12.
49. Scott, *Adoption as Sons of God*, 233.
50. Scott, *Adoption as Sons of God*, 233.
51. Wright, *Romans*, 418.
52. Wright, *Romans*, 417-18.

descent from David[53] and establishes the genealogical background for the Davidic Messiahship of Jesus.[54]

Additionally, Jipp attests, "For Paul, the messianic tradition that developed in biblical and later Judaism based on the oracle of 2 Samuel 7 was a promise, a promise which, like that to Abraham, was spoken to a seed—the seed of David (2 Sam 7:12; cf. Ps 89:4; 18:50)."[55] The coming of God's Son is qualified with "ἐκ σπέρματος Δαυὶδ κατὰ σάρκα," which is "a clear allusion to the messianic stature of the Son."[56] God's decree for the Davidic king, identified in 2 Samuel 7:12 as "ἀναστήσω τὸ σπέρμα σου μετὰ σέ," is expected in this formula in Romans 1:3-4. Paul clearly describes Christ's physical descent from Abraham with "ἐκ σπέρματος Δαυὶδ," connected with Abraham as in Romans 11:1 or 2 Corinthians 11:2.[57] The stream of interpretation is that Paul "sees Jesus—as Messiah—as both 'seed of David' (cf. Rom 1:3), and 'seed of Abraham' (cf. Gal 3:16, etc.)."[58] Jeremiah 33:22 demonstrates the application of the promises to Abraham to the seed of David: "Just as the host of heaven cannot be numbered and the sands of the sea cannot be measured, so I will multiply the seed of my servant David and the Levites who minister to me." The *Targum* of Psalm 89:3-4 shows this relationship: "I have made a covenant with Abraham my chosen one, I have sworn to my servant David: I will establish your seed forever."[59] The Davidic Messiah should be recognized in terms of "γενομένου ἐκ σπέρματος Δαυὶδ" within the big picture of the salvation history, which is related to God's promise to Abraham.

The Spirit of Holiness

Paul's wording, "*according to the Spirit of Holiness*" (κατὰ πνεῦμα ἁγιωσύνης), supports the Davidic Messiah's feature of Jesus.[60] In addition, the Davidic

---

53. Novenson, *Christ among the Messiahs*, 169n127; Hays, "'Have We Found Abraham to Be Our Forefather according to the Flesh?' A Reconsideration of Rom 4:1," 76-98; BDAG, 916.

54. Novenson, *Christ among the Messiahs*, 169; Scott, *Adoption as Sons of God*, 238.

55. Whitsett, "Son of God, Seed of David," 671.

56. Moo, *Romans*, 46.

57. Calhoun, *Paul's Definitions of the Gospel in Romans 1*, 101.

58. Whitsett, "Son of God, Seed of David," 675.

59. ארום אמרית עלמא בחסדא יתבני שמיא תתקין קושטך בהון: גזרית קיים לאברהם בחירי קיימית לדוד עבדי:

60. The History of Religions School paradigm suggests that Paul related more to the mission to the Gentiles and diminished the Jewish messianism of Jesus with a redaction of the confession in the σάρκα-πνεῦμα contrast in Rom 1:3-4. As noted above, the

messianic figure is presupposed to have the anointing of the Spirit to rule his people, as noted in the previous chapters. The anointing of the Spirit of the Lord means that the king has a peculiar relationship with Yahweh, too. While "πνεῦμα ἁγιωσύνης" is not employed to designate the Holy Spirit in the New Testament, and it does not appear in the LXX, it can be a literal translation for "רוּחַ קָדְשׁ."[61] The peculiar relationship with Yahweh has been shown to be his bearing God's Spirit.

The anointing of oil manifests that the king bears the Spirit of the Lord (1 Sam 10:1–13; 16:1–13).[62] God's presence, which is the result of bearing the Spirit, represents his glory, which is splendor, and he is praised as the "King of Glory" (Ps 24:7–10).[63] The Davidic Messiah can be anticipated as anointed with the Holy Spirit. God elected David to rule for the sake of God himself, and granted his Spirit and his presence to him, so that the endowing of the Holy Spirit designates the Davidic kingship. The messianic king presented in the Second Temple Jewish writings appears with the terms of Spirit and power, which are well-known characteristics of the Davidic Messiah in the Old Testament (*T. Levi* 18:11; *Ps. Sol.* 17:37).[64] Furthermore, *T. Levi* 18:11 used the form πνεῦμα ἁγιωσύνης, a recognized term in Hellenistic Jewish eschatology for the Holy Spirit in Greek.[65]

---

scholars of this school from Bousset through Bultmann have fit Paul's understanding to their agenda with its non-Jewish categories. They hold that Paul stresses the *kyrios* Christology for Jesus in his teaching, rather than the messiahship of Jesus. In their interpretation of the σάρκα-πνεῦμα contrast, the existence of human beings is understood to be subordinate to the heavenly realm. Paul chooses a creed, accepting the dialectic of the contrast of flesh versus spirit accepted by Hellenistic Christians. Jewett, "The Redaction and Use of an Early Christian Confession in Romans 1:3–4," 108. As noted above, though, God's Son is defined as the Davidic Messiah in the Old Testament and the Second Temple Jewish writings. There is no contrast between 1:3 and 1:4, and the parallel between σάρξ and πνεῦμα in Rom 1:3–4 focuses on the christological ideas concerning the Messiah, instead of on the contrast between the words themselves. Calhoun, *Paul's Definitions of the Gospel in Romans 1*, 100. Balancing "κατὰ σάρκα" with "κατὰ πνεῦμα" in Rom 1:4, Paul provides a messianic description. What is stressed in these two verses is not the contrast between the two abstract ideas of σάρξ and πνεῦμα. Cranfield, *A Critical and Exegetical Commentary on the Epistle to the Romans*, 1:60; Becker, *Auferstehung der Toten im Urchristentum*, 21–22.

61. 1QH 7:6–7; 9:32; 1QS 4:21; 8:16; 9:3; CD 2:12; *T. Levi* 18:11. Fitzmyer, *Romans*, 236; Schreiner, *Romans*, 43; Moo, *Romans*, 42–43.

62. John D. W. Watts writes, "Anointing (1 Sam 12:13) is intended to impart the gift of the spirit." Watts, *Isaiah 1–33*, 209. Isa 11:2 shows that "God's spirit speaks and acts through his Anointed One."

63. Jipp, *Christ Is King*, 153; Newman, *Paul's Glory-Christology*, 44–52.

64. Eskola, *Messiah and the Throne*, 240; Becker, *Auferstehung der Toten im Urchristentum*, 130.

65. Eskola, *Messiah and the Throne*, 238; Longenecker, *Romans*, 73.

While Paul explains Jesus "was appointed to be the Son of God 'in power'" (ἐν δυνάμει), "ἐν δυνάμει" related to "κατὰ πνεῦμα" modifies "υἱοῦ αὐτοῦ" in Romans 1:4.[66] Moreover, Aquila Lee presents the meaning of ἐν δυνάμει:

> With regard to the phrase ἐν δυνάμει, it seems better to connect it with υἱοῦ θεοῦ than with the verb. In support of this it may be said that the sense which results from taking "in power" with "Son of God" accords well, while the sense which results from taking it with ὁρισθέντος, accords ill, not only with Paul's teaching elsewhere but also with the presence of "his Son" at the beginning of v. 3. We understand the first part of the clause to mean "who was appointed Son-of-God-in-power," that is, in contrast with his being Son of God in apparent weakness and poverty during his earthly existence.[67]

Moo also remarks, "The power that has shown the transition from v. 3 to v. 4, then, is not a transition from a human messiah to a divine Son of God (adoptionism) but from the Son as Messiah to the Son as both Messiah and powerful, reigning Lord."[68] Thus, the Spirit characterizes the Davidic Messiah, who has a close relationship with God as the Son, and it is a feature of the eschatological Messiah with the presence of God in the Old Testament and Jewish writings.

Appointment as God's Son

A result of the Messiah being granted the Spirit is his appointment as the Son of God, as well. While Paul emphasizes that God's Son is appointed (ὁρισθέντος), according to the spirit of holiness, the term "ὁρίζειν" has the meaning of the enthronement of Jesus, who is the Davidic Messiah in his resurrection. His use of "ὁρίζω" shows that the reason for the Davidic Messiah's enthronement is the fact of his divine sonship.[69] Schreiner writes,

---

66. Moo, *Romans*, 48; Eskola, *Messiah and the Throne*, 240; Lee, *From Messiah to Preexistent Son*, 268; Cranfield, *Romans*, 1:62; Dunn, *Romans 1–8*, 14; Fitzmyer, *Romans*, 235.

67. Lee, *From Messiah to Preexistent Son*, 268.

68. Moo, *Romans*, 48.

69. Some scholars believe that "ὁρίζω" is recognized as "declare" by the theory for adoptionist Christology. Pertaining to adoptionist Christology, see Schweizer, "πνεῦμα," in *TDNT*, 6:416–17; Hahn, *The Titles of Jesus in Christology*, 248–58; Schmidt, "ὁρίζω," in *TDNT*, 5:452; Stuhlmacher, "Theologische Probleme des Römerbriefpräskripts," 382; Bultmann, *Theology of the New Testament*, 1:49–50; Dunn, *Christology in the Making*, 33–36; Jewett, "The Redaction and Use of an Early Christian Confession in Romans

"The appointment of Jesus being described here is his appointment as the messianic king."[70]

While "ὁρίζω" should be translated as "appoint," "determine," or "decide" as employed in the New Testament (Luke 22:22; Acts 2:23; 10:42; 11:29; 17:26, 31; Heb 4:7), the meaning of "appointment" is based on 2 Samuel 7:12, 14, "which promises that the Messiah from the 'seed' of David would be adopted as Son of God."[71] Christ's appointment is additionally supported by the Old Testament background because the Davidic Messiah is decreed in Psalm 2:7, and "ὁρίζειν" and "προορίζειν" are connected with "the theme of Jesus' resurrection as his appointment" (e.g., Acts 10:42).[72] It shows that Jesus was appointed as the Son of God when he was resurrected from the dead as the Davidic Messiah. Paul realizes the accomplishment of God's promises in 1:2 to be through Christ's resurrection in the royal investiture in 1:4.[73]

Resurrection

The point in Romans 1:3–4 is surely to describe Jesus as the messianic king, while "his Son" (υἱοῦ αὐτοῦ) in 1:3 focuses on the seed of David with reference to his messianic kingship, instead of to his elevation as a divine being through resurrection. According to Eskola,

> On theological grounds we can say that the epitheths used here fit well in the Royal messianology exploited in the formula. Jesus is Messiah as well as κύριος when he is being exalted to the universal kingship. According to Psalms 2 and 110 these are the epiteths or metaphors for the Davidide who shall fulfill the eschatological expectations of God's kingdom.[74]

While he lives as a human being, but as the Messiah and the Son of God, too. his installation as the messianic king, who rules as the Lord and Christ on the heavenly throne occurs in the event of the resurrection. The messianic king position is closely connected with the resurrection, as Peter

---

1:3–4," 99–122; Jewett, *Romans*, 103; Moo, *Romans*, 45n31.

70. Schreiner, *Romans*, 42.

71. Scott, *Adoption as Sons of God*, 241.

72. Whitsett, "Son of God, Seed of David," 677. For Paul's employment of προορίζειν as an interpretation of Psalm 2, see Allen, "Old Testament Background of (pro)horizein in the New Testament," 104–8; Marcus, *The Way of the Lord*, 63.

73. Whitsett, "Son of God, Seed of David," 677.

74. Eskola, *Messiah and the Throne*, 242.

concludes with respect to the crucifixion and resurrection of Jesus that "God has made him both Lord and Christ" (Acts 2:36).⁷⁵ As mentioned above, the phrase, "The Son of God in power according to the Spirit of holiness" in 1:4, presents a unique closeness with God because the Messiah is in the background of the statement of Psalm 2:7.⁷⁶ In addition, Paul cites Psalm 2:7 to relate the resurrection of Jesus to his installation in Acts 13:33 that "he has fulfilled to us their children by raising Jesus, as also it is written in the second Psalm, 'You are my Son, today I have begotten you.'"⁷⁷ Paul proclaims the Messiah Jesus with his installation as God's Son in his citation of Psalm 2:7 in Acts 13:33.⁷⁸ The interpretation of Psalm 2:6 in early Christianity, as Christ's exaltation and enthronement in connection with the concept of Zion as the heavenly Jerusalem, provides support for Christ's divine sonship in the light of Acts 13:33, as well.⁷⁹

Messiah's Enthronement

The enthronement can be implied in Christ's resurrection (cf. Rom 8:34). The Messiah's enthronement is clearly a feature of the Davidic Messiah. God's throne is shared with the Davidic king. Psalms 44:7 in the LXX, reads, "ὁ θρόνος σου, ὁ θεός, εἰς τὸν αἰῶνα τοῦ αἰῶνος, ῥάβδος εὐθύτητος ἡ ῥάβδος τῆς βασιλείας σου." In both LXX Psalms 44 and 109, then, the Davidic king is God's agent—who shares God's throne, rules on his behalf, and is worthy of hymnic honors. Eskola notes, "Sitting 'at the right hand' expresses both the great significance of the throne of God and the special status of the enthroned one."⁸⁰ The Davidic king is a representative of the heavenly King, and the throne of the Davidic king is Yahweh's throne; he is described as exalted according to Chronicles (1 Chr 28:5; 29:23; 29:25). Consequently, κατὰ πνεῦμα designates the enthronement of the Davidic Messiah, who shares God's glory as a representative of the heavenly King.

Some suggest that the apostle deliberately defused or neutralized the messianic hope because its radical and political implications were a

---

75. Moo, *Romans*, 48.
76. Schreiber, *Gesalbter und König*, 410.
77. Moo, *Romans*, 48.
78. Schreiner, *Romans*, 42.
79. Lee, *From Messiah to Preexistent Son*, 270. As Collins and Collins mention, the Qumran texts include a reference to divine begetting and the sonship of the Messiah, who is the Son of God and has features of preexistence in LXX Psalms. Collins and Collins, *King and Messiah as the Son of God*, 48–74. The preexistence of the Messiah is especially shown in *1 Enoch* 48, 4 Ezra, and 11Q13. Collins, *The Scepter and Star*, 75–100.
80. Eskola, *Messiah and the Throne*, 61.

THE GOSPEL OF THE DAVIDIC MESSIAH   127

hindrance to Paul's mission in the center of the Roman Empire. However, the Messiah, Jesus—whom Paul recognized to be the fulfillment of the messianic hope—is already in heaven at the right hand of God's throne as the one to whom all beings, at all levels of the cosmos, have to do homage as their Lord (Phil 2:6–11).[81] Jipp rightly asserts,

> It can be stated with little exaggeration that Wilhelm Bousset's influential *Kyrios Christos* and its positing of a division between Palestinian and Hellenistic Christianity, with the latter valuing the title "Lord" but devaluing Jewish Davidic traditions, has provided the historical foundations for Paul's supposed disinterest in Jesus' Davidic descent.[82]

The believers in Rome are being called to submit to the kingship and lordship of Jesus—a call that is the crux of Paul's gospel with regard to the Davidic Messiah (Rom 1:5).

Hence, the Messiah, Jesus—who is the fulfillment of messianic hope—is the one risen from the dead, the exalted one at God's right hand. The resurrection and enthronement of the messianic king demonstrate the authority of the Messiah, Jesus, whom Paul serves as "δοῦλος." Because the term "δοῦλος" means service to a greater authority, Paul shows himself as a humble and dedicated servant of Christ, the Messiah.[83] Furthermore, Christ's messiahship is involved with Paul's apostleship, which is granted through the Messiah (1:5). While he presents himself as called to be an apostle, Paul posits himself as specially commissioned by the risen Messiah.[84] The apostolic calling is reminiscent of the prophetic ministry (Isa 49:1; Jer 1:5), and Paul holds that he proclaims "the fulfillment of what was prophesied in the OT (Rom 1:2; 16:26)."[85] Paul's description of himself, "set apart for the gospel of God" (ἀφωρισμένος εἰς εὐαγγέλιον θεοῦ), may allude to the prophetic calling for his apostolic task.[86] His calling as apostle is serving the gospel, which elaborates the Davidic Messiahship of Jesus in verses 2–4.

Therefore, the salvation history interpretation can be derived from Paul's presentation of this parallel in God's gospel, as noted above, and it supports the consistent Davidic Messiahship theme in Romans 1:3–4.[87]

---

81. Zeller, "Zur Transformation des Christos bei Paulus," 163.
82. Jipp, *Christ Is King*, 4.
83. Schreiner, *Romans*, 32.
84. Dunn, *Romans 1–8*, 9.
85. Schreiner, *Romans*, 33.
86. Moo, *Romans*, 42.
87. Eskola, *Messiah and the Throne*, 61.

Κατὰ σάρξ and κατὰ πνεῦμα should be understood within identification for the Davidic Messiah's enthronement. The raising of David's seed is promised in the divine decree in 2 Samuel 7:12. Both the LXX and MT correspond to this reasoning.[88] God's promises, which were assured by the prophets (1:2), are fulfilled in terms of both Messiahship and divine sonship (1:3-4).[89] Christ's resurrection from the dead is the start of the new age, "the age to come."[90] The new redemption history era begins with the Davidic Messiah.[91] Douglas Moo comments, "In this new stage of God's plan Jesus reigns as Son of God, powerfully active to bring salvation to all who believe (cf. I: 16)." Christ's resurrection reveals the inauguration of the new age in Paul's letters.[92] Paul's description alludes to God's announcement that he has raised up the Davidic descendant to be enthroned as the Davidic king.[93] In Romans 1:3-4, placing "τοῦ υἱοῦ αὐτοῦ" in front of two participles, Paul announces in the gospel pertaining to Jesus—who was descended from David, resurrected, and appointed to be the Son of God—that Jesus was already His Son prior to these events.[94] It is undeniable that Paul suggests the Davidic Messiahship of Jesus in the introduction of Romans. Paul is the servant of Jesus, who is the Messiah and Lord (1:4). The Davidic Messiah's authority as the expected king is supported with the parallel in 1:3-4. Paul offers further grounding of God's gospel with the content of God's Son, who is the Davidic Messiah, in this formula in Romans 1:3-4. All of this corresponds to the

---

88. Eskola, *Messiah and the Throne*, 235. M. A. Knibb attests, "The fact remains, however, that the Septuagint has introduced messianic references in places where such do not exist in the Massoretic Text and even if messianic expectation was less pervasive at the turn of the era than is often assumed, Greek-speaking Christians found it natural to apply numerous passages in the Septuagint to their interpretation of the significance of the life and death of Jesus." Knibb, "The Septuagint and Messianism: Problems and Issues," 123.

89. Eskola, *Messiah and the Throne*, 61; Stuhlmacher, "Theologische Probleme des Römerbriefpräskripts," 378-86; Moo, *Romans*, 50; Schreiner, *Romans*, 43.

90. Wright, *Romans*, 419.

91. Moo, *Romans*, 50.

92. Moo, *Romans*, 50; Schreiber, *Gesalbter und König*, 411.

93. Jipp, "Ancient, Modern, and Future Interpretations of Romans 1:3-4," 258. The placement of the parallel in Rom 1:3-4, with two participles for the statement about God's Son, is understood as a formula that—in the opinion of many scholars—supports the idea that this is a pre-Pauline confession. For a survey of scholars, see Jewett, "The Redaction and Use of an Early Christian Confession in Romans 1:3-4," 103-13. Poythress maintains that Paul used traditional expressions and ideas, which were included in early creeds. Poythress, "Is Romans 1:3-4 a Pauline Confession After All?," 180-83. In addition, Scott asserts that vocabulary, style, and theology in this parallel based on Paul's own. Scott, *Adoption as Sons of God*, 227-36.

94. Cranfield, *Romans*, 1:58; Wilckens, *Der Brief an die Römer*, 1:64-65.

Davidic messianic language in the Old Testament and the Second Temple Jewish writings as noted in earlier chapters.

JUDGMENT THROUGH THE MESSIAH IN THE GOSPEL OF GOD

Paul's gospel articulation, with the echoes of the Davidic Messiah, is intended as a thematic notion that appeals to the recipients in Rome.[95] Paul's Davidic Messiah echoes in his gospel are an important theme of God's judgment through the Davidic Messiah in Romans.[96] Although the Messiah's faithfulness can be suggested as related to the gospel concerning the Messiah in Romans 1:3–4, it is not a significant feature of the Davidic Messiah, Jesus, and it does not explain the reason Paul focuses on God's judgment through the Davidic Messiah in the discourse about righteousness in the judgment in Romans.

Judgment through the Davidic Messiah in the Gospel

Even though the gospel of God has been understood as God's invitation for his glorious victory over opponents and deliverance of his people from their enemies, God's judgment is included in the announcement of the good news. Another vital feature of the good news, which has been shown in the messianic texts in the Old Testament and Jewish writings, is judgment through the messianic figure. While the gospel means "the good news," especially victory, it includes his vengeance and vindication.[97] The Davidic Messiah's gospel reveals divine wrath over the whole world (1:18).[98] In other words, the gospel is related to eschatological divine judgment of the world[99] because the content of the εὐαγγέλιον cannot only be "grace," but also "judgment" (Rom 2:16; Rev 14:6–7, etc.).[100]

---

95. The echo in Paul's letter "does not have the specificity of allusion but is reserved for language that is thematically related to a more general notion or concept." Porter, "Allusion and Echoes," 40.

96. Contra the thematic conception for Israel's exile or new exodus, see Seifrid, "Romans," 619. Concerning the Exodus tradition in Romans, see Keesmaat, *Paul and His Story*, 55–65.

97. Cranfield, *Romans*, 1:55.

98. Consider that the gospel in 1:17 is related to God's wrath in 1:18, a verse that opens with γάρ. I will examine this in the next part.

99. Käsemann, *Romans*, 7.

100. Strecker, "εὐαγγέλιον," in *EDNT*, 2:71.

The anointed—the Davidic messianic figure in Isaiah 61:1—who is the herald of good news to the poor (Πνεῦμα κυρίου ἐπ' ἐμέ, οὗ εἵνεκεν ἔχρισέν με, εὐαγγελίσασθαι πτωχοῖς, in LXX Isa 61:1), will proclaim the year of the Lord's favor, as well as the day of God's vengeance (Isa 61:2; נָקָם in the MT, ἀνταπόδοσις in the LXX). "Vengeance" (ἀνταπόδοσις) denotes divine retribution in the last judgment.[101] This term ἀνταπόδοσις is employed in one of the ancient texts of Romans 2:5, A, suggesting ἀνταπόδοσις for God's judgment.[102] In Romans 2:5, Paul utilizes the term, "*day of wrath*," which is the quasi-technical term for the time of final judgment.[103] The direct allusion to the judgment in Isaiah 61:2 might not be presented in Romans 2:5. It seems that a function of the anointed is the proclamation of God's judgment in Isaiah 61:1–4, and the day of judgment is included in the message of the gospel, though.

Joel announces God's salvation, which includes his judgment, in Mount Zion in LXX Joel 3:5.[104] The survivors of God's people (πᾶς ὅς ... σωθήσεται, in LXX 3:5) are described as "receiving the announcement" (εὐαγγελιζόμενοι) of God's salvation. The announcement of God's salvation for God's people is in his coming for judgment (LXX Joel 3:3–4). In LXX Nahum 2:1, the announcement of Judah's salvation is proclaimed to the people (οἱ πόδες εὐαγγελιζομένου καὶ ἀπαγγέλλοντος εἰρήνην).[105] This good news connects to the announcement of God's judgment as in the opening of this book (LXX Nah 1:1–6). The Lord will destroy his enemies (LXX Nah 1:8–14; 2:1–4, 19). God's good news includes his imminent judgment over all of his enemies in these passages, as well.

In the Second Temple Jewish writings, the gospel is clearly related to God's judgment in terms of the Messiah. As noted above, the Messianic figure cannot be excluded from the gospel in the Second Jewish writings (*Ps. Sol.* 11:1; 1QS 4:6–7; 1QH 18:14; 4Q521; 11Q13). The messianic figure, the anointed Melchizedek—who is the announcer of good tidings (מבשׂר) in 11Q13 2:18—has the significant role of God's agent for the last judgment as the anointed one in Isaiah 61:1, along with the messenger of the good news in Isaiah 52:7.[106] While he will proclaim liberty for the captives

---

101. Moreover, Ps 69:21 presents God's retributive punishment (68:22 in the LXX). Büchsel, "ἀνταπόδοσις," in *TDNT*, 2:169.

102. Although the variant ἀνταποδόσεως does not look like perceptive, it is an attempt to match the verb "ἀποδώσει" in Rom 2:6. Schreiner, *Romans*, 110; Cranfield, *Romans*, 1:145n2.

103. Moo, *Romans*, 134.

104. Williams, *For Whom Did Christ Die?*, 139.

105. Williams, *For Whom Did Christ Die?*, 139.

106. Horbury insists, "The identification of this coming announcer with

(11Q13 2:6), he will carry out the vengeance of God's judgment on the day of judgment (11Q13 2:13). In this text, the announcer of good tidings, the priest-king Melchizedek, "shall give judgment in the midst of gods: as David said in Psalm 82:1–2 (11Q13 2:9–12)."[107] This is combined with the *Psalms of Solomon* 11:1 and presents the avenging in the day of vengeance as an interpretation of Isaiah 61:1, which is connected with Isaiah 52:7.[108]

As a result, God's judgment cannot be excluded from the content of the good news, according to the employment of εὐαγγέλιον and its verbal forms in the Old Testament and Jewish writings. A further factor that should be considered is the good news is closely linked with the messianic king, who is the agent of God's judgment. This is surely related to the idea that there were expectations for God's visitation, salvation, and ruling through the Davidic Messiah, the agent of God's judgment in the Old Testament and Jewish writings, as shown in the previous chapters.

God's Judgment in Romans 1:3–4

Considering the gospel that includes God's judgment through the Davidic Messiah, Paul's emphasis in Romans 1:3–4 is related to God's judgment through the agent, the Davidic Messiah, as in the Old Testament and the Second Temple Jewish writings. Paul's sequence of thought clearly parallels that of the Psalm. The judgment through the Messiah is inseparably toed to the content of God's gospel in Romans 1:3–4. Paul recognizes the Messiah's sonship on the basis of Psalm 2; it is presupposed that the judgment through the Messiah (Rom 2:16) is executed on all the nations who rebel against Yahweh and his Messiah (Ps 2:2). The inheritance of all the nations (2:8) should be accomplished while he judges all the nations "with a rod of iron" (cf. 2:9–12). Paul's sequence of thought paralleled with Psalm 2 can be found in Romans 1:18–2:16, which will be examined later.

In addition, the Davidic Messiah will destroy all opposition to his rule (Ps 110:5–7), which is clearly illustrated in the Messiah's enthronement that is described with resurrection and enthronement in Paul's understanding (cf. 4:25 and Rom 8). In Romans, Paul concentrates on presenting his gospel via the category of justification through his death and resurrection. It

---

Melchizedek as anointed of the spirit and the 'god' who 'judges in the midst of gods' also coheres with later views of Melchizedek as a great spiritual being linked with Christ." Horbury, *Herodian Judaism and New Testament Study*, 99.

107. Horbury, *Herodian Judaism and New Testament Study*, 99.
108. Horbury, *Herodian Judaism and New Testament Study*, 99.

is clearly revealed in Christ's atoning death and resurrection, which bring about justification of all believers as in 4:25. Mark Seifrid posits,

> It is "in the gospel" that the "righteousness of God" is revealed.... And it is God's righteousness which has been revealed: in Christ's resurrection God has been vindicated and has defeated his enemies. Salvation comes through destruction, justification through condemnation. Moreover, the gospel is "the power of God unto salvation" because the "righteousness of God" revealed in it entails nothing less than the resurrection from the dead.[109]

God's saving through the Davidic Messiah, Jesus, cannot be disconnected from his judgment in the gospel of God; the coming Messiah was assumed to be a deliverer.

Jesus is "the one appointed by God to be judge of the living and the dead" (Acts 10:42). It is plainly shown in the appointment of the Davidic Messiah in Romans 1:4. The syntax of the aorist participle in Romans 1:4, "ὁρισθέντος," corresponds with the syntax of Acts 10:43.[110] Moreover, the role of the eschatological judge appears in Acts 17:31 since "he has fixed a day on which he will judge the world in righteousness by a man whom he has appointed, and of this he has given assurance to all by raising him from the dead." Because this concept of Jesus as the eschatological judge corresponds to the Davidic Messiah's role in the Old Testament and the Second Temple Jewish writings examined in the previous chapters, he is expected to judge in righteousness.

Furthermore, the context of passages adjacent to the introduction that include Davidic messianism (1:3-4) should be considered in determining the function of the Davidic Messiah within Paul's argument. In addition, other passages regarding the Davidic Messiah can explain Paul's contention connected with the function of the Davidic Messiah, Jesus, who is the eschatological messianic king according to the Davidic line in Romans. The Davidic Messiah role in Romans is clearly demonstrated to be the agent of God's judgment. It is additionally connected to the message in God's gospel concerning his Son, which includes the message of judgment in 1:3-4.

---

109. Seifrid, *Christ, Our Righteousness*, 46-47.

110. Eskola, *Messiah and the Throne*, 224. "Οὗτός ἐστιν ὁ ὡρισμένος ὑπὸ τοῦ θεοῦ κριτὴς ζώντων καὶ νεκρῶν" (Acts 10:42). Calhoun writes, "The notion of Jesus being 'appointed' or 'designated' by God seems to have currency in multiple strands of early Christianity, a point which weighs against the supposition of compound simplex iteration in v. 4. The author of Acts views this 'appointment' as pertaining to the specific task of executing divine judgment, as in 10:42." Calhoun, *Paul's Definitions of the Gospel in Romans 1*, 134.

The relationship between the introduction (1:3–4) and the summary of the gospel (1:16–17) must be considered, as well.[111] According to Seyoon Kim,

> It is then not difficult to understand the unity of the two definitions of the gospel in Rom 1:3–4 and 1:16–17. We can see that, similarly to 1 Cor 15:23–28 (cf. 15:51–57) and Col 1:13–14, with the two definitions side by side in Rom 1 Paul is affirming God's installation of Jesus as his Son to exercise his kingship (1:3–4), in terms of God's righteousness (1:16–17).[112]

Paul's cases for justification and righteousness in Romans are firmly related to his "reflection upon biblical texts, foremost of which are the Psalms and Isaiah—the portions of the LXX most susceptible to a royal-messianic interpretation given their depiction of righteous royal figures who suffer and are vindicated by God."[113] Paul maintains that God's righteousness is revealed in the gospel (1:16–17), which will be examined more in the next chapter. While he designates the gospel concerning the Davidic Messiah "as centering upon a resurrected, royal Son of God, this divine justice must be understood as an outworking of God's resurrection of his Messiah from the dead and subsequent enthronement."[114] The believers in Rome are introduced to the Davidic Messiah God's gospel (1:3–4). Paul's gospel stresses the language of divine justice, judgment, God's wrath and righteousness mediated by the Davidic Messiah.

Paul's point is based on God's execution of righteous judgment through the agent, the Davidic Messiah, to offset God's wrath toward ungodliness and unrighteousness (Rom 2:16). Christ's Davidic Messiahship is clearly related to the idea of the execution of God's judgment, which is manifested in the Old Testament and the Jewish Second Temple writings. In his execution of God's judgment, his impartial judgment and righteousness are emphasized in Romans, too. Paul articulates the impartial judgment and justifying righteousness in the Messiah's role as agent of God's judgment, rather than the Messiah's faithfulness in God's judgment through the Davidic Messiah in 1:18–4:25, which will be examined in the next chapter.

---

111. Bornkamm, "Paul's Christology," 12–13.
112. Kim, "Jesus the Son of God as the Gospel (1 Thess 1:9–10 and Rom 1:3–4)," 132.
113. Jipp, *Christ Is King*, 213.
114. Jipp, *Christ Is King*, 213–14.

The Faithful Messiah?

The Messiah Christology in Romans 1:3-4 can hardly be separated from the arguments of this letter, especially from 15:12, because Romans 1:3 and 15:12 form a messianic inclusio surrounding Paul's larger contention in Romans.[115] Both of these passages manifest the kingship of Jesus "on the basis of Jesus' resurrection and with reference to Christ's reign over Gentiles."[116] Wright cites "Romans 1:3 and 15:12, in both of which there is clear reference to Jesus as the Davidic king." Romans 15:12 presents the Davidic Messiah as "the root of Jesse." Wright understands that Paul returns to the theme of God's faithfulness in 15:8, and Paul's cases as he uses the Davidic Messiah's confession is coherent from the beginning to the end of this letter. The Davidic Messiah, who—according to Old Testament prophecy—would arise to rule the Gentiles (15:12), was appointed as the Son of God with the resurrection. And he was "exalted" at God's right hand that he might rule with sovereignty based on Psalm 110:1.[117]

Christopher Whitsett focuses on God's faithfulness based on the Messiah's birth in the Davidic line, as well.[118] From his view, Paul cites Isaiah 11:10 in Romans 15:12 in accordance with his argument. He writes,

> The whole of Rom 1:3b states and restates Jesus' fleshly descent from David, the precise element of the promise of 2 Sam 7 that plays a role in Paul's argument; Christ's physical descent demonstrates God's faithfulness. The limitations of space prohibit any adequate discussion of κατὰ σάρκα here. . . . Thus Jesus' Davidic heritage fits into the complex of promise and seed in Paul's arguments. Jesus' Davidic descent plays the same role—in an anticipatory way—in 1:3 as in 15:12; it confirms Gods promise to David and thus confirms God's truthfulness to the seed of Abraham. Very much like Ps 89:19-37, Paul answers the present unhappy plight of Israel (Rom 9:1-3) by citing God's faithfulness to the promise of 2 Sam 7; God's trustworthiness toward David (now fulfilled in David's seed, Jesus) confirms God's faithfulness in all things.[119]

---

115. Jipp, "Ancient, Modern, and Future Interpretations of Romans 1:3-4," 258.
116. Whitsett, "Son of God, Seed of David," 673.
117. Wright, *Paul: In Fresh Perspective*, 44.
118. Whitsett, "Son of God, Seed of David," 673.
119. Whitsett, "Son of God, Seed of David," 674-75.

While Paul carefully designs his theological argument in 15:1-13, the resurrected Davidic king's role is ruling the nations as in 1:3-4, which resonates with the second chapter of Psalms.[120]

It seems that Whitsett follows the argument of Richard Hays, who states,

> It is no accident that this nexus of ideas fits perfectly into the argument that Paul is bringing to a climax in Rom 15:7-13. Paul cites the Psalm's line about singing praise among the Gentiles to evoke the image of a suffering and vindicated Christ whose deliverance from death confirms God's faithfulness to Israel (cf. Rom 15:8) and establishes God's merciful sovereignty over nations (Rom 15:9a). Significantly, the chain of four quotations in Rom 5:9-12 ends with an explicit pointer—this time from Isaiah—to a "shoot of Jesse" who will "rise up to rule the Gentiles."[121]

The inclusion of Christology in Romans is understood as the evocation of Davidic messianic themes, when Hays emphasizes the famous theme of God's faithfulness.[122]

God's faithfulness is characterized by these scholars as linked to the Messiah's faithfulness in Romans texts. Wright holds,

> This theme [vis. The messiahship of Jesus] makes it very likely, in my view, that when Paul speaks in Galatians and Romans of *pistis Christou*, he normally intends to denote faithfulness of the Messiah to the purpose of God.... Precisely as Messiah, he offers God that representative faithfulness to the plan of salvation through which the plan can go ahead at last, Abraham can have a worldwide family (chapter 4), and the long entail of Adam's sin and death can be undone (5.12-21) through this *obedience*, which as we know from 1.5 is for Paul very closely aligned with faith, faithfulness or fidelity.[123]

The Isaianic passage that is one of the great messianic oracles states with the Messiah "becoming 'a servant to the circumcised on behalf of God's trustfulness, to confirm the promises of the patriarchs, and that the Gentiles would glorify God for his mercy.'"[124] Wright goes on to say, "By speaking

---

120. Wright, *Paul and the Faithfulness of God*, 819.
121. Hays, "Christ Prays the Psalms," 135.
122. Keck, "Christology, Soteriology, and the Praise of God (Romans 15:7-13)," 93.
123. Wright, *Paul: In Fresh Perspective*, 47.
124. Wright, *Paul and the Faithfulness of God*, 819.

of the Messiah's 'faithfulness,' Paul clearly intends to relate the action (or passion) of the Messiah to the purpose of God to which Israel had been unfaithful. . . . But this points to a second feature: by speaking of the Messiah's death as an act of 'faithfulness' Paul makes it clear that what is accomplished through the Messiah (through the-Messiah-as-Israel-in-person) is the faithfulness of the active will and the purpose of the covenant God."[125] The Messiah's faithfulness accomplishes God's covenantal promise.[126] The faithfulness of the Davidic Messiah, Jesus, resolves Israel's failure to be "faithful."[127] Romans 15:1–13 "begins with a reference to *ho Christos* as the one who, according to Psalm 68, did not please himself, but took on himself the reproaches of the people."[128] In Wright's view, the Messiah's reproach is an act of "faithfulness."[129] Through the obedience of the Messiah, the Messiah fulfills "the active will and purpose of the covenant God."[130] Through the obedience of the Messiah, his faithfulness, God's purpose of "redemption" is accomplished.[131]

However, although God's faithfulness in covenantal relationship is clearly illustrated in Paul's discourse in 15:7–13, this does not guarantee that the Messiah's faithfulness is included in a correct understanding of God's gospel in 1:3–4, which is closely related to 15:12. Instead, God's judgment through the Davidic Messiah is Paul's point in his discourse in these passages, not the Davidic Messiah's faithfulness.

The Davidic Messiah of Isaiah 11 in Romans 15:12

God's judgment is presupposed in the gospel pertaining to the Davidic Messiah in the introduction of Romans, and God's judgment through the Davidic Messiah connects to Romans 15:12 in Paul's argument. In the first part of Romans 15:12, God's faithfulness in covenantal relationship clearly appears. The "faithfulness of God" (ἀλήθεια θεοῦ) in Romans 15:8 refers to his covenant faithfulness because God is faithful to his covenantal promises of salvation for Israel.[132] The Messiah came as an executor of God's cov-

---

125. Wright, *Paul and the Faithfulness of God*, 842.
126. Wright, *Paul and the Faithfulness of God*, 830–31.
127. Wright, *Paul and the Faithfulness of God*, 830.
128. Wright, *Paul and the Faithfulness of God*, 820.
129. Wright, *Paul and the Faithfulness of God*, 842.
130. Wright, *Paul and the Faithfulness of God*, 842.
131. Wright, *Paul and the Faithfulness of God*, 830.
132. Schreiner, *Romans*, 754–55.

enantal promises to save his people.¹³³ In Romans 15:8, in Davidic Messiah as the servant of the circumcision, there are echoes of the Isaianic Servant Songs.¹³⁴ The Davidic Messiah's role in the Servant Songs (Isa 42:1–4; 49:1–6; 52:13–53:12) is the saving of the nations.¹³⁵

However, as noted above, 15:7–12 is an inclusio of Romans 1:3–4, but judgment through the Davidic Messiah is focused on, rather than the Davidic Messiah's faithfulness. It is construed with Paul's citation of Isaiah 11, in which impartial judgment in righteousness is stressed in God's judgment through the Messiah as noted in the previous chapters.

Judgment through the Davidic Messiah

With respect to Paul's the citation of Isaiah 11:10 in Romans 15:12, it should be understood as well that Isaiah chapter 11 concentrates on God's judgment through the Davidic Messiah, as noted in earlier chapters. While Isaiah 10:5–11:6 contains a pattern of the earlier "messianic passages,"¹³⁶ The tenth chapter of Isaiah resonates with Isaiah 2:6–7 in the broader pattern of God's judgment. Also, Isaiah 10:33–34 eschatologically summarizes Isaiah chapter 11.¹³⁷ Randall Heskett explains,

> Therefore, the eschatological nature of 11:6–9 offers a balance to the generalizing nature of 10:33–34 and thereby frames Isa 11:1–5 within this vast perspective. Like 2:2–3, the ending of ch. 10 now situates the events of within this larger pattern of God's eschatological judgment whereby ch. 11 follows immediately with messianic prophecy.¹³⁸

The Davidic Messiah's role in Isaiah 11:3–5 is doubtlessly judicial, and he will judge with righteousness and equity.¹³⁹ Novenson declares, "Numerous texts from this period provide evidence that Gen 49:10; Num 24:17; and Isa 11:1–10 were reworked and transformed into royal expectations for a king and judge who would bring justice."¹⁴⁰ As noted above, in Second

---

133. Schreiner, *Romans*, 755.
134. Seifrid, "Romans," 688.
135. Seifrid, "Romans," 688.
136. Wenger, *An Examination of Kingship and Messianic Expectation in Isaiah 1–35*, 259.
137. Heskett, *Messianism within the Scriptural Scroll of Isaiah*, 126.
138. Heskett, *Messianism within the Scriptural Scroll of Isaiah*, 126.
139. Williamson, "The Messianic Texts in Isaiah 1–39," 258.
140. See, for example, *Sib. Or.* 3. 767–808; *T. Levi* 17:2–11; 18:2–9; *T. Jud.* 24 1Q28b;

Temple Jewish writings, the eleventh chapter of Isaiah is interpreted as God's judgment.

The work of the "root of Jesse" stands to rule the nations (Rom 15:12). While this verse can describe the promise of restoration, it is fulfilled after his judgment.[141] Seifrid comments,

> Although the entire line of David will be removed by the judgment of the Lord, the Lord will begin afresh and create a new David out of the "stump of Jesse," which will be left behind. Unlike the prior line of David who preceded him, he will judge righteously, defending the poor and needy (11:2–5). . . . The remnant of Israel will be restored from the nations (11:11–16).[142]

Moreover, the eschatological judgment under the Davidic Messiah is clearly shown in the context of Romans 15:12 because Davidic Psalms, which are alluded to in Romans 15:9, 12, are founded in his victory over his enemy.[143] David's victories can anticipate the great victories in the Davidic Messiah, Jesus.[144] In sum, Paul's citation of Isaiah 11 in Romans 15:12 is more likely not a clue for the Messiah's faithfulness because God's judgment is more stressed in this allusion. It is more suitable as a reference to the Davidic Messiah, who is the agent of God's judgment.

The "Strong" and "Weak"

Romans 15:7–13 conclude 14:1—15:6, in which Paul exhorts the "strong" and the "weak."[145] The significant ending in presenting the Davidic Messiah (Rom 15:5–7) shows Paul's main concern is God's judgment about the distinction between Jews and Gentiles. Dissension (14:1) and mutual judgment (14:3) between Jewish Christians and Gentile Christians shall be banned due to the Davidic Messiah's lordship (14:9). In accord with his opening admonition (14:1), Paul warns against mutual judgment (14:10): "Why do you pass judgment on your brother? Or you, why do you despise

---

1QM 11:6–7; 4Q161; 4Q252; 4QFlor; Philo, *Moses*. 1. 290; Josephus, *War*. 6. 310–12; 1 Enoch 49:1–4. Novenson, *Christ among the Messiahs*, 57–58.

141. Seifrid, "Romans," 690.
142. Seifrid, "Romans," 690.
143. Schreiner, *Romans*, 757.
144. Schreiner, *Romans*, 757.
145. Schreiner, *Romans*, 753.

your brother?"¹⁴⁶ In addition, Paul confirms that God will judge all people on the last day in his citation of Isaiah 45:23.¹⁴⁷ Moo maintains,

> On the one hand, as Paul has emphasized earlier (vv. 4, 10), it shows why it is wrong for a Christian to stand in judgment over another: "Do not judge your brother, for God will judge him." But the fact of judgment to come also reminds believers that they will have to answer before the Lord for their own behavior: "Do not judge your brother (and so sin), for God will judge you."¹⁴⁸

Furthermore, Schreiner observes,

> In the concluding verses (Rom. 14:10–12) Paul draws the implications from the lordship of Christ. Since Christ is Lord and judge, it is totally inappropriate for some believers to judge or despise other believers (v. 10). All believers will stand before God's judgment Seat.¹⁴⁹

In this passage, the Messiah, who is described as the Lord of both the dead and the living, fulfills God's judgment through his death and resurrection (14:9).¹⁵⁰ This is the main content of Paul's gospel in Romans. Being justified by virtue of the Messiah's death and resurrection, believers—regardless of the distinction between Jews and Gentiles—can glorify "the God and Father of our Lord Jesus Christ" (15:7). Before the Messiah's redemption, they sinned and fell short of the glory of God (3:23). Robert Jewett argues,

> In the love feasts where Christ played the role of host and in the kerygma in which Christ's death for sinners was declared, each member of the various congregations had experienced such unearned welcome. A reminder of this basis was provided in 15:3 and will be reiterated in 15:8, but it also needs to be recognized that this clause succinctly summarizes the main argument of Romans, namely, that God accepts sinners who formerly made themselves into his enemies.¹⁵¹

The phrase, "for the glory of God," (15:7) is attached to Paul's exhortation to "accept one another," instead of judging one another in 14:1–15:7.

---

146. Seifrid, "Romans," 684.
147. Moo, *Romans*, 848.
148. Moo, *Romans*, 848.
149. Schreiner, *Romans*, 722.
150. Schreiner, *Romans*, 722.
151. Jewett, *Romans*, 889.

Paul's intention is that believers should accept one another for the glory of God just as Christ accepted believers for God's glory. Paul encourages mutual acceptance, rather than mutual condemnation, especially between Jews and Gentiles.[152]

Judgment and reconciliation of the Gentiles

The Davidic Messiah's judgment is presupposed to extend over the nations. The Messiah's faithfulness in the covenant boundary loses meaning in this concept for the Davidic Messiah's judgment in Romans 15. In Paul's mind, there is no distinction between Jews and Gentiles related to mutual condemnation in Romans 14:1–15:6. In the rendering of Isaiah 11:1, God's judgment over nations cannot be denied. The impartiality of God's judgment is implied in presenting the Davidic Messiah. Horbury additionally notes that the later influence of the star-prophecy (Num 24:17), combined with the Jesse-oracle (Isa 11:1–2), in both Christian and Jewish circles suggests "a long-standing association" of these two prophecies, already current in the Second Temple period. This is suggested by its emergence (*Ps. Sol.* 17:1; 1QSb, col. V; *T. Jud.* 24; and Rev 22:16).[153] It is quite plausible that the link between Isaiah 11 and Numbers 24 existed in the mind of the translator and made its way into the rendering of Isaiah 11:1.[154] God's judgment over nations appears in this connection between Isaiah 11 and Numbers 24. Seifrid attests,

> Various early Jewish texts in some measure echo the promise of the Messiah found in this verse and its context. . . . As is typical of the Qumran writings, 4Q 161 8–10 III, 18–25 interprets Isa 11:10 to speak of the Messiah "ruling" (cf. the LXX) all the Gentiles (*gôyim*) and Magog (see Ezek. 38:2; 39:6). His sword will judge all peoples. Here the Gentiles appear as the enemies of the Lord and his people: the Messiah rules by the sword.[155]

---

152. Jewett, *Romans*, 754.

153. Horbury, *Jewish Messianism and the Cult of Christ*, 92–93.

154. In Qumran texts, the Davidic Messiah's judgment is emphasized in messianic texts, which are based on Num 24:7 and Isa 10:34–11:5. Cf. 4QpIsa[a] (4Q161) and 4Q285; 1QM 1:3; 11:4-7. Horbury explains, "Later in this fragment ([4QpIsa[a]] lines 16–18) 'he shall slay the wicked' is interpreted of the branch of David who will slay 'his [en]emy' (singular). The description of his rule and judgment includes a mention of Magog (line 20), which recalls the role of God and Magog as the foe of the messiah." Horbury, *Jewish Messianism and the Cult of Christ*, 60.

155. Seifrid, "Romans," 690.

In Romans 15:9, Paul presents the larger context of Psalm 18, which is one of thanksgiving. Paul cites, "Therefore I will praise you among the Gentiles, and sing to your name" (Rom 15:9; cf. Ps 18:49). In this Psalm, David offers praise to Yahweh for salvation from enemies. Yahweh delivers him from death because of David's righteousness (18:6–24).[156] David judges his enemies and destroys them (18:31–42).[157] David becomes the head of nations, and Yahweh places nations under his rule (18:46–48). David praises, "For this I will praise you, O LORD, among the nations, and sing to your name." (18:49). Paul's citation presents the risen Messiah as standing in the place of David.[158] While all people, who sinned, were opposed to God, and were apart from God's glory, bringing about God's wrath—the Davidic Messiah judges their sins through his death and resurrection. The Messiah brings the Gentiles salvation because of the execution of the Messiah's judgment.[159]

Paul's focus in Romans 15:9 is including the Gentiles in God's people (15:9; cf. 3:21–31; 4:12–17; 9:24–25, 30; 10:9–13; 11:28–30).[160] The inclusion of the Gentiles is a result of God's judgment through the Davidic Messiah, and the covenantal barrier is excluded in this judgment and inclusion. By including the Gentiles, Paul's intention in Romans 15:8–9 is highlighting the responsibility of the nations to glorify God.[161] This is related to a welcome of their fellow Christians glorifying God, appealing to Christ's model.[162] In light of the Messiah's role, Paul recognizes his own role as gathering the Gentiles for the worship of God. Paul employs the verb "προσλαμβάνω" in describing the Messiah's redemptive role of welcoming the extended congregations, who are not solely Jews.[163] The Messiah destroys the ethnic barrier, as well as the distinction between the "strong" and the "weak."

The context of Deuteronomy, cited in Romans 15:10, is similar to this context of Psalm 18:50.[164] After he judges his people (Deut 32:19–33), Yahweh will judge his enemies (Deut 32:42–43). The rejoicing of the nations is placed between announcements of Yahweh's judgment on the nations.[165]

156. Seifrid, "Romans," 689.
157. Seifrid, "Romans," 689.
158. Seifrid, "Romans," 689.
159. Seifrid, "Romans," 689.
160. Moo, *Romans*, 874.
161. Shum, *Paul's Use of Isaiah in Romans*, 251.
162. Shum, *Paul's Use of Isaiah in Romans*, 251.
163. Jewett, *Romans*, 889.
164. Seifrid, "Romans," 689.
165. According to Deut 32:42, "I will make my arrows drunk with blood, and my

In this citation, Gentiles and Jews praise God together. The inclusion of Gentiles in praising God is part of God's purposes in his victory over the nations.[166] The Gentiles' hope of salvation is accomplished after the Davidic Messiah's judgment in the context of Isaiah 40–55 (see Isa 45:7).[167] Moo says that "the basic meaning of the text is the same in both versions; either would allow Paul to make the point he wants to make: that the Gentiles' participation in the praise of God (vv. 9b–11) comes as a result of the work of 'the root of Jesse,' a messianic designation."[168] Correspondingly, in this context, the Davidic Messiah's role is the agent of God's judgment in the Isaian text, as noted above. Therefore, Paul's citation of these verses is an affirmation of the Davidic Messiah because David praises God "among the Gentiles" due to God's victory over Gentile nations through the Davidic Messiah.[169] God's judgment over the covenantal barrier is implied in the Davidic Messiah in Romans 15:12. It effects the Gentiles' inclusion in glorifying God (15:9–12).

The offering of Gentiles.

Paul emphasizes that the inclusion of Gentiles results from God's judgment through the Messiah, in which Paul's focus is not the Messiah's faithfulness in covenantal relationship. Instead, Paul argues justification by faith in the Messiah's death and resurrection even for the Gentiles. In Romans 15:16–21, Paul again presents his apostolic mission within a citation of the Servant Song (Isa 52:15). While Paul identifies the Davidic Messiah in Isaiah 53 as Christ, he testifies to his apostolic mission regarding Christ, the Davidic Messiah, in Romans 15:16–21. Paul offers righteousness through faith in the Davidic Messiah as the solution to God's judgment. It is not described as the Messiah's obedient death, his covenantal faithfulness. This is clearly shown in Romans 1:18–4:25, which the next chapter will examine. The Davidic Messiah is the answer for sinners in terms of God's judgment. Justification by faith is the result of the Davidic Messiah's sacrificial role. His death is not just his faithful death in covenantal relationship; rather, it is the object of

---

sword shall devour flesh—with the blood of the slain and the captives, from the long-haired heads of the enemy." And, Deut 32:43 reads, "Rejoice with him, O heavens. . . . for he avenges the blood of his children and takes vengeance on his adversaries."

166. Moo, *Romans*, 878.
167. Seifrid, "Romans," 689.
168. Moo, *Romans*, 880.
169. Moo, *Romans*, 878–89.

God's judgment. Paul's ministry consists of "serving the gospel of God" as a priestly ministry.[170] According to Moo,

> But the sacrificial language in the last part of the verse makes it more likely that he intends the term to connote *priestly* ministry specifically. Thus Paul goes on to describe his "ministry" here as consisting in "serving the gospel of God as a priest." The purpose of this ministry, further, is that "the offering of the Gentiles might be acceptable."[171]

In Paul's understanding of his ministry, based on Moses's song and the Davidic psalms, Gentiles turn from being sinners to being acceptable offerings (Rom 15:16) for the worship and praise of God. This results from God's judgment through the Davidic Messiah. Through faith in the Davidic Messiah's death and resurrection, Gentiles are justified and reconciled with God, so that they can be acceptable sacrifices to God (Rom 12:1). Consequently, Paul's citation of the Davidic Messiah in Romans 15:12 means that the Messiah's ruling over the Gentiles includes his salvation and judgment, so Paul's intention in this passage is that believers should accept one another. Hence, the point in Paul's Isaiah citation in this passage is the Messiah's judgment, instead of his faithfulness.

For this reason, the gospel concerning the Davidic Messiah in Romans 1:3–4, related to Romans 15:12, supports his role as the executor of God's judgment. The Davidic Messiah in God's judgment is clearly implied in the gospel of God, and he is the executor of God's judgment in the heavenly court (Rom 2:16; 8:34). The Messiah's covenantal faithfulness is not Paul's emphasis in God's judgment through the Davidic Messiah as is shown in Romans 15:12. Rather, the justifying righteousness language in God's judgment through the Davidic Messiah is emphasized in the gospel of God. In addition, while equity and righteousness in God's judgment are included as judgmental themes in Isaiah 11, the Davidic Messiah's faithfulness in Romans 1:3–4 is not crucial within Paul's citation of Isaiah 11 in Romans 15:12.

CONCLUSION

In Romans 1:3–4, Paul announces God's gospel, which mainly concerns God's Son—a statement of Paul's significant purpose in writing his letter to the believers in Rome. While the content of the gospel includes God's invitation for the salvation of his people in 1:3–4, it additionally includes

---

170. Moo, *Romans*, 889.
171. Moo, *Romans*, 889.

the message of God's judgment through the Davidic Messiah. The Davidic Messiah was resurrected and enthroned to be the agent of God's judgment. This is announced in Paul's letter to the believers in Rome for their justification in Paul's gospel in 1:3–4 as an allusion to Psalms 2 and 110. As a result, Paul does not deny or refuse the descent from the Davidic line because, as mentioned above, the Jewish messiahship is included in the Messiah Christology in Paul's letters.

In Romans 15, Paul focuses on the Davidic Messiah's role as God's judgment. After God's judgment through the Davidic Messiah, the Gentiles are included to glorify God. There is no distinction between Jews and Gentiles. The reconciliation of Gentiles is a significant theme in the argument of Paul pertaining to the "weak" and "strong." After justification that crosses over the covenantal barrier, which is God's impartial judgment through the Davidic Messiah's death, the Gentiles can be God's people. Paul's mission, the offering of the Gentiles, in Romans 15:16 is based on the Davidic Messiah's judgment (15:12). Therefore, Paul's focus in the gospel of God is God's judgment through the Messiah, instead of rather than the Messiah's covenantal faithfulness.

Chapter 5

The Judgment of God and the Davidic Messiah

in Romans 1:18–4:25

INTRODUCTION

Modern Pauline scholars explain that the Messiah's faithfulness to God's covenantal promises is the center of Romans' Christology. Yet, if, as I suggested in the previous chapter, the Davidic Messiah Jesus is the agent of God's judgment in Romans, this covenantal language is not the focus of Paul's attention in this passage. Despite the Messiah's covenantal faithfulness mentioned by several New Testament scholars, Paul's main emphasis in Romans 1:18–4:25 is God's judgment through the Davidic Messiah, Jesus.

This chapter illustrates that God's judgment through the Davidic Messiah is evident by the righteousness language; righteousness consequently cannot be identified with the term *"faithfulness."* Because, in Romans 1:18–3:20, Paul's purpose for presenting God's righteousness is linked to God's wrath against sin, Paul does not use the terms *"covenant"* and "faithfulness" for the Messiah in this passage. The Davidic Messiah—the agent of God's judgment—is demonstrated in Romans 2:16 as "according to my gospel, God judges the secrets of men by Christ Jesus." The Davidic Messiah, as perceived in the Old Testament and Second Jewish literature, is employed in Paul's argument of God's judgment in Romans 1:18–4:25. The first section of this chapter establishes the Messiah as an instrument of God's judgment. The second section of this chapter illustrates that Jesus Christ's death is God's unique method to answer his wrath and judgment toward sinners. In Romans, Paul concentrates on the intertwined role of the Davidic Messiah, consisting of receiving God's punishment on the cross and the executing of God's judgment. This execution of God's judgment toward the Messiah is especially shown in 3:21–26; the Messiah's faithfulness is not described. Therefore, the third section contends that the justifying righteousness of the Davidic Messiah occurs in the Davidic Messiah's death and resurrection in 4:25. This wording of Paul articulates the righteousness by faith in the Davidic Messiah, Jesus, instead of the Messiah's covenantal faithfulness.

JUDGMENT THROUGH THE DAVIDIC MESSIAH: ROMANS 2:16

Paul stresses that Jesus, the Davidic Messiah, is the agent of God's judgment in his gospel (2:16). This emphasis is placed on Paul's argument of God's wrath toward all human beings (1:18–3:20). Opening his argument, Paul shows God's wrath is revealed against all ungodliness and unrighteousness of men (1:18). Paul relates the justifying righteousness (1:17) to God's wrath with judgmental language. Moreover, Paul focuses on God's impartial judgment (1:18–2:16). God righteously judges Jews and Gentiles, regardless of covenantal boundary. The Messiah's faithfulness does not fit in this flow of Paul's argument with regard to God's judgment.

Revelation of God's Wrath

Paul starts this passage with God's wrath "revealed from heaven against all ungodliness and unrighteousness of men" (Rom 1:18).[1] God's wrath is clearly judgmental in Paul's thought.[2] This is in accordance with the

---

1. The wrath and judgment in Paul's letters are usually future (Rom 2:5, 8; 3:5; 9:22; Eph 5:6; Col 3:7; 1 Thess 5:9). However, God's righteousness is presently revealed with this verbal form. Bockmuehl, *Revelation and Mystery in Ancient Judaism and Pauline Christianity*, 141. While the verb παρέδωκεν describes the manifestation of God's wrath with past tense, the wrath of God began and is continuing up to the present time. Schreiner, *Romans*, 84–85.

2. There is pervasive forensic language and imagery based on the δικ-stem in this passage (1:18–3:20). Seifrid, "Unrighteous by Faith," 108.

prophets who prophesied the day of God's judgment in the Old Testament (Joel 2:1f; Amos 5:18f). It is the day of wrath when the righteous judgment of God is revealed, and the day of judgment on Jerusalem is equivalent to the day of wrath (Job 20:28; 21:20, 30; Isa 13:9, 13; Ezek 7:19; Zeph 1:15, 18; 2:2).[3] Furthermore, Paul qualifies the "day of wrath" as the time of judgment (2:5).[4] For example, the pouring out of God's wrath—"righteous judgment" (δικαιοκρισία)—revealed on that day is a central theme in this section.[5]

In the Second Temple literature, the eschatological judgment is identified with the revealing of God's wrath (1 *En.* 84:4; 91:7–9).[6] The wrath of God is judgment against sin (Sir 5:6; 36:8), and it concerns his punishment for sin (Wis 11:9; 16:5; 18:20).[7] As ungodliness brings about God's retribution (Ezek 23:28–30; Wis 11:15–16; *T. Gad.* 5:10), Paul identifies the reason for God's wrath, establishing the intrinsic relation between sin and punishment.[8]

God's Wrath toward All Human Beings

The fundamental reason that God pours out his wrath is people's refusal to honor and worship him and their turn to idolatry (1:19–23).[9] The handing over (παραδίδωμι, 1:24, 26, 28) of God is a response to the exchanging of the glory of God for idolatry (1:23, 25, 26), which is a "divine retribution."[10] God's retributive wrath is to be executed against the overt idolatry of the Gentiles, who are described as having no covenantal relationship.[11] Ellen Christiansen maintains, "The alternative Paul suggests is belonging defined not in narrow particularistic terms of covenant or election."[12] Because covenant is not an obvious category for Gentiles, Paul does not utilize διαθήκη in this section.[13] The relationship of Gentiles with God is more distant than

---

3. Eskola, *Theodicy and Predestination in Pauline Soteriology*, 118.
4. Moo, *The Epistle to the Romans*, 134–35.
5. Moo, *The Epistle to the Romans*, 135.
6. Eskola, *Theodicy and Predestination in Pauline Soteriology*, 119.
7. Eskola, *Theodicy and Predestination in Pauline Soteriology*, 119.
8. Fitzmyer, *Romans*, 284.
9. Schreiner, *Paul, Apostle of God's Glory in Christ*, 105.
10. Bell, *No One Seeks for God*, 54.
11. The Jewish people were not characterized by overt idolatry after the exile. McFadden, *Judgment According to Works in Romans*, 34.
12. Christiansen, *The Covenant in Judaism and Paul*, 230.
13. Christiansen, *The Covenant in Judaism and Paul*, 230–32.

that of Jews. Paul does not argue toward a covenantal identity for Gentiles.[14] Nonetheless, Paul describes God as executing his retributive wrath on Gentiles' idolatry.

In his subsequent charge, Paul explains the final judgment of God's wrath that shall be executed on the hypocritical judges, represented as Jews (2:1-6).[15] He employs the judgment motif against the Jewish people in Romans 2.[16] Paul interacts with an interlocutor, a Jew who relies on the law for deliverance from God's wrath. This interlocutor is also presupposed as the pretentious judge in the diatribe of 2:1-16.[17] In his dialogue with his Jewish partner, Paul charges persuasively that Israel is "steeped in sin."[18] Indeed, the verdict in 2:1 with the logical connective "διό" echoes the inexcusable human beings' status in 1:21-32: "Therefore (διό) you have no excuse, O man, every one of you who judges. For in passing judgment (ἐν ᾧ γὰρ κρίνεις) on another you condemn yourself, because you, the judge, practice the very same things (τὰ γὰρ αὐτὰ πράσσεις)."[19] While interpreters mainly assume that 1:18-32 characterizes the sins of non-Jews, considering Paul's sequent charge against Jews and his conclusions (3:9, 19-20, 23), he additionally considers God's impartial judgment on Jews in Romans 1:18-32.[20] John Barclay asserts, "A close reading of 1:18-32 suggests that there are echoes here of a biblical rebuke of Israelite idolatry (LXX Ps 105:20 in Rom 1:23), and as we know from Pseudo-Philo and 4 Ezra, even substantial distinctions between Jews and Gentiles can be accompanied by a general critique of Israel's waywardness and corruption."[21]

In presenting an accusation against the Jewish people, Paul clearly presents the judgmental concept with the "God's righteous judgment" (δικαιοκρισία, 2:5). This means "God judges righteously."[22] He attests that God "will render each according to his works" (ὃς ἀποδώσει ἑκάστῳ κατὰ

---

14. Christiansen, *The Covenant in Judaism and Paul*, 230-32.

15. Bornkamm, *Early Christian Experience*, 59; Seifrid, "Unrighteous by Faith," 108.

16. McFadden, *Judgment According to Works in Romans*, 43.

17. Berkley, *From a Broken Covenant to Circumcision of the Heart*, 110. Concerning diatribe, see Stanley Stowers, *The Diatribe and Paul's Letter to the Romans*; Song, *Reading Romans as a Diatribe*. Many scholars understand a Jewish dialogue partner in 2:1-16. McFadden, *Judgment According to Works in Romans*, 56; Schreiner, *Romans*, 103; Wilckens, *Der Brief an die Römer*, 1:121; Dunn, *Romans 1-8*, 90; Wright, *Romans*, 437.

18. Gathercole, "Justified by Faith, Justified by His Blood," 2:150.

19. Elliot, *The Rhetoric of Romans*, 120.

20. Barclay, *Paul and the Gift*, 462-63.

21. Barclay, *Paul and the Gift*, 463.

22. McFadden, *Judgment According to Works in Romans*, 44.

τὰ ἔργα αὐτοῦ; 2:6), as well. As in Romans 1, the retribution formula, παρέδωκεν αὐτοὺς ὁ θεὸς appears.²³ Bassler holds,

> This same idea is to be found in 2:1–11 where not only is the reference to wrath picked up again (2:5, 8) and the theme of παρέδωκεν ὁ θεὸς mirrored in the ὃς ἀποδώσει of 2:6, but the link between wrath and justice is now stressed in the new emphasis on the judgment of God (2:2, 3), alternatively expressed as his righteous judgment (δικαιοκρισία; 2:5).²⁴

In addition, Joseph Fitzmyer explains,

> Here it (righteous judgment) has the connotation of God's condemnatory judgment, stressing the equity of the divine sentence to be issued on the day of the Lord. . . . Dikaiokrisia finds its Qumran Hebrew counterpart in משפטי צדק (*mispete sedeq*), "just judgment" (1QH 1:23; cf. 1:30; 1QS 4:4), before which the sectarian stood in dread.²⁵

God's wrath is characterized as God's righteous judgment (2:5) and impartial judgment (2:11; προσωπολημψία).

With God's impartial judgment, Paul delineates that there is no exemption of Jews in God's truthful and impartial judgment (τὸ κρίμα τοῦ θεοῦ ἐστιν κατὰ ἀλήθειαν ἐπὶ τοὺς τὰ τοιαῦτα πράσσοντας, Rom 2:2), while the interlocutor presumes his election as God's people who will be delivered from judgment because of the riches of God's kindness (2:4). Paul's argument is that those Jews, in passing judgment on Gentiles, will face God's wrath because they practice the same things (2:1). Barclay contends,

> The connection with The Wisdom of Solomon extends into Romans 2, for in 2:1–5 Paul turns against a form of exceptionalism evidenced in that text. . . . Because the "we" of Wisdom was not explicitly identified as Jewish (only as 'the righteous'), Paul directs his attack in 2:1–5 not at "Jews," but at self-confident critics in general. But his close engagement with this Jewish debate shows that Jewish exceptionalism is here at least partly in view. Indeed, Paul finishes this paragraph with a double repetition of the motif in 1:16, emphasizing the common position of Jew and Greek, and the priority of the Jew and Greek, and the priority of the Jew in both salvation and judgment (2:9, 10). He thereby destabilizes an assumption that the distinction between Jew and

---

23. Bassler, *Divine Impartiality*, 128.
24. Bassler, *Divine Impartiality*, 128.
25. Fitzmyer, *Romans*, 301–2.

non-Jew is liable to count favorably for the former in the "just judgment" (δικαιοκρισία) of God (2:5).[26]

Thus, Paul's position is that God executes his wrath on the Jews and Gentiles. God's impartial judgment is executed on all human beings without distinction, whether or not they are included in the covenantal relationship. God's just judgment falls truthfully (2:2) and impartially (2:11) on those who do evil.[27] The theme of God's impartial judgment of all people, Jews and Gentiles, according to works is clearly shown in 2:1–16.[28] Yinger also states, "However, his particular use of the doctrine of divine impartiality in this text, namely to relativize Jewish covenant advantage before God, may have been surprising to first-century Jews."[29] While the impartiality of God's judgment in the Old Testament for his people seems a little changed in Paul's assertion, his judgment is impartial due to the sinful situation of all individuals including Jews and Gentiles (3:9–10). God's judgment (τὸ κρίμα τοῦ θεοῦ) is essentially condemnation and an adverse sentence (3:8; 13:2; Gal 5:10) on the sinner, rather than restoration of his covenantal people, as κρίνεις does in 2:1.[30] Hence, impartial judgment over all humanity is emphasized, instead of covenant relationship, while God's judgment may be realized as effecting the recovery of covenantal relationship.

God's judgment through the Messiah

Paul concludes his argument of Romans 1:18–2:15 with God's judgment through the Davidic Messiah. Paul's concern is God's judgment through the Messiah on the "secrets of men" on the day of judgment (2:16).[31] In Paul's

---

26. Barclay, *Paul and the Gift*, 463–64. Regarding the language of *The Wisdom of Solomon* in Rom 2:1–5, see Dunn, *Romans 1–8*, 82–83; Moo, *Romans*, 133; Jewett, *Romans*, 201–2.

27. Das, *Paul, the Law, and the Covenant*, 171.

28. Seifrid, "Unrighteous by Faith," 123. While the works of the law have been acutely disputed, pertaining to the meaning of the works of the law I am following Schreiner's arguments in his book, Schreiner, *The Law and Its Fulfillment*, 41–71. The works of law have the meaning of the actions that are demanded by the law; they are identified with the whole law. The phrase "the works of the law" is meant to be the whole law in the Qumran writings (4QFlor 1:7, similarly in 1QS 5:21; 6:18; 1QpHab 7:11; 8:1; 12:4; 11QTa 56:3; 4QMMT^a). Fitzmyer, *According to Paul: Studies in the Theology of the Apostle*, 18–35. Contra Dunn, "Works of the Law and the Curse of the Law (Galatians 3.10–14)," 523–42; Dunn, *The Theology of Paul the Apostle*, 354–71; and, Dunn, *Romans 1–8*, 154–55.

29. Yinger, *Paul, Judaism, and Judgment according to Deeds*, 156.

30. Fitzmyer, *Romans*, 300.

31. Barclay, *Paul and the Gift*, 471.

thought, God will judge the secrets of all on the day of judgment. The present work of conscience described in 2:15 "will reach its consummation, full validity, and clarification on the day of judgment, when God will judge the secrets of all."[32] Regardless of Jews or Gentiles, God will judge one's works, an expression meaning the "secrets of men."[33]

The phrase "through Christ Jesus" depends on "the christological element in the judgment."[34] Romans 2:16 is closely parallel to the *Similitudes* of Enoch by the judgment of the Son of Man, who shall judge the secret things (1 *En.* 49:6; 61:9).[35] 1 Corinthians 4:5 may deserve particular attention due to the analogous phrases "the secret things in darkness" (τὰ κρυπτὰ τοῦ σκότους) and "the purpose of the heart" (τὰς βουλὰς τῶν καρδιῶν).[36] Paul presents Jesus Christ as the judge, which is reminiscent of the judge, the Davidic Messiah, in *1 Enoch*. God's judgment through the Davidic Messiah (2:16) corresponds with the phrase "the wrath of God is revealed from heaven" (1:18) because the "judgment seat" (βῆμα) is identified as God's throne of glory, which is located in the heavenly court.[37] All the people of God will stand before the judgment seat, where judicial processes are executed. "For we will all stand before the judgment seat of God" (πάντες γὰρ παραστησόμεθα τῷ βήματι τοῦ θεοῦ, Rom 14:10).[38] In this verse, God's judgment seat (14:10) is identified with the judgment seat of Christ, too.[39] Dunn observes, "For Paul, evidently, there is no essential difference between the judgment seat of Christ (2 Cor 5:10) and that of God (here)."[40] According to Gathercole,

> Romans 2:16 talks of God as active in judgment, and this verse also gives the lie to the theological objection that divine condemnation would be an "unchristological" divine action. Rather, Paul thinks in terms of the 'wrath of the lamb' (as also

---

32. Schreiner, *Romans*, 125.

33. Stuhlmacher, *Paul's Letter to the Romans*, 46.

34. Moo, *Romans*, 155.

35. Stuhlmacher, *Romans*, 43. Paul presents the idea of a judgmental court as in *1 Enoch*.

36. Konradt, *Gericht und Gemeinde*, 509. Paul also notes, "For all of us must appear before the judgment seat (βῆμα) of Christ, so that each one may receive a recompense (κομίσηται) what he has done in the body, whether good or evil" (2 Cor 5:10). 2 Corinthians 5:10 has the image of the judgment scenes. BDAG, 557.

37. Eskola, *Messiah and the Throne*, 275. Heaven is God's judgment seat (cf. Ps 76:9; 2 Thess 1:7 ff.). Stuhlmacher, *Romans*, 36.

38. Eskola, *Messiah and the Throne*, 274.

39. Stuhlmacher, *Romans*, 274–77; see Dunn, *Romans 9–16*, 809; LSJ, II. 2.

40. Dunn, *Romans 9–16*, 809.

in Revelation 6:16), of a judgment in which Christ is installed as the judge: "on the day when God judges . . . through Jesus Christ" (2:16; cf. 2 Cor 5:10; 2 Thess 1:8-9).[41]

The Messiah represents God, who is the judge, in the heavenly court.

Consequently, Paul's concern in this passage is God's judgment through the Davidic Messiah, Jesus. Paul presents God's wrath toward all human beings' idolatry (1:18-32). Some Jews believe in God's partiality toward them (2:11), and expect preservation on the day of God's wrath (2:12-20).[42] Yet, Paul's argument is proceeding to the assertion that the Jews will be judged because of their sin, despite their covenant with God, due to the fact that God will judge them according to what they have done.

God's Wrath and Righteousness in the Gospel

Paul presents God's "wrath" (ὀργή, 1:18) as related to justifying righteousness in Romans 1:17. Romans 1:17 and 1:18 juxtapose the revelation of God's wrath and his righteousness.[43] In 1:18, Paul explains the reason that he proclaims the gospel related to God's wrath (1:16-17) by beginning with the term "for" (γάρ).[44] The justifying righteousness supports the judgmental concept of God's "wrath." This matches Paul's argument about God's judgment through the Davidic Messiah in Romans 2:16. Paul shows that justifying righteousness comes through faith in the Messiah, while the wrath of God is over sinners, regardless of Jews and Gentiles, as noted above. While the righteousness of God has been extremely controversial in New Testament scholarship,[45] the justifying righteousness—which is God's wrath—fits well in Romans 1:16-17.[46] The present tense of ἀποκαλύπτεται in 1:17

---

41. Gathercole, "Justified by Faith, Justified by His Blood," 174.

42. Schreiner, *Paul*, 108.

43. Seifrid, "Romans," 611; Cranfield, *Romans*, 1:106-10; Wilckens, *Römer*, 1:102-3; Barclay, *Paul and the Gift*, 462.

44. C. H. Dodd understands γάρ as a simple transitional particle or as an adversative particle. Dodd, *The Epistle of Paul to the Romans*, 18. Yet, the γάρ explains the meaning of 1:17. Seifrid, "Romans," 611; Seifrid, "Unrighteous by Faith," 109.

45. It is can be interpreted as (1) possessive genitive ("a righteousness belonging to God" or "God's own righteousness"); (2) a genitive of source ("righteousness from God"); (3) an objective genitive ("righteousness that is valid before God"); or (4) a subjective genitive ("God's saving power"). See Moo, *Romans*, 74-79. While scholars have asserted the combined options for the righteousness of God, many scholars suggest the faithfulness of God in covenantal relationship. Dunn, *Romans 1-8*, 40-41; Wright, *Romans*, 424-26; Campbell, *The Rhetoric of Righteousness in Romans 3.21-26*, 138.

46. BDAG, 247, s.v., 1 a-b; LSJ 429, s.v., I-II. Calhoun, *Paul's Definitions of the*

indicates that the righteousness of God, God's justifying activity, is being manifested in preaching the gospel.[47] In Romans, God's righteousness has been revealed in the event of the Messiah Jesus (1:17, ἀποκαλύπτεται) because, through his death and resurrection, the Messiah justifies those who have faith in him (4:25).[48]

Paul widely uses ὀργή and σωτηρία in a forensic sense, while God's judgment is described as his wrath in the Old Testament.[49] The legal logic of the gospel is retained in the term "ὀργή" and "σωτηρία."[50] Calhoun rightly remarks, "The gospel's primary functionality according to the second definition therefore lies in the area of forensic eschatology, with σωτηρία signifying acquittal at the divine trial, and ὀργή condemnation."[51] Additionally, the gospel has the role of God's power to save his people at the eschatological judgment, as Paul says in 1:16, "δύναμις θεοῦ ἐστιν εἰς σωτηρίαν παντὶ τῷ πιστεύοντι."[52] This supports the judgment aspect in the gospel and faith as the medium for believers' salvation from God's judgment, instead of the meaning of the Messiah's faithfulness in the gospel.

As a result, Paul's argument regarding God's wrath is that in the day of judgment, sinners will be judged, although believers have the hope of being protected from God's wrath through the Messiah Jesus.[53] Paul describes God's deliverance in the eschatological trial, which invokes God's impartial righteousness in his judgment (2:5-11).[54] Fitzmyer rightly notes, "The justification of the Christian is accompanied by an assurance of deliverance

---

Gospel in Romans 1, 157–58; Bultmann, *Theology of the New Testament*, 1:270–87; Moo, *Romans*, 222.

47. Moo, *Romans*, 222. With respect to this term, see, Brown, *The Semitic Background of the Term "Mystery" in the New Testament*; Bockmuehl, *Revelation and Mystery in Ancient Judaism and Pauline Christianity*, 140–41.

48. The term 'ἀποκαλύπτεται' is eschatological in Paul (Rom 1:18; 8:18; 1 Cor 3:13; Gal 3:23; 2 Thess 2:3, 6, 8). Schreiner, *Romans*, 61. See Oepke, "καλύπτω," in *TDNT*, 3:583.

49. Eskola, *Theodicy and Predestination in Pauline Soteriology*, 118. God's wrath against his enemies is related to the judgment and victory of the Davidic Messiah (Pss 2:12; 110:5). Schreiner, *Romans*, 84–85.

50. Calhoun, *Paul's Definitions of the Gospel in Romans 1*, 152. Foerster insists that deliverance resolves a legal difficulty. "But ישׁע and שׁפט are not co-extensive, since the ref. of the former is not to securing justice, but to a work of liberation from legal oppression." Foerster, "σῴζω," in *TDNT*, 7:974.

51. Calhoun, *Paul's Definitions of the Gospel in Romans 1*, 150.

52. That deliverance from God's final wrath is salvation is fundamental in Jewish understanding. Seifrid, *Justification by Faith*, 212. See especially Rom 13:11; 1 Thess 5:8, 9. See Cranfield, *Romans*, 1:88–89.

53. Eskola, *Theodicy and Predestination in Pauline Soteriology*, 117.

54. Calhoun, *Paul's Definitions of the Gospel in Romans 1*, 151.

from the wrath to come (5:9-10; 1 Thess 1:10; 5:9); the verdict of acquittal has already been pronounced in what Christ Jesus has achieved for humanity, and there is no longer any condemnation of it (8:1, 30-34)."[55] For this reason, Paul testifies that "we have now been justified by his blood, much more shall we be saved by him from the wrath of God" (5:9). Paul states that all the people will stand before the divine judgment (14:10), as well. Yet, they have the opportunity to believe the gospel that offers σωτηρία from God's judgment.[56]

Correspondingly, Paul presents God's judgment through the Messiah Jesus "according to my gospel" in Romans 2:16. In this phrase, Paul's proclamation of judgment "inseparably belongs to the gospel."[57] Paul's comment of "according to my gospel" (κατὰ τὸ εὐαγγέλιόν μου, 2:16) means the coming judgment because the proclamation of judgment belongs to the gospel.[58] Consequently, the agent of God's judgment, the Messiah Jesus in Romans 2:16, is related to judgmental language in the flow of Paul's contention.

Messiah's Faithfulness?

Paul proclaims, "ὁ δὲ δίκαιος ἐκ πίστεως ζήσεται" (the righteous shall live by faith, 1:17). Several scholars render πίστις as "faithfulness" in Romans 1:16-17. Campbell affirms that the Pauline quotation of Habakkuk 2:4 is to be understood as messianic-christological in Romans 1:17.[59] When the term "πίστις" can signify "*faithfulness*," based on Josephus and the LXX, the "faithfulness of Christ" in this verse can denote the entire passion of Jesus.[60] Campbell maintains, "So the Christological reading will be adopted here: Christ's fidelity, that Paul explicates elsewhere in particular relation to the story of his crucifixion, is functioning in 1:17 and 3:22 to reveal or disclose some righteous characteristic of, or action by, God."[61]

---

55. Fitzmyer, *Romans*, 306-7.
56. Calhoun, *Paul's Definitions of the Gospel in Romans 1*, 153.
57. Käsemann, *Commentary on Romans*, 68.
58. Käsemann, *Commentary on Romans*, 68; Stuhlmacher, *Romans*, 36.
59. Campbell, *The Rhetoric of Righteousness in Romans 3:21-26*, 67-68; Campbell, "Romans 1:17-A Crux Interpretation for Pistis Christou Debate," 273; Williams, "'Righteousness of God' in Romans," 277; Hays, *The Faith of Jesus Christ*, 151-57.
60. Campbell, *The Deliverance of God*, 610-11.
61. Campbell, *The Deliverance of God*, 613.

In addition, the term "ὁ δίκαιος" indicates the messianic figure with a messianic reading of Habakkuk.[62] Because Habakkuk 2 itself is a messianic text, "ὁ δίκαιος" is a messianic title (as in Ps 17:32; Isa 53:1; Wis 2:12-20; 1-7). Campbell holds,

> Our first cluster of observations focuses on the adjective δίκαιος, which is present in Hab 2:4 in an arthrous, substantive form. A reference to Christ as ὁ δίκαιος integrates smoothly with Paul's elevated use of this word elsewhere—and perhaps integrates more smoothly than a reference to humanity, since Paul so sternly and repeatedly characterizes humanity in the early chapters of Romans as ἄδικος and ἀδικία. ὁ δίκαιος may also be functioning in Hab 2:4 as a more stereotyped, titular reference to Jesus as the Messiah. . . . Paul's evident fondness for articular substantives as titles for Christ—again, particularly well attested in Romans—lends still further support to a titular use of ὁ δίκαιος in 1:17 as a reference to Christ.[63]

In this article, Campbell suddenly connects the messianic title "ὁ δίκαιος" to the faithfulness of Christ. He adds,

> The crafted parallelism between ὁ ερχόμενος and ὁ δίκαιος suggests this (cf. Isa 35:4; Matt 3:11; 11:3; John 1:15, 27; cf. also Hab 2:3, which is included in the citation), as does the inversion of the pronoun to produce the distinctly messianic phrase ὁ δίκαιος μου. Admittedly, chap. 11 of Hebrews discusses anthropocentric faith rather extensively, but what is less often noticed is that this long discussion is grounded in chap. 12 on the faithfulness of Christ; . . . τον της πίστεως ἀρχηγόν και τελειωτήν Ἰησοῦν (Heb 12:2).[64]

Campbell emphasizes that Paul presents the centrality of the death of Jesus on the cross, "which is the perceptible historical point where God's eschatological salvation has finally become apparent."[65] Moreover, Campbell declares that Paul places Christ's covenantal faithfulness "at the center

---

62. Campbell interprets this term "*righteous one*" (ὁ δίκαιος) as a christological designation (Acts 3:14; 7:52; 22:14; Heb 10:37; Jas 5:6; 1 Pet 3:18; 1 John 2:1). Campbell, *The Rhetoric of Righteousness in Romans 3:21-26*, 67-69; Hays, *The Faith of Jesus Christ*, 151-57.

63. Campbell, "Romans 1:17–A Crux Interpretation for Pistis Christou Debate," 282-83.

64. Campbell, "Romans 1:17–A Crux Interpretation for Pistis Christou Debate," 284.

65. Campbell, "Romans 1:17–A Crux Interpretation for Pistis Christou Debate," 284.

of the gospel."⁶⁶ Consequently, Paul does not express the faith as believers' "belief" but the Messiah's "faithfulness" in Romans 1:17.

However, while "ὁ δίκαιος" may be recognized as a messianic title, this term "ὁ δίκαιος" usually describes the Messiah as the executor of God's judgment in righteousness. Therefore, this term especially does not support a christological reading of Romans 1:17, the Messiah's faithfulness. Paul utilizes this term as describing believers' faith in the Messiah, and this agrees God's judgment in Paul's continuous argument.

Πίστις as Believers' Faith

The term "πίστις" refers to the faith of believers in 1:17.⁶⁷ The phrase "ἐκ πίστεως εἰς πίστιν" is emphatic in its focus on the centrality of faith in 1:17,⁶⁸ and it is in accord with salvation for the one who believes (τῷ πιστεύοντι) in 1:16.⁶⁹ "Πίστις" in 1:17 is occasionally recognized as "my faithfulness," based on the LXX. Wright holds that God's faithfulness is the key feature of "my" (μου) in the LXX Habakkuk 2:4.⁷⁰ He concentrates on God's faithfulness in the gospel—the proclamation of the crucified and risen Messiah.⁷¹ Another fragmentary text of Greek Habakkuk 2:4, 8ḤevXIIgr, though, translates the Hebrew exactly: "[καὶ δί]καιος ἐν πίστει αὐτοῦ ζήσετ[αι]" (and [the] upright one will live by his fidelity, 17.29–30).⁷² Aquila, Theodotion, and Symmachus additionally render this as "his (or 'its') faithfulness" rather than "my faithfulness."⁷³ Seifrid posits that this term is used with the meaning of "faith." He says,

> Paul clearly uses the term in the latter sense: "the righteous person lives by faith." He thus varies from the Hebrew text, which speaks of the "faithfulness" (אֱמוּנָה) by which the righteous one lives. The placement of the preposition phrase "by faith" after

---

66. Campbell, *The Rhetoric of Righteousness in Romans 3:21–26*, 208.

67. Ulrichs, *Christusglaube*, 182; Davies, *Faith and Obedience in Romans*, 39–46; Fitzmyer, *Romans*, 264; Silva, *Philippians*, 161; Galington, *Faith, Obedience, and Perseverance*, 49–50; Schreiner, *Romans*, 74–75; Seifrid, "Romans," 609–10.

68. Cranfield, *Romans*, 1:100; Moo, *Romans*, 71; Schreiner, *Romans*, 72; Byrne, *Romans*, 54.

69. Schreiner, *Romans*, 72.

70. Wright, "Romans," 425.

71. Wright, "Romans," 426.

72. Tov, Kraft, and Parsons, eds., *The Greek Minor Prophets Scroll from Naḥal Ḥever: 8ḤevXIIgr*, 52–53.

73. Seifrid, "Romans," 609.

the noun next to the verb favors reading it adverbially (cf. Gal 2:20), as with both the Hebrew text and septuagintal readings.[74]

Paul intentionally takes off μου from the LXX to emphasize the faith of believers and hence amends the "faithfulness reading."[75]

Another significant tradition supports this general conception, which is clearly different from that of the Messiah's faithfulness. It can be seen in 1QbHab 8:1–3. In the interpretation of Habakkuk 2:4, the righteous are "all observing of the law in the house of Judah" (8:1). God will "save" them (8:2) because of "their faithfulness to the teacher of righteousness" (8:2–3), who is the Messiah.[76] These readings for πίστις as "faith" sufficiently encourage the faith of believers in Romans 1:17.

God's judgment and believers' faith

Paul's flow of argument in Romans 1:18–2:16 and God's judgment through the Messiah in his gospel (2:16) prove his emphasis that the salvation from God's judgment is through "πίστις," the faith, in Romans 1:17. In other words, the christological reading—the Messiah's faithfulness—does not fit Paul's contention in the next passage (1:18–3:20). The main theme in 1:18–3:20 clearly supports "believers' faith in the Messiah," instead of "the Messiah's faithfulness" in 1:17. Believers' faith corresponds to God's wrath toward all human beings in the next passage. According to Bassler,

> There the development of the primary theme of impartial recompense for all who do wrong, whether Jew or Greek (1:18–2:9), is juxtaposed with the initial announcement of the gospel as the power of salvation to all who believe, whether Jew or Greek (1:16). . . . A further clue to the correlation Paul perceived between impartiality in judgment and in grace is provided by the somewhat enigmatic phrase κατὰ τὸ εὐαγγέλιόν μου of 2:16. . . . But this same disregard for external differences is a central feature of the message of salvation entrusted to Paul. We must therefore regard this as the significance of the phrase κατὰ τὸ εὐαγγέλιόν μου in v. 16. By judging the hidden things of men God cuts through the externals that distinguish Jew from

---

74. Seifrid, "Romans," 608–9.

75. Schreiner, *Romans*, 74; Eskola, *Theodicy and Predestination in Pauline Soteriology*, 106–10; Stuhlmacher, *Romans*, 29; Jewett, *Romans*, 146. Contra Dunn, *Romans 1–8*, 45.

76. Ulrichs, *Christusglaube*, 188.

Gentile and renders a truly impartial judgment over all—and this is in complete accord with Paul's gospel.[77]

While God's righteousness is revealed in the gospel concerning the Messiah, the gospel is the power of salvation to faith of believers from God's wrath. Das additionally maintains,

> One simply cannot assume from the phrase "righteousness of God" that Paul has covenant loyalty toward Israel in mind. . . . Not surprisingly, Paul employs διαθήκη at that point in the letter. In view of the argumentative trajectory of the letter, one should not assume that the "righteousness of God" in Rom 1:16–17 means a covenantal faithfulness to Israel for which Paul has yet to contend. In Romans 1–4, God is acting not just on Israel's behalf but on behalf of all humanity.[78]

In other words, God's judgment through the Davidic Messiah implicates impartial judgment that is different from covenantal faithfulness, which is Paul's gospel not only for Jews, but for Gentiles, as well. The phrase "παντὶ τῷ πιστεύοντι" with "Ἰουδαίῳ τε πρῶτον καὶ Ἕλληνι" (1:16) designates the universality of the gospel.[79] The Messiah's covenantal faithfulness comes into conflict with impartial judgment over covenantal relationship. Instead, the faith of believers—who are Jews and Gentiles—fits more with salvation from God's impartial judgment.

The righteous one

The "righteous one" (ὁ δίκαιος) should not be perceived as a specific designation for the Messiah in Romans 1:17. In Habakkuk 2:4, צַדִּיק / δίκαιος is defined as the "just one," rather than as the "faithful one."[80] In the context of Habakkuk 2:4, this term does include judgment. The fact is that the judgment theme in Habakkuk supports the understanding of the righteous one as believers, rather than the Messiah. Moreover, the Messiah's faithfulness is unfamiliar in this judgmental context.

Furthermore, the language of God's judgment in Habakkuk is undeniable.[81] If, in the context of Habakkuk, God's judgment is the thematic emphasis, the Messiah's obedient faithfulness does not fit in this judgment

---

77. Bassler, *Impartiality*, 157–58.
78. Das, *Paul and the Stories of Israel*, 69.
79. Calhoun, *Paul's Definitions of the Gospel in Romans 1*, 153.
80. Ulrichs, *Christusglaube*, 188.
81. Seifrid, "Romans," 610.

language. In Habakkuk, immediate judgment is coming upon Judah through the Babylonians. Seifrid explains,

> Habakkuk 2:4 applies to the whole of the argument which follows. That means, of course, that Paul announces that the world of "Jew" and "Greek" stands immediately before the hour of judgment just as the "Chaldean" invasion once impended over Israel. The significance of this observation should not be lost on us. The story-line runs directly counter to N. T. Wright's proposal that the apostle's thought is built around Israel's return from exile. Moreover, it is not merely Israel to which Paul applies the text from Habakkuk, but all of humanity.[82]

In the description of the judgment on Babylon, the covenantal faithfulness language is more distant.[83] The deliverance of God's people is accomplished alongside the judgment of God in Habakkuk.[84] Habakkuk concentrates on delaying the time for salvation (Hab 2:3) because God's judgment is impending. The narrative context of Romans 1:17 illustrates that the message of Paul's gospel in Romans points to salvation in "the impending hour of judgment, not the end of exile (see also 9:25–33; 10:19–21)."[85] As a result, God's judgment through the Messiah and salvation from God's wrath by faith are surely anticipated in these judgmental expressions.

For this reason, the meaning of the "righteous" (δίκαιος) in 1:17 clearly has a judgmental meaning, considering the context of Paul's subsequent argument, as noted in the previous chapters. The "righteous one," who is justified by faith, corresponds to human beings described as ἄδικος and ἀδικία in the following passage.[86] In the previous verse (1:16) because the πᾶς explicitly indicates the generic meaning, the δίκαιος in 1:17 is supposed to mean the believer as a righteous man.[87] Although Romans 1:17 may effect the accomplishment of God's covenantal promise, the Messiah's faithfulness is unfamiliar in Paul's thought in this passage. Paul's focus in 1:17 is the faith of God's people in the Messiah for salvation under God's impending judgment, instead of the Messiah's faithfulness.

---

82. Seifrid, "Unrighteous by Faith," 118–19.
83. Seifrid, "Romans," 608–9. Contra Wright, *Romans*, 425–26.
84. Seifrid, "Romans," 611.
85. Seifrid, "Romans," 608–9.
86. Ulrichs, *Christusglaube*, 188.
87. Ulrichs, *Christusglaube*, 188.

JUDGMENT ON THE DAVIDIC MESSIAH: ROMANS 3:21–25

Christ's death overcomes God's wrath against sinners, which is Paul's argument in 1:18–3:20. In Romans 3:21–25, Paul focuses on the Davidic Messiah's role as the atonement to resolve the problem of God's judgment over Jews and Gentiles. The Messiah's faithfulness is not suggested in this point of God's judgment on the Messiah. Paul's main emphasis is not God's righteousness through the Messiah's covenantal faithfulness in this passage. Rather, God's righteousness through faith in the Messiah is Paul's main concentration in Romans 3:21–25. God's wrathful judgment is executed on the place of the cross for the salvation of sinners—even those beyond the covenantal relationship in 1:18–3:20.

God's Righteousness through Faith in the Messiah

In Romans 3:21, Paul begins with God's righteousness—the "justifying activity of God"—as in Romans 1:17.[88] God's righteousness through the Messiah in Romans 3:21–26 is Paul's answer concerning God's wrath on both the Jews and Gentiles in 1:18–3:20.[89] What the Davidic Messiah achieves by God's judgment through him is God's righteousness, instead of his covenantal faithfulness. In these verses, Paul stresses faith in the Davidic Messiah, rather than the Messiah's faithfulness, by whom sinners can become righteous (Rom 3:22–23).[90] The language in this argument is not covenantal, but clearly judgmental, and Paul emphasizes faith in the Messiah, instead of the Messiah's faithfulness.

---

88. Moo, *Romans*, 222. The conjugation, "but now" in 3:21, demonstrates the new era that God has initiated. Piper, "The Demonstration of the Righteousness of God in Romans 3:25, 26," 7–9; Campbell, *The Rhetoric of Righteousness in Romans 3:21–26*, 45–57. The change of these two eras is the fundamental theme of Pauline theology. Moo, *Romans*, 221. The righteousness of God dominated the new era. Schreiner says that "most commentators correctly detect a temporal sense here. Indeed, the temporal dimension of the argument is crucial, indicating a salvation-historical shift between the old covenant and the new." Schreiner, *Romans*, 178.

89. Dunn, *Romans 1–8*, 164.

90. Even though the subjective genitive is grammatically possible, "all who have faith" in 3:22 illustrates that Paul points to the faith of believers, rather than to the faithfulness of Christ. The grammatical argument for faithfulness is not decisive. See Jewett, *Romans*, 278; Dunn, *Romans 1–8*, 166; Cranfield, *Romans*, 1:203; Moo, *Romans*, 224–35; Schreiner, *Romans*, 182–87. The genitive Χριστοῦ is designated as the object of faith (Rom 3:26; Gal 2:16, 20; 3:22; Eph 3:12; Phil 3:9; Col 2:12). Cranfield, *Romans*, 1:203; Seifrid, "Romans," 618; Dunn, *Romans 1–8*, 166–67.

Judgment language in this passage is related to God's righteousness through the Messiah. Paul implements the juridical verdict of "δικαιόω" (justify) to describe the redemption of all the people who have sinned in 3:23. The participle "being justified" modifies those who "sinned" and "are falling short."[91] This verb means "to declare righteous" in a legal sense, not "to make righteous" or "to treat as righteous."[92] Moo contends, "No 'legal fiction,' but a legal reality of the utmost significance, 'to be justified' means to be acquitted by God from all 'charges' that could be brought against a person because of his or her sins."[93] Also, this verb is also employed in a forensic sense in Romans 8:33, "Who shall bring any charge against God's elect? It is God who justifies." The judicial images in Romans 8:33 support this term as the justifying verdict given to believers in God's judgment.[94]

In addition, the forensic meaning for "justify" fits with the phrase "apart from the law" (3:21) and with the flow of Paul's argument from the previous chapter. Schreiner holds,

> Those who keep the law "will be justified," that is, vindicated in the divine law court on the last day (Rom 2:13). On the other hand, no one who is of the "works of the law" will be justified before God because vindication before God is only available by faith (Rom 3:20, 24, 26, 28, 30; 5:1; Gal 2:16-17; 3:11, 24; 5:4).[95]

The "righteousness of God" is characterized by the phrase "apart from the law" (χωρὶς νόμου, 3:21), in which God's vindication of his people is clearly presented "apart from" the law by the Messiah's atoning death.[96]

The context of Romans 3:24-26 encourages the position that the righteousness of God refers to God's judgment of sin because justification (Rom 3:21-22) is attained for sinners through the Messiah's atoning death.[97] God inflicts his punishment on Christ on the cross rather than compromising his righteousness.[98] Describing that "God put forward [Christ] as 'ἱλαστήριον' by his blood, to be received by faith. This is to show God's righteousness" (3:25), Paul provides the answer to God's wrath toward sinners with God's

---

91. He employs δικαιούμενοι, a participle of "δικαιόω," as a modifier of "ἥμαρτον" and "ὑστεροῦνται" within a subordinate clause. Moo, *Romans*, 227.

92. Moo, *Romans*, 228.

93. Moo, *Romans*, 228.

94. Moo, *Romans*, 542.

95. Schreiner, *Paul*, 204.

96. Moo, *Romans*, 223.

97. Schreiner, *Paul*, 202.

98. Schreiner, *Paul*, 202.

righteousness shown in the previous passage (1:18–3:20).[99] Wright recognizes that God's covenant has its "fulfill[ment] in the death and resurrection of the Messiah, and . . . was being implemented through [Paul's] own apostolic mission."[100] God's covenantal faithfulness, his righteousness, is the framework in which Paul focuses on righteousness and justification.[101] Moreover, he integrates the forensic and participatory characteristics of God's righteousness into his covenantal faithfulness.[102] Wright emphasizes that the "faith" of the Messiah is his covenantal faithfulness and obedience, leading to believers' justification.[103] In this section, though, Paul does not suggest the Messiah's faithfulness with "πίστις Χριστοῦ." Additionally, Paul no longer constrains God's righteousness through the Messiah's atoning death to stay within the boundary of the covenantal relationship. Charles Irons asserts, "Although God's a God of love and mercy, he could only forgive and justify sinners in a manner consistent with his holiness and righteousness by means of the propitiatory death of Christ for our sins which satisfied the demands of God's justice."[104] God's righteousness, which is an attribute of God's justice, is demonstrated by Christ's atoning death.[105]

God put forward a "ἱλαστήριον" to show his justifying righteousness in his forbearance through the passing over of former sins (3:25).[106] The word "passing over" (πάρεσις) is applied within the judicial context for sins to refer to the "postponement of punishment" or "neglect" of persecution.[107] Furthermore, God's passing over the sins on account of his "patience" is expressed as "the forbearance of God intended to lead human beings to repentance" (2:4).[108] Dunn defines "ἀνοχῇ" in Romans 2:4 as God's forbearance—a "delay of wrath." This cites God's suspension of his wrath (1 Tim 1:16; 1 Pet 3:20; 2 Pet 3:9, 15).[109] While God endured—and still endures—Gentiles' sins, which are described as spoiling the creation

---

99. Schreiner, *Paul*, 202.

100. Wright, *Paul and the Faithfulness of God*, 1263.

101. Wright, *Paul and the Faithfulness of God*, 993, 1013.

102. Wright, *Paul and the Faithfulness of God*, 846, 875, 900.

103. Wright, *Paul and the Faithfulness of God*, 847.

104. Irons, *The Righteousness of God*, 280.

105. Cranfield, *Romans*, 1:22–23.

106. Schreiner, *Paul*, 202.

107. Moo, *Romans*, 238.

108. Seifrid, *Christ, Our Righteousness: Paul's Theology of Justification*, 65.

109. Dunn, *Romans 1–8*, 81; Gathercole, "Justified by Faith, Justified by His Blood," 181.

(1:18-32),[110] God's righteousness is demonstrated through the ἱλαστήριον because justification is available to sinners, including Gentiles.[111]

Because God's righteousness in the justification of sinners and his forbearance in the passing over of sins through the Davidic Messiah are manifested in the "ἱλαστήριον," he may be said to be the righteous and the justifier (εἰς τὸ εἶναι αὐτὸν δίκαιον καὶ δικαιοῦντα, 3:26). He is righteous in his judgment.[112] Moo notes, "Paul's point is that God can maintain his righteous character ('his righteousness' in vv. 25 and 26) even while he acts to justify sinful people ('God's righteousness' in vv. 21 and 22) because Christ, in his propitiatory sacrifice, provides full satisfaction of the demands of God's impartial, invariable justice."[113] The righteousness of God is characterized by the involvement of judgment in this passage, in which Paul states that "God is also righteous in condemning sinners in judgment (cf. also Rom 2:5; 3:4; 2 Thess 1:6-10)."[114]

This corresponds to the righteousness of God in 3:5. God's righteousness should be understood with the cognate verb, "be in the right," when he judges in 3:4.[115] God's righteousness is displayed in judgment, and Paul demonstrates that God is not "unjust" in his judgment of sin. Moo goes on to say,

> On the other hand, if v. 5 is attributed to Paul, with v. 5b the logical conclusion to be drawn from the assertion of God's punitive righteousness in v. 5a, these difficulties are avoided, but others are encountered.... The only way to make sense of the sequence of thought, then, is to view the issue in v. 5 as the "justness" of God's condemning Jews for sins that manifest his righteousness.... Paul has already used dik-language in this broader sense in 2:5, where he affirmed that the judgment of God will be just, being based on the works of each person.[116]

While God's covenantal faithfulness in Romans 3:2-3 can anticipate God's righteousness in 3:5, it cannot be identified as God's righteousness in his judgment. The righteousness of God and faithfulness to his covenant are

---

110. Seifrid, "Romans," 621.
111. Schreiner, *Paul*, 202-3.
112. Wilckens, *Römer*, 1:198; Cranfield, *Romans*, 1:213; Moo, *Romans*, 242.
113. Moo, *Romans*, 242.
114. Schreiner, *Paul*, 202.
115. Moo, *Romans*, 189.
116. Moo, *Romans*, 191.

related, but not the same. Instead, God's righteousness is defined as relating to his judgment of sinners.[117] Schreiner attests,

> God's righteousness surely fulfills his covenantal promises, but it does not follow from this that we should define righteousness as covenantal faithfulness.... Romans 3:5 is often introduced as evidence for defining "righteousness of God" as "covenantal faithfulness," since in Romans 3:1–8 God's righteousness is parallel to his "faithfulness, truth and reliability."... it is doubtful that righteousness of God should be rendered "covenantal faithfulness" in Romans 3:5. Paul's argument here assumes that "our unrighteousness demonstrates God's righteousness." It is quite likely that the righteousness in view here does not refer to salvation but to God's judgment of sinners. If this is the case, then interpreting God's righteousness as his covenantal faithfulness is singularly ill-fitting, for God's covenantal faithfulness to his people does not consist in his judgment of them. It is true that Paul reminds his readers of God's covenantal faithfulness to the Jews in Romans 3:1–8, but he also reminds them of God's righteous judgment of their sins.[118]

Therefore, Paul does not describe God's wrath toward his covenant people, but explains God's righteousness toward all human beings.[119] God is presupposed to judge the "world, especially the Gentiles who were outside the covenant."[120] As his judgment over all human beings, God's righteousness is identified as his judging righteousness in Romans 3:3–5.

Consequently, Paul points out God's righteous judgment over Jewish sinners, and he expands God's righteous judgment to Gentiles in this passage. Paul's reference does not stress God's faithfulness to his covenantal promises. Instead, he focuses on God's judgment of sinners.[121] Gathercole additionally maintains,

> Thus, better sense is achieved by seeing the atoning work of Christ as revealing God to be both just (in that our sin is dealt with in Christ) and the justifier (who saves us in Christ). Not that there is a sharp distinction between God's punitive righteousness and his salvific righteousness: rather, God saves the righteous precisely by his punitive removal of the wicked, as

---

117. Schreiner, *Paul*, 199.
118. Schreiner, *Paul*, 199.
119. Schreiner, *Paul*, 190–91.
120. Schreiner, *Romans*, 158.
121. Schreiner, *Paul*, 199.

elsewhere in Paul (e.g., 2 Thess 1:5–10) and frequently in the OT (most clearly in Psalms, e.g., Ps 7; 9:3–4; 10:12–15).[122]

The concept of the righteous judge corresponds to the righteousness in God's judgment through the Davidic Messiah in the Jewish tradition, as well. Paul primarily utilizes judgmental terms in this passage to proclaim the answer to God's wrath. He concentrates on God's judgment over sinners and on God as the One who is righteous and the justifier, instead of on God in covenantal relationship. While God's covenantal faithfulness might be imagined in his judgment to place his people in a righteous relationship with him, in this passage, Paul's concern is God's universal wrath toward sinners, along with the solution to that wrath. In this argument, God's mercy is displayed in the wrath poured out on the Messiah. Paul emphasizes the justifying righteousness fulfilled for all sinners, including Jews and Gentiles, through the Messiah, rather than the Messiah's faithfulness.

There is no distinction

God's universal judgment through the Messiah is connected in Paul's argument in the phrase that "there is no distinction" (οὐ γάρ ἐστιν διαστολή, 3:22). Although God's faithfulness in his covenantal relationship with his people may be suggested by the judgmental language in Romans 3:21–26, the scope of the passage goes beyond that relationship. This weakens the covenantal meaning for the faithfulness of the Messiah, as noted previously.[123] Paul argues that the righteousness of God is given to all who believe, because there is no distinction (3:22). This corresponds to the fact that God's judgment is a broader concept than is covenantal wrath in his covenantal relationship.

"All" (πάντες) in 3:23 is formally part of the explanation of "οὐ γάρ ἐστιν διαστολή," which itself supports the πάντας of 3:22."[124] Bassler holds, "The initial development of the idea of justification by faith for all who believe (3:21–22a) is grounded by the phrase, 'There is no distinction' (v. 22b: οὐ γάρ ἐστιν διαστολή); a warrant that points back to the more traditional formulation in 2:11; οὐ γάρ ἐστιν προσωπολημψία."[125] The phrase that "there is no distinction" corresponds to Paul's insistence in Romans 1:18–3:20 that all human beings are condemned, and they cannot evade

---

122. Gathercole, "Justified by Faith, Justified by His Blood," 180–81.
123. Bassler, *Impartiality*, 156.
124. Cranfield, *Romans*, 1:205.
125. Bassler, *Impartiality*, 156.

God's wrath. Paul demonstrates that all people, Jews and Gentiles, stand under God's judgment, and the need for justification is anticipated.[126]

It is summarized as well in Paul's contention that "all have sinned and fall short of the glory of God" (3:23).[127] As in Romans 1:18, Paul affirms universal sinfulness.[128] Stephen Chester maintains,

> In fairness, Wright is not in this passage directly discussing the meaning of justification, but the point remains that Paul's statements do not easily lend themselves to understanding justification itself as a declaration of covenant membership. . . . While the term "covenantal" appropriately captures things that are essential in any interpretation of Paul's texts—continuing divine commitment to promises to Israel, Paul's commitment to Israel's Scriptures as God's word, and the importance for Paul of both Jews and Gentiles together now constituting God's people in Christ—it does not in contemporary usage communicate very clearly the radical nature of Paul's theology of grace that informs his teaching about justification and assaults all notions of human worthiness.[129]

Righteousness through the Messiah embraces all human beings; this "copes with the universality of sin among them."[130] The connection exists between "δικαιοσύνη θεοῦ" and "παντὶ τῷ πιστεύοντι, Ἰουδαίῳ τε πρῶτον καὶ Ἕλληνι" in Romans 1:16-17."[131] Seifrid argues,

> Correspondingly, as in 1:17, Paul again announces that the cross performs its saving work in and through faith alone. The "righteousness of God" is mediated "through the faith of Jesus Christ" (3:22). God set forth Christ as a "place of propitiation, through faith in his blood" (verse 25). He justifies "the one who believes in Jesus" (verse 26). Accordingly, this "righteousness of God" is for all who believe. The loss of the divine glory—Paul's characterization of idolatry—extends to all human beings (1:23; 3:23). Correspondingly, because faith alone justifies, the distinction between Jew and Gentile has been overcome (verse 24).[132]

---

126. In this view, "δίκαιοι" and "δικαιωθήσονται" are forensic in Romans 2:13. Berkley, *From a Broken Covenant to Circumcision of the Heart*, 113.

127. Bassler, *Impartiality*, 156.

128. Chester, *Reading Paul with the Reformer*, 399.

129. Chester, *Reading Paul with the Reformer*, 398-99.

130. Fitzmyer, *Romans*, 346.

131. Cranfield, *Romans*, 1:203.

132. Seifrid, *Christ, Our Righteousness*, 64.

Paul thinks primarily of two groups of humanity, one of which is confined within the boundary of covenantal relationship, while the other goes beyond this boundary. While Paul's wording can recall Israel's past experiences—such as disobedience and the departure of the divine glory (1 Sam 4:21; Ezek 11:23)—all human beings fall into idolatry (1:23), despite having been created to participate in God's glory (2:7).[133]

The impartiality of God's judgment flows through Paul's argument in Romans 4. The "no distinction," with reference to the covenantal boundary, supports the importance of faith in him because the Messiah's role is mainly justification of the ungodly through faith in the Messiah. These ungodly people cannot exclude Gentiles, who are apart from the covenantal relationship. Abraham's faith is presented as an example of the justification of the ungodly through faith in the Messiah in Romans 4. Ungodly individuals include all sinners, even those beyond Israel's covenantal relationship. This much is shown in Paul's designation of justification of the ungodly by faith in Romans 4. Abraham's justification, which is God's judicial verdict, was not "'on the basis of' his obedience (Rom 4:2), but rather 'on the basis of' faith (4:3), of grace (4:4), by the God who justifies the ungodly (4:5); at the point of his justification, Abraham was in the 'ungodly' category."[134] Abraham, who is one of the ungodly, is a tool for God's saving purpose due to the fact that all human beings fall under divine judgment (Gen 12:10–14:24).[135]

The flow of Paul's argument proceeds to include the following: God put forward Jesus as "ἱλαστήριον by his blood through faith" (3:25), and "justification of ungodly" (4:5), and "justification by his blood" (5:9). Brian Vickers writes,

> Paul's point is to give more evidence that Abraham brought nothing to the table that contributed to his justification. Moreover, we can safely say that the "ungodly" are justified ultimately because Christ died for them (3:25; 5:6); God's just wrath against sin has been met; the guilty did not get off scot-free. In the Old Testament texts, the idea is that justice cannot be suspended or brushed aside, that guilt must be punished, and that right must be upheld. All these criteria are met in the substitutionary death of Christ.[136]

On the basis of their own virtue, the ungodly cannot present their justification. The Messiah died for the ungodly while they were still sinners

---

133. Seifrid, "Romans," 618.
134. Gathercole, "Justified by Faith, Justified by His Blood," 157.
135. Seifrid, "Romans," 622.
136. Vickers, *Jesus' Blood and Righteousness*, 100.

(5:8). In Paul's mind, the ungodly are composed of two groups: the Jews and the Gentiles. The Gentiles, particularly, are apart from members of the covenant family (additionally shown in 3:22–24); they are justified from sin by Christ's blood.

The significant sentence that "there is no distinction" directly leads to Paul's contention in Romans 3:27–31 that "there is no boasting."[137] Paul continuously argues that the righteousness is by faith in Romans 3:27–31. The only thing that God demands for Jews and Gentiles to be justified is faith (3:29–30).[138] Paul concludes with "οὖν" in Romans 3:27, so that "boasting is ruled out because righteousness is obtained by faith in Jesus Christ, not by works of law."[139] Boasting is excluded because the righteousness of God is based on the Messiah and faith in him—not on works of the law.[140] The verb "ἐξεκλείσθη" supports this understanding.[141] Schreiner maintains,

> Righteousness cannot be obtained through the Mosaic covenant but only through the death of Jesus Christ. . . . In verses 27–28 Paul reiterates twice why boasting is excluded, emphasizing the polarity between "works" and "faith." The evidence supporting the notion that ἔργα νόμου focuses on "boundary markers" separating Jews from Gentiles is unpersuasive as I argued at 3:20. The term embraces all that is contained in the Mosaic law. . . . Boasting is excluded because righteousness is obtained not by keeping the law but by faith in Christ.[142]

With respect to boasting in 3:27, God's salvation of the Gentiles (3:29) by their faith guides the flow of Paul's argument.[143] He addresses the matter of "boasting" based on Romans 2:17–23, and he continues this topic in 4:1–8; 5:1–11; and 8:12–39.[144] The justification of Gentiles in Romans 3:29 runs through with the exclusivity of faith and the universality of the gospel.[145]

Some scholars assert that this diatribe style supports a covenantal reading of Romans 4:1, but the key themes—being "καύχημα" and the

---

137. Tatum, "Law and Covenant in Paul and the Faithfulness of God," 320.
138. Schreiner, *Romans*, 200.
139. Schreiner, *Romans*, 200.
140. Schreiner, *Romans*, 200.
141. Ποῦ οὖν ἡ καύχησις; ἐξεκλείσθη. διὰ ποίου νόμου; τῶν ἔργων; οὐχί, ἀλλὰ διὰ νόμου πίστεως (Rom 3:27).
142. Schreiner, *Romans*, 204.
143. Seifrid, "Romans," 622.
144. Seifrid, "Romans," 622.
145. Seifrid, "Romans," 622.

justification "χωρὶς ἔργων νόμου" in 3:27-28—are explained in 4:1-8.[146] Connections exist between 3:27-28 (καύχησις, 3:27) and 4:1-8 (καύχημα, 4:2), and "χωρὶς ἔργων νόμου" is echoed in 4:6.[147] Paul's most vital christological-eschatological perspective appears in this context, "both for the notion of 'boasting' and of 'faith.'"[148] It is explicable as "faith-dependence upon a divine decision irrespective of inherent human worth."[149] Romans 3:27-31, the thematic introduction of Romans 4, encourages justification as mainly connected with faith; a person can be justified by faith (3:27-28).[150] God justifies Jews and Gentiles, regardless of their covenantal membership (3:29-30). Vickers rightly proposes,

> So the life of Abraham, rather than proving an exception to Paul's discussion thus far as the Jewish interpretations of Abraham seem to argue, is the supreme example that verifies exactly what Paul is saying. The boasting Paul excludes in 3:27 is denied to Abraham as well. While acknowledging the difficulties in the conditional sentence, whether Abraham could boast of his works before men is not really the ultimate issue in this verse. The point seems to be that Abraham, the ungodly (v. 5), cannot be justified before God on the basis of works; therefore he has no grounds for boasting. Since Paul's larger aim is to show that justification is on the basis of faith, and since "work(s)" are here contrasted with faith, and, moreover, since God is clearly the one who judges (reckons) a person's status, it is fair to say that whatever respect works gain in the eyes of men is hardly the issue.[151]

Paul focuses on boasting in this passage, and the boasting before God is already excluded (3:27).[152] The righteousness of God is a gift for the un-

---

146. Schliesser, *Abraham's Faith in Romans 4*, 311. Contra Wright, *Paul and the Faithfulness of God*, 1003. Wright opposes a soteriological understanding of faith and boasting in Rom 4:1. He follows Hays' argument. Hays, "'Have We Found Abraham to Be Our Forefather according to the Flesh?' A Reconsideration of Rom 4:1," 76–98. The description of Abraham, "our forefather according to the flesh," is modified by the description of his lineage. However, his reading is difficult to explain the definite article "Ἀβραὰμ τὸν προπάτορα." It is not in accord with his assertion that this term "*forefather*" is a predicate. There are other objections. See Engberg-Pedersen, *Paul and the Stoics*, 363n3.

147. Barclay, *Paul and the Gift*, 482.

148. Schliesser, *Abraham's Faith in Romans 4*, 332.

149. Barclay, *Paul and the Gift*, 482.

150. Barclay, *Paul and the Gift*, 482.

151. Vickers, *Jesus' Blood and Righteousness*, 92–93.

152. Vickers, *Jesus' Blood and Righteousness*, 93.

godly, which is through faith in the Messiah, as shown in Paul's statements in Romans 3:21–26. In addition, God's righteousness is a judgmental term, instead of a covenantal term in Romans 4.

Righteousness, gift by faith

Paul stresses that the justifying verdict has the characteristics of a gift.[153] The prominence of "faith" is critical in this passage (noun in 3:22, 25, 26; verb in 3:22).[154] This gift of justification supports the definition of faith as faith in the Messiah's role within God's plan for justification. The righteousness of God is related to "faith in Jesus Christ," which explains God's righteousness is a gift.[155] According to Schreiner, "δικαιοσύνη θεοῦ διὰ πίστεως Ἰησοῦ Χριστοῦ indicates that people experience God's salvation through the faith in Jesus Christ."[156]

Because Paul never refers to Jesus as "faithful," and he offers Abraham as the foundational and paradigmatic model of faith (not faithfulness) in Romans 4, πίστις in 3:21–26 is the faith of believers.[157] God's righteousness affects sinners, who have faith while their condition is totally sinful and far from God, regardless of whether they are Jews or Gentiles.[158] John Barclay contends,

> Human beings do not give the costliest gifts to worthless people; the death of Christ for the ungodly confounds the normal expectation of the congruous gift. Thus, as a divine gift, given to all in the death of Christ, an act of love for the wholly unworthy, Paul figures the Christ-gift as the ultimate incongruous gift.[159]

All who believe—whether Jew or Gentile—despite their sinful status (3:22–23), demonstrate their dependence on God's gift "without discrimination and without regard to worth."[160] All sinners "can only receive by faith the gift of God offered in Christ Jesus."[161] Romans 3:22 clearly says that God's righteousness is given by faith in the Messiah to "εἰς πάντας τοὺς

---

153. Moo, *Romans*, 228.
154. Barclay, *Paul and the Gift*, 476.
155. Schreiner, *Romans*, 181.
156. Schreiner, *Romans*, 181.
157. Barclay, *Paul and the Gift*, 476; Dunn, *Romans 1–8*, 1:166.
158. Barclay, *Paul and the Gift*, 476.
159. Barclay, *Paul and the Gift*, 479.
160. Barclay, *Paul and the Gift*, 476.
161. Schreiner, *Romans*, 181.

πιστεύοντας." Paul emphasizes faith of all believers, both Jews and Gentiles with this phrase.

The characteristic of the gift in God's righteousness is suggested in 3:24: "justified by his grace as a gift through the redemption" (δικαιούμενοι δωρεὰν τῇ αὐτοῦ χάριτι διὰ τῆς ἀπολυτρώσεως). Moreover, Schreiner writes,

> The gift character of God's righteousness is communicated in the phrase δωρεὰν τῇ αὐτοῦ χάριτι (freely by his grace, v. 24). Those who place their faith in Christ are in the right before him, not on the basis of their own work but simply by virtue of their faith in Christ Jesus. Ἀπολυτρώσεως (v. 24) modifies the participle δικαιούμενοι. The gift of righteousness communicated by God's grace was accomplished through (διά, dia) redemption.[162]

Paul highlights the gift-character of justification in this participle, "δικαιούμενοι" (3:24).[163] He continues the theme of "righteousness by faith" from 3:22 in this participial clause. Bassler rightly observes,

> Those being justified contribute nothing to their justification, though they receive it passively through faith, which too is a gift (see e.g., Rom 4:16; 9:16; Eph 2:8-9). The cause of their justification is not from within themselves but rather God's "free grace." Christ's penal death accounts believers not guilty and not worthy of condemnation, and they are credited with God's righteousness.[164]

Because justification has the characteristic of total grace on God's side, and Paul emphasizes the gift of justification, it requires faith on the human side.[165] Righteousness is provided through faith in Jesus, whose death "liberated from the slavery of sin and satisfied God's judging righteousness."[166] Hence, because the justification of God comes through his grace (δωρεὰν τῇ αὐτοῦ χάριτι; 3:24), which is an absolutely free and unmerited gift, justification can be attained only through faith in the Messiah.

---

162. Schreiner, *Romans*, 189.
163. Moo, *Romans*, 227.
164. Bassler, *Impartiality*, 483-84.
165. Moo, *Romans*, 228.
166. Schreiner, *Romans*, 200.

Faithfulness of the Messiah?

While Paul shows the righteousness of God "through faith in Jesus Christ" in Romans 3:22, many scholars interpret "faith of Christ" (πίστις Χριστοῦ) as the subjective genitive, "faithfulness of Christ."[167] Recently, Richard Longenecker has asserted that the faithfulness of Christ is the meaning of "πίστις Χριστοῦ" in his commentary on Romans.[168] He writes,

> All of these, as I've argued elsewhere, speak in a functional manner of Jesus' faithfulness of the will of God in effecting human redemption through his earthly ministry, sacrificial death, and physical resurrection. Further, it may be postulated that as a Jewish believer in Jesus, whose faith was rooted not only in the person and work of Jesus Christ but also in the Jewish (OT) scriptures, Paul's thought was impacted formatively by the messianic prophecy of Isa 11—particularly the words of Isa 11:5 regarding "The Branch from Jesse," which affirm: "Righteousness (MT צדק) will be his belt and faithfulness (MT אמונה) the sash around his waist."[169]

Longenecker understands that Christ's faithfulness is associated with Paul's messianic Christology.

Campbell feels that the faithfulness of Christ "fits smoothly into the downward martyrological trajectory in the story of Jesus' passion."[170] His basis for this assertion is that faithfulness is an ingredient in the martyrdom theology.[171] The image of a sacrificial death is employed in Isaiah 53 to describe the death of a martyr.[172] The sacrificial language of the atoning death of martyrs is used in 4 Maccabees 17:21–22.[173] Desta Heliso explains,

> The Mother of the Seven Brothers is referred to as ἡ δικαία τοις τέκνοις (4 Macc 18:7) and her seven children are also described

---

167. Johnson, "Rom 3:21–26 and the Faith of Jesus," 77–90; Williams, "'Righteousness of God' in Romans," 272–78; Hays, *The Faith of Christ*, 170–74; Campbell, *The Rhetoric of Righteousness in Romans 3:21–26*, 66; Wright, *Romans*, 469–77; Longenecker, *The Epistle to the Romans*, 412.

168. Longenecker, *Romans*, 412.

169. Longenecker, *Romans*, 412.

170. Campbell, *The Deliverance of God*, 611.

171. Campbell, *The Deliverance of God*, 611.

172. Schreiner, *Romans*, 192.

173. "And through the blood of those devout ones and their death as an atoning sacrifice (ἱλαστηρίου), divine providence saved Israel that previously had been suffered" (4 Macc 17:22). In addition, in 2 Macc 6:13–16; 7:18, 32–33, 37–38; 4 Macc 6:27–29; 9:20; 10:8.

as δίκαιοι, whose obedience to their Mother, their loyalty to the law and their faithfulness to God led them to martyrdom (15:10; 16:22; cf. 15:24; 17:22). In their faithful action, the martyrs not only became instrumental for the purification of their nation and punishment of the tyrant (17:17–22), but also they imitated Δαωιηλ ὁ δίκαιος, his three friends (16:21; cf. 18:15).... All this seems to support the view that Jesus' obedience-to-death probably is the same thing as his faithfulness-to-death.[174]

Because numerous martyrologies mention faithfulness explicitly (see 4 Macc 15:24; 16:22; 17:2), Paul considers Jesus' death to be an essentially martyrological story, which includes the element of faithfulness.[175]

Wright insists that the Messiah's faith in 3:22 must be defined as the Messiah's faithfulness to the divine plan for Israel, as well.[176] The faith (πίστις) is faithfulness, which is always supposed to be the badge of Israel and the badge of Jesus.[177] The answer in Romans 3:21–31 to the question in previous chapters is that the Messiah is faithful to death and, through his obedient death, God's faithfulness in the covenantal relationship with his people is displayed.[178] He notes,

> Once we understand Christos as the Messiah, Israel's representative, Israel-in-person if you will, the logic works out immaculately. (a) The covenant God promises to rescue and bless the world through Israel. (b) Israel as it stands is faithless to this commission. (c) The covenant God, however, is faithful, and will provide a faithful Israel, the "faithful Israelite," the Messiah. It is the tight coherence of this train of thought, rather than any verbal arguments about subjects and objects, prepositions and case-endings on the one hand, or preferential theological positions on the other, that persuaded me many years ago that Romans 3:22 speaks of the Messiah's faithfulness.[179]

In Wright's comprehension, covenantal faithfulness presents the larger category that includes God's judging righteousness. He maintains, "The covenantal perspective on election, and its redefinition through Jesus the Messiah, provides the larger category within which 'juridical'

---

174. Heliso, *Pistis and the Righteous One*, 226.
175. Heliso, *Pistis and the Righteous One*, 226.
176. Wright, *Paul and the Faithfulness of God*, 839.
177. Wright, *Paul and the Faithfulness of God*, 840.
178. Wright, *Paul and the Faithfulness of God*, 841.
179. Wright, *Paul and the Faithfulness of God*, 839.

and 'participationist' categories can be held together in proper Pauline relation."[180]

In addition, Wright connects the Messiah's faithfulness to martyrdom theology:

> Jesus' faithfulness unto death is here, as in some other Pauline passages, described in sacrificial terms (for the details, see the comments below). This is one of the trickiest passages in Paul in terms of precise nuances, but the context appears to be that reappropriation of the Levitical sacrificial language, particularly from the Day of Atonement scene in Leviticus 16, which we also find in, for instance, the Maccabean literature (4 Macc 17:22).... And, like the Maccabean passage, this one arguably carries overtones also of that other great reworking of Levitical themes, the fourth Servant Song of Isaiah (Isa 52:13–53:12).[181]

Paul's sacrificial terms are a rearrangement of the Levitical sacrificial terms from the Day of Atonement in Leviticus 16. This background is in accord with the Maccabean literature, which carries the fourth Song of Isaiah.

As noted above, some scholars recognize ἱλαστήριον as a hint of martyrdom theology for the Messiah's faithfulness based on Isaiah 53. The Messiah's faithfulness is suggested in the martyrdom theology. Although the idea of the "noble death" of the righteous was probably known to Paul,[182] the date of 4 Maccabees makes it questionable that its martyrdom theology could have influenced Paul's writing, especially about "ἱλαστήριον." Klauck notes that 4 Maccabees was written about 90 or 100 AD.[183] Furthermore, "noble death" does not have a cultic meaning as in Romans 3:25.[184] Inserting the idea of martyrdom in Paul's thought is misguided "since ἱλαστήριον does not denote the act of sacrifice, nor are the martyrs compared with victims of sacrifice (such as those on the Day of Atonement)."[185] Marinus de Jonge holds,

> Again the model of interpretation reflected in these accounts of the Maccabean martyrs elucidates only certain aspects of Jesus' mission culminating in his death and resurrection. In his solidarity with others, Jesus died for their sins, and not for his own.

180. Wright, *Paul and the Faithfulness of God*, 846.

181. Wright, "Romans," 467.

182. Haacker, *Der Brief des Paulus an die Römer*, 91n40, 41. He understands that the pagan Roman conception suggests the idea of "noble death."

183. Klauck, *4 Makkabäerbuch*, 669.

184. Stuhlmacher, *Reconciliation, Law, and Righteousness*, 102–3.

185. Bailey, "Jesus as the Mercy Seat," 158.

He was not just a martyr bringing about reconciliation with God and peace for Israel on earth. He appeared as a unique servant of God, God's final envoy. His death brought a definitive turn in the relationship between God and those who truly serve him. His resurrection was not only a sign of his personal vindication and the beginning of a blessed life in heaven, it underscored that God's rule is about to be fully realized on earth. It meant the end of all oppression, enmity to God, sorrow and death. As one type of early formulas emphasizes: "Χριστός, the Messiah, died for us (our sins)."[186]

The concept of the Messiah's obedience, which is expressed in ἱλαστήριον, misses the cost of its atoning significance, which is clearly related to God's judgment on the Messiah.

While the wording of Paul concerning the Messiah's death in Romans 3:25 corresponds to the Suffering Servant in the Old Testament, the Messiah's faithful obedience is not included in Paul's argument. Rather, the death of the Messiah is the place of God's wrathful judgment, and the Messiah himself is the propitiatory sacrifice, in which God provides the "solution" for his wrath over all human beings.

The Messiah—God's Ἱλαστήριον

In Romans 3:25, Paul moves to Christ's cross. Paul subsequently manifests the meaning of believing in the Messiah, especially ἱλαστήριον in 3:25. The Messiah is the object of belief, instead of the subject of faithfulness in his sacrificial death on the cross. In the interpretation of this passage, the Messiah's faithfulness is usually understood as his obedience on the cross related to ἱλαστήριον. Ἱλαστήριον functions, however, as the object of faith, which is the resolution of God's wrath.

The primary focus of the Messiah's atonement is the resolution of God's wrath. How is God's wrath suspended? God can neither accept sin, nor simply forgive it. His judicial righteousness, on the contrary, requires a punishment equivalent to the guilt. All human beings, as sinners and ungodly people, fall under God's righteousness and his wrath.[187] While sinful man cannot accomplish this satisfaction, the Son of God comes to present himself to the holy God for atonement.[188] With his death on the cross, Jesus

---

186. de Jonge, "Jesus' Death for Others and the Death of the Maccabean Martyrs," 151.
187. Hofius, *Paulusstudien*, 34.
188. Hofius, *Paulusstudien*, 34.

makes the indispensable satisfaction for God's judging righteousness.[189] This interprets the Pauline concept of the righteousness of God in the sense of judicial justice.[190]

Ἱλαστήριον

The righteousness of God is not, during Paul's time, a new concept because the Davidic Messiah was expected as the royal, as well as the priestly, Messiah in terms of God's judgment. Although the Davidic Messiah was mainly expected as the messianic king for the salvation of his people, he was expected as the High Priest with the atonement role, too. The atoning and judging functions are combined in the death of the Messiah in Romans. Jens Schröter relates, "In his interpretation, Paul places this cultic metaphor into the horizon of the simultaneous revelation of the wrath and righteousness of God, and thereby into a context that is characterized by judgment metaphors."[191] Paul proclaims this image of the Davidic Messiah in Romans 3:24–25, that "they are justified by his grace as a gift, through the redemption that is in Christ Jesus, whom God put forward as ἱλαστήριον by his blood by faith."

The crucial point is that justification, the judicial verdict, has been accomplished with the ransom of Christ's death, which is the atonement sacrifice. Paul, in turn, argues with a series of images—the lawsuit, the ransom, and the altar.[192] The meaning of "ἀπολύτρωσις" (redemption) is "liberation through payment of a price."[193] Applying this meaning to Christ's death, Paul utilizes it for the ransom of blood to pay for the sins of all human beings under God's wrath. The death of Jesus Christ is the apex of the fulfillment of redemption to atone for sins. Paul's presentation of ἱλαστήριον denotes the redemption for the sins of all those who would be saved (3:24–25).[194]

This chief emphasis is that God's righteousness is satisfied through the ἱλαστήριον by punishing Jesus Christ. Schreiner contends, "Thus, through Jesus' atoning sacrifice, God's judging righteousness (Rom 3:25–26) has

---

189. Hofius, *Paulusstudien*, 34.

190. Hofius, *Paulusstudien*, 34.

191. Schröter, *From Jesus to the New Testament*, 195–96.

192. Black, *Romans*, 65.

193. Paul utilizes the theme of Israel's exile, the Isaianic theme of redemption. Seifrid, "Romans," 619; Morris, *The Apostolic Preaching of the Cross*, 22–26.

194. Many scholars support the pre-Paul tradition (3:24–25a) theory. Even if Paul employs traditional language, he fashions this tradition with his own theological statement. See Moo, *Romans*, 220n7; Schreiner, *Romans*, 187–88.

been vindicated."[195] The ἱλαστήριον presents the ground for advocating that God is the righteous justifier because he did not taint his holiness by passing over sins in the old covenant and by forgiving sin in the present.[196] God maintains his righteousness as the righteous justifier through the ἱλαστήριον, which is the redemption of sinners.

The Day of Atonement.

Ἱλαστήριον figures prominently in the role of the high priest on the Day of Atonement to atone for God's people. Commentators have widely understood it as having the sense of "mercy seat," although some scholars also support the idea of propitiation or of expiation.[197] The cultic image of "ἱλαστήριον" refers to the sacrificial blood of the Day of Atonement. "Ἱλαστήριον" should be recognized as the "mercy seat" as evinced by the LXX and Hebrews 9:5 in an allusion to the Day of Atonement.[198] It is effective by faith in the Messiah's sacrificial blood (διὰ πίστεως ἐν τῷ αὐτοῦ αἵματι, 3:25). Schreiner comments,

---

195. Schreiner, *Paul*, 236.

196. Schreiner, *Paul*, 236.

197. Ἱλαστήριον denotes "mercy seat" and the operation of the cover of the ark in the LXX (Exod 25:17, 18, 19, 20, 21, 22; 31:7; 35:12; 38:5, 7, 8; Lev 16:2, 13, 14, 15; Num 7:89). Bailey understands this term in the context of the meaning, "mercy seat," in Lev 16. See Bailey, "Jesus as the Mercy Seat"; Gathercole, "Justified by Faith, Justified by His Blood," 178; Seifrid, "Romans," 619-22. Some scholars understand ἱλαστήριον as "propitiation." Deissmann, *Bible Studies*, 127; Morris, *The Apostolic Preaching of the Cross*, 144-78; Morris, *The Epistle to the Romans*, 180-82; Cranfield, *Romans*, 1:214-18. It refers to a "propitiatory gift or offering," or "gifts of appeasing," in nonbiblical Greek literature. The suggestion of "propitiation" is supported through the idea that the "ἱλασ-" word group and "ἱλάσκεσθαι" show the wrath of God. Morris, *The Apostolic Preaching of the Cross*, 145-47. "Expiation" has been maintained by several scholars against "propitiation" because they assert that there is no idea of placating the wrath of God in the Old Testament. Dodd, *Romans*, 54-55; Dodd, *The Bible and the Greeks*, 82-95; Tobin, *Paul's Rhetoric in Its Contexts*, 130-32; Ziesler, *Paul's Letter to the Romans*, 111-12; Fitzmyer, *Romans*, 348-50. In particular, these scholars argue that the verb "ἱλάσκεσθαι" does not have God as its object, but that sin is the object of this verb, and that כפר—that is translated "ἱλάσκεσθαι"—often has the meaning of "to cover," or "to wipe off"; thus, "to conceal" or "to cleanse." The chief emphasis of these scholars is that God does not capriciously show wrath to his people. However, Paul does not oppose the character of expiation and propitiation with "mercy seat" in ἱλαστήριον. The "mercy seat" could contain the "wiping out" of sins within the Day of Atonement because the cultic idea in the Old Testament has made it possible to "wipe away" sins, along with God's wrath. Moo, *Romans*, 235; Seifrid, "Romans," 620.

198. Seifrid, "Romans," 619.

> Such a notion was presumably not grotesque to Paul because he did not conceive of propitiation as the satisfaction of a law that was above God but the satisfaction of God's own holy justice and anger. The presence of propitiation does not exclude the concept of expiation. Both are present in 3:25. The death of Jesus removed sin and satisfied God's holy anger.[199]

Paul presents ἱλαστήριον as the resolution of God's wrath and justifying righteousness because ἱλαστήριον is the place of propitiation and expiation. The righteousness of God effects deliverance from God's wrath (3:24); expiation is contingent on propitiation.[200]

While God's wrath is propitiated with ἱλαστήριον, God forgives his people through the blood sprinkled on the "mercy seat" on the Day of Atonement. As Daniel Bailey notes:

> The combination of God's righteousness and redemption in Exodus 15:13 (ὡδήγησας τῇ δικαιοσύνῃ σου τὸν λαόν σου τοῦτον, ὃν ἐλυτρώσω) closely parallels Romans 3:24 (δικαιόω and ἀπολύτρωσις). Furthermore, Exodus 15:17 promises that the exodus would lead to a new, ideal sanctuary established by God himself. God's open setting out of Jesus as the new ἱλαστήριον— the centre of the sanctuary and focus of both the revelation of God (Exod 25:22; Lev 16:2; Num 7:89) and atonement for sin (Leviticus 16)—fulfills this tradition.[201]

On this day, the high priest entered the "holy of holies" to atone for God's people by pouring blood on the "mercy seat."[202] In the seventeenth chapter of Leviticus, the high priest sprinkled the sacrificial blood to accomplish the atonement for the sins of God's people.[203] The order of God's justification originates from God's new ἱλαστήριον. The forgiveness of sins is clearly related to the citation to the blood in Romans 3:25, in which "his blood" is connected with ἱλαστήριον.[204] Because Paul elsewhere defines Christ's blood as the price of redemption (Eph 1:7; cf. Acts 20:28; 1 Cor 6:20; 7:23), the blood of redemption is an allusion to the blood sprinkled on the "mercy seat" as the rite of the Day of Atonement in the Old Testament.

---

199. Schreiner, *Romans*, 192.

200. Seifrid, "Romans," 620.

201. Bailey, "Jesus as the Mercy Seat," 156.

202. Moo, *Romans*, 232; Stuhlmacher, *Romans*, 60.

203. According to Stuhlmacher in *Romans*, 58, "The Christian's *kapporet* no longer exists hidden in the holy of holies of the temple, but is revealed to all in the form of Christ hanging on the cross."

204. Schreiner, *Romans*, 193–94.

The sprinkling of blood can make believers, who were sinners and apart from the glory of God, to be in the presence of God. On the ἱλαστήριον the sacrificial blood was poured out, and Yahweh appeared (Lev 16:2).[205] The fact is that the "כפרת" (mercy seat) represents, on the one hand, the place of the appearance and the presence of YHWH (Exod 25:22; 30:6; Lev 16:2; Num 7:89), and on the other hand, the Yom-Kippur place of atonement (Lev 16:14 ff.).[206] The Messiah is the place God's wrath is poured out against sinners, who deserve the condemnation of God.[207]

Additionally, the Messiah is the "propitiatory sacrifice" that is ἱλαστήριον itself. Beale posits,

> What was done in the old temple in the secrecy of the holy of holies is now "displayed publicly." Part of the core of the temple, the mercy seat of the ark, is identified with Jesus, likely portrayed as the beginning of the eschatological temple, to which the old temple ark pointed (so that, perhaps, there is a nuance of Christ as the atonement, which consecrates the new temple). Likewise, the animal sacrifice, the blood of which was sprinkled on the mercy seat, pointed to the greater sacrifice of Christ. . . . This fits with the overall purpose of the Levitical sacrifices to keep Israel as a set-apart people for God (Exod 19:5-6) and to allow God to continue to dwell in his tabernacle among them (Exod 29:38-46).[208]

While the meaning of Jesus Christ's death is expressed in the cultic image of blood sacrifice—which was a significant part of the Day of Atonement rite in the Old Testament—the cultic idea of the atonement sacrifice was widely spread in the diaspora churches.[209] The Messiah's death is a sin offering, in which God's righteousness has been revealed. The sacrifice for sin, which is the substitutionary atonement, takes place under the judgment of God.[210] Romans 3:25 highlights the righteousness of God, which is not convincingly identified with God's covenantal faithfulness.[211]

---

205. The "mercy seat" presents the present of the Lord. Stuhlmacher, "Recent Exegesis on Romans 3:24-26," 100.

206. Kraus, *Der Tod Jesu als Heiligtumsweihe*, 31.

207. Beale, *A New Testament Biblical Theology*, 489.

208. Beale, *A New Testament Biblical Theology*, 489.

209. Mark 14:24; Heb 9:11-14; 1 Pet 1:19; see Taylor, *The Atonement in New Testament Teaching*, 63-64; Davies, *Paul and Rabbinic Judaism*, 236; Dunn, *Romans 1-8*, 171.

210. Vickers, *Jesus' Blood and Righteousness*, 183.

211. Vickers, *Jesus' Blood and Righteousness*, 183.

In addition, Jesus, the Davidic Messiah, assumes the role of the High Priest for God's judgment in Romans. Moreover, he is the perfect sacrifice and the great High Priest.[212] Paul presents Christ as the "sin offering" (Rom 8:3). Ἱλαστήριον has a cultic meaning in Romans 3:25,[213] as the phrase "through his blood" illustrates. Paul's comparison of Jesus to a sin offering in Romans 8:3—which includes the phrase περί αμαρτίας, a reference to a "sin offering" in the LXX—supports this typological language in Romans 3:25.[214] Additionally, the heavenly Messiah is our intercessor (8:34), along with the sacrifice for our sin. The portrayal of the exalted Davidic Messiah, who sits at God's right hand, as such is consistent with the account of our intercessor, the High Priest in Hebrews 7:25.[215] According to Hengel,

> This formulation (Rom 3:25) comes close to the cultic terminology and the ideational world of Hebrews, where only ἱλαστήριον in the sense of *kapporet* in the earthly sanctuary appears again (Heb 9:5). For Hebrews the "place of expiation" in the heavenly sanctuary and the "throne of grace" (4:16) are connected with one another: in a similar fashion Christ as the once-for-all atoning sacrifice and the heavenly high priest, who is enthroned at the right hand of God, are identical.[216]

The resurrected Christ, who is the High Priest at God's right hand, brings to the forefront the Day of Atonement symbolism.[217]

> According to the story, the Davidic priest-king enters the heavenly Temple as a high priest par excellence. He offers a sacrifice for sins and sprinkles blood upon the mercy seat. After this the priest-king is enthroned on the very same seat, God's throne of Glory in the heavenly Holy of Holies.[218]

Christ completes the Old Testament, specifically its sacrificial system.[219] The Old Testament ritual is fulfilled in Christ's "once-for-all" sacrifice.[220]

---

212. Vickers, *Jesus' Blood and Righteousness*, 167n25. See 1 Pet 1:19.

213. As mentioned above, while some scholars support "expiation" and "propitiation" for ἱλαστήριον, these include the cultic idea with 'by his blood' within Romans 3:25. Wright, *Romans*, 474.

214. Bailey, "Jesus as the Mercy Seat," 156.

215. Käsemann, *Romans*, 248; Behm, "παράκλητος," in *TDNT*, 5:809–14; Hengel, *Studies in Early Christianity*, 160–61.

216. Hengel, *Studies in Early Christianity*, 161.

217. Eskola, *Messiah and the Throne*, 253.

218. Eskola, *Messiah and the Throne*, 261.

219. Vickers, *Jesus' Blood and Righteousness*, 167n25.

220. Moo, *Romans*, 232.

The atonement of the Messiah Jesus consistently appears with early exaltation Christology. Paul implements a reference to Psalm 110 in his cultic interpretation. God exalted the Messiah, who is the High Priest, to the heavenly throne in Romans 4:25.[221] The themes of atonement by the Davidic Messiah, and believing in one who atones and justifies sinners, are allusions to Isaiah 53. They correspond to the main themes in Romans 3:21-26: righteousness and atonement. Schreiner attests, "There is an allusion to Isaiah 53, since through the atoning sacrifice of the Davidic Messiah, sinners are justified."[222] Furthermore, Hebrews 9 mentions Christ's death as representing the blood in the Spirit (9:14), and Jesus is considered of both as sacrifice and as high priest.[223] This corresponds to the Davidic Messiah in Isaiah 53, who shall sprinkle many nations and is an offering for guilt (אָשָׁם, περὶ ἁμαρτίας). As noted, above, it is employed in Romans 8:3, too. The Davidic Messiah is described in Isaiah 53 as causing many to be accounted righteous.

In addition, while the faithfulness of the Messiah in the covenantal relationship is presupposed in the Messiah's obedience in his sacrificial death, no clear language depicts the faithfulness of the Davidic Messiah in his agency within judgment and atonement. Again, the Messiah's faithfulness does not appear in God's judgment through the Davidic Messiah, even in the Messiah's suffering for atonement. Instead, God's righteousness is in view in his judgment through the Davidic Messiah. Similarly, Paul emphasizes God's judgment on the Davidic Messiah for the justification of God's people, especially as in Isaiah 53. From this perspective, faith in the Davidic Messiah related to the Suffering Servant in Isaiah 53 corresponds to Paul's argument in the next chapter.

Consequently, Paul stresses the righteousness in the Messiah's atonement, rather than God's or the Messiah's covenantal faithfulness in Romans 3:21-26, in which God's judgment on the cross is shown as the place for solving God's wrath. The Davidic messiahship, in the Old Testament and the Second Temple Jewish writings, can fully explain the cultic and judgment concepts in Romans 3:21-26. God's righteousness is accomplished through the ἱλαστήριον. Christ's death is punitive in Paul's understanding that the Davidic Messiah "bore the act of divine condemnation of sin in his own death."[224] The Davidic Messiah's atoning death is full payment for human sins because he bore God's wrath and judgment through his death.

---

221. Eskola, *Messiah and the Throne*, 267.
222. Schreiner, *Paul*, 236.
223. Kraus, *Der Tod Jesu als Heiligtumsweihe*, 154.
224. Jonge, "Jesus' Death for Others and the Death of the Maccabean Martyrs," 179.

In the context of Isaiah 53, the atoning death for the justification of sinners is related to sinners' belief in the Messiah in the gospel, instead of to the Messiah's faithfulness. As a result, the justification of sinners is God's gift for those who believe in the Messiah's atoning death to resolve God's wrath. The fourth chapter of Romans clearly shows this connection between faith in the Messiah and his justification of sinners.

JUSTIFICATION THROUGH THE DAVIDIC MESSIAH: ROMANS 4:25

The passage treated in the previous section indicates that the prominent role of the Davidic Messiah, Jesus, is the execution of God's judgment (3:21–26). The theme of God's judgment through the Messiah coherently continues in Romans 4. In this role, the Messiah's faithfulness is not Paul's concern. Paul delineates justification through the death and resurrection of the Messiah (4:25) with the Messiah's justifying work in view

The Justifying Messiah

Paul's language in Romans 4:25 is clearly punitive in his description of God's judgment through the Davidic Messiah.[225] Concluding his discourse about God's wrath toward sinners (Rom 1:18–4:25), both Jews and Gentiles, Paul plainly utilizes judgmental wording to support his contention. While some scholars suggest that the Suffering Servant in Isaiah 53 related to Romans 4:25 is employed to manifest the Messiah's faithful obedience to God's covenantal promises, Paul's argument of justification by faith continues with his emphasis on the justifying Messiah in Romans 4.

Handing over His Son

At the end of Romans 1:18–4:25, Paul presents God's handing over of the Messiah for the justification of sinners in Romans 4:25. Because the term "*handing over*" (παραδίδωμι) refers to "handing over to execution," Paul's usage of this term has the "ironic sense in which Jesus receives punishment because of our sins."[226] "Handing over" for our trespasses (παραπτώματα) is a punitive idea pertaining to Christ's death. The word "transgressions,"

---

225. Gathercole, "Justified by Faith, Justified by His Blood," 182.

226. Gathercole, "Justified by Faith, Justified by His Blood," 182; BDAG, 762; W. Popkes, "παραδίδωμι," in *EDNT*, 3:18.

rather than "sins," additionally fits Paul's rhetorical purpose, which covers violations of both Jews and Gentiles in 1:18–3:20. And παράπτωμα occurs six times "in the subsequent discussion of Adam's transgression (5:15–20)."[227] It evokes "the wider context of the servant's receiving punishment on behalf of the people."[228] Paul underlines the punishment of the Messiah for the people's sins with his reference to LXX Isaiah 53.[229] The language of death—"handing over" (παραδίδωμι)—with "for our trespasses" (διὰ τὰ παραπτώματα ἡμῶν), is a strong reference to LXX Isaiah 53:5 and 53:12.[230]

Wright declares that God has done this through the Messiah's faithfulness, and the Messiah is the figure in Isaiah 40–55.[231] He explains,

> His obedience leads to a shameful and shocking death, shocking partly because of its shamefulness, partly because of its vicarious character and partly because, uniquely in Israel's scriptures, it constitutes a human sacrifice (Isa 53:10). . . . This highlights once more the theme we saw earlier: the faithfulness of the Servant Messiah as the quality through which all this has been accomplished.[232]

Wright connects the Servant's death to a greater "exile" envisioned in Isaiah 49.[233] From this view point, God's righteousness—which is questioned by Israel's failure—is effective through the Messiah's faithfulness in the covenantal relationship.[234]

---

227. Jewett, *Romans*, 343.
228. Gathercole, "Justified by Faith, Justified by His Blood," 182.
229. Gathercole, "Justified by Faith, Justified by His Blood," 153.
230. Stuhlmacher attests that handing over "Jesus our Lord" to death διὰ τὰ παραπτώματα ἡμῶν and raising him from the dead διὰ τὴν δικαίωσιν ἡμῶν (4:25) are from the Hebrew text of Isaiah 53:5, 11. Stuhlmacher, "Isaiah 53 in the Gospels and Acts," 154. He explains that if the LXX had been the basis of 4:25, "it would have suggested speaking of ἁμαρτίαι, 'sins,' instead of παραπτώματα, 'transgressions' (which goes back to the transgressors, פֹּשְׁעִים of Isa 53:12), and of the justification of the Servant himself (cf. 1 Tim 3:16) instead of the justification of the many." Stuhlmacher, "Isaiah 53 in the Gospels and Acts," 154. For the differences between the Hebrew and Greek, see Sapp, "The LXX, 1QIsa, and MT Versions of Isaiah 53 and the Christian Doctrine of Atonement," 173–76. Some scholars insist that Semitic structure and Aramaic parallel of παρεδόθη δια τα παραττώματα "delivered because of our transgressions" appear in the Targums of Isa 53:5b. Bruce, *The Letter of Paul to the Romans*, 113; Jeremías, *New Testament Theology*, 296–97.
231. Wright, *Paul and the Faithfulness of God*, 999.
232. Wright, *Paul and the Faithfulness of God*, 999.
233. Wright, *Paul and the Faithfulness of God*, 1000.
234. Wright, *Paul and the Faithfulness of God*, 1000.

However, while the Messiah's death and resurrection are explicated in echoes of the Suffering Servant in Isaiah 53, Paul presents the Messiah as the solution for God's judgment on sinners through his death and resurrection. This is completely in accord with the Davidic Messiah, the agent of God's judgment, as shown in the previous chapters. Fitzmyer rightly states, "The clause alludes to Isa 53:4–5, 11–12 and reveals the vicarious character of Christ Jesus' suffering in his role as the Servant of Yahweh who takes away human sin and achieves justification for human beings."[235] Stuhlmacher says, as well,

> When Isaiah 53:10–12 stands in the background of Paul's Christological texts . . . then the point is that Christ effects justification for sinners as the vicariously Suffering Servant. He bore their iniquities and punishment vicariously and went to death for them while they were still ungodly (cf. Rom 4:25; 5:6–8).[236]

Paul's conclusion in Romans 1:18–4:25 is that for the justification of sinners, God punished his Son, the Davidic Messiah, by "handing him over" to deal with human sin.

Resurrection of the Messiah.

Resurrection necessarily implies enthronement and judgment in the heavenly court in Romans 4:25. His resurrection cannot be separated from Christ's cross, by which the Messiah's vindication for believers is proclaimed in 4:25.[237] Paul instructs that "he was handed over for our trespasses and raised for our justification" (4:25).[238] This verse is "so formulated in a literary parallelism; both effects are to be ascribed to the death and the resurrection."[239] The resurrection of Jesus is dependent on Isaiah 53, because Isaiah 53:11 in the LXX and at Qumran says that the righteous Messiah "will see light" (δεῖξαι αὐτῷ φῶς). This verse is considered to refer to the resurrection.[240] Moreover, it is in accord with the righteous Messiah in Isaiah 52:13 that "he shall be high and lifted up, and shall be exalted."

---

235. Fitzmyer, *Romans*, 389.

236. Stuhlmacher, *Revisiting Paul's Doctrine of Justification*, 58.

237. Schreiner, *Romans*, 462.

238. For the meaning of διά in Rom 4:25, see Bird, "'Raised for Our Justification': A Fresh Look at Romans 4:25," 39–46. I follow Schreiner's understanding of causal sense, "because of." Schreiner, *Romans*, 243–44.

239. Fitzmyer, *Romans*, 389.

240. Schreiner, *Paul*, 190.

The Messiah justifies sinners by his death and resurrection. This act quenches God's wrath on their behalf. The royal and priestly Messiah, who is clearly portrayed in 3:25, appears too in 4:25. While he is characterized as the Davidic Messiah, his death, resurrection, and enthronement are additionally linked with the High Priest described in 8:34—an allusion to Psalm 110:1 and 5. His enthronement "at the right hand" of God, in 8:34, illustrates his function in God's judgment. As mentioned above, Acts 17:31 alludes to Christ enthroned as a heavenly judge because "he has fixed a day on which he will judge the world in righteousness by the man whom he has appointed, and of this he has given assurance to all by raising him from the dead" (Acts 17:31). The enthroned Messiah is now participating in God's judgment at the right hand of God (Rom 8:34). Judicial images continue to appear in 8:34. Christ's intercession means "ensuring that the justifying verdict for which he died is applied to us in the judgment."[241] Christ's intercession should be seen alongside his resurrection. His intercession first proves his priestly ministry as in Psalm 110, and it is demonstrated as well in the Davidic Messiah of Isaiah 53:12. The new Davidic Messiah was resurrected and enthroned to execute the priestly role, according to the order of Melchizedek, as described in Psalm 110.

For this reason, Paul teaches that Jesus was "handed over" for our trespasses and raised for our justification (Rom 4:25), which corresponds to the suffering of the Servant, the Davidic Messiah in Isaiah 53. All this is due to God's judgment. In other words, Paul stresses the judgment of God through the Davidic Messiah against sinners and the solution to God's wrath in Romans 1:18—4:25, rather than the Messiah's faithfulness, although some scholars think that Messiah's covenantal faithfulness is manifest because it is based on his obedience in his suffering. These scholars feel that in Romans 5:19, Paul's focus is that Jesus' death is primarily the ultimate act of obedience.[242] But Christ's obedience cannot be identified with his covenantal faithfulness itself. Schreiner writes,

> Granted, the obedience of Christ is an important element in Pauline theology. But there is not a shred of evidence anywhere else that he speaks of that obedience as Christ's πίστις. The parallel between Rom 5:15–19 and πίστις Ἰησοῦ Χριστοῦ is hardly as strong as proponents of the subjective interpretation claim.[243]

---

241. Moo, *Romans*, 542.
242. Moo, *Romans*, 344; Vickers, *Jesus' Blood and Righteousness*, 148.
243. Schreiner, *Romans*, 185.

Paul does not draw attention to Christ's covenantal faithfulness with his obedience. Instead, the central issue is that God's righteousness operates over all humanity. Paul concentrates on all human beings—whether Jew or Greek, as in 3:22.[244] Paul observes that Christ's "one act of righteousness results in justification leading for all men" (5:18). "One act of righteousness" is identified as a verdict that is just.[245] Paul connects this forensic idea with the next verse. Romans 5:19 reads that Christ's "obedience makes many righteous" (5:19).[246] Christ's obedience as one righteous act makes all human beings righteous, including Jews and Gentiles, beyond the covenantal relationship.

Thus, while some believe Messiah's covenantal faithfulness, which is obedience, the Messiah's obedience cannot be identified as covenantal faithfulness. Rather, this is righteous conduct that results in a forensic verdict. Vickers rightly remarks, "While Christ's life and death cannot be separated, it does seem that Paul's main focus is on Christ's death as the supreme act of righteousness, his act of obedience that secures the status of 'righteousness' for those identified with him."[247] While Christ's obedience can be the grounds for justification, it cannot be identified with covenantal faithfulness itself. Paul suggests Christ's obedience as redemptive death, which is the consummation of redemptive history.[248]

The Messiah's resurrection is the main point in these verses, so πίστις summarizes the narrative of the Messiah's resurrection. The Messiah's death is presented for the justification of the ungodly in Romans 4:25, which is in allusion to Isaiah 53. This verse is connected to Isaiah 53:1: "Who has believed what he has heard from us?"[249] The juxtaposition of Romans 10:16 and Isaiah 53 concerns the report of the Messiah.[250] As an apostle, he encounters the unbelief of Jews. With Isaiah 53:1, Paul points out Isaiah's proclamation of the gospel, calling for faith: "But they have not all obeyed the gospel. For Isaiah says, 'Lord, who has believed what he has heard from

---

244. Vickers, *Jesus' Blood and Righteousness*, 113. The universal dominion of death is described as apart from the presence of the law in Rom 5:13–14. Moo, *Romans*, 332.

245. Fitzmyer, *Romans*, 420; Moo, *Romans*, 345; Schreiner, *Romans*, 287.

246. Forensic meaning for "καθίστημι," see Fitzmyer, *Romans*, 421; Moo, *Romans*, 344–46; Schreiner, Romans, 223–24; Bühner, "καθίστημι," in *EDNT*, 2:225–26.

247. Vickers, *Jesus' Blood and Righteousness*, 147–48.

248. Vickers, *Jesus' Blood and Righteousness*, 150–52. Jesus Christ's obedience is a different idea from the faithfulness of Wright's Messiah.

249. Betz, "Jesus and Isaiah 53," 75.

250. Betz, "Jesus and Isaiah 53," 75.

us?'" (Rom 10:16).²⁵¹ Now, Paul's point is inverted in Romans 15:21.²⁵² In the context of Isaiah 52, in which "nations" and "kings" have not heard Yahweh's Word, they who have not heard Yahweh's Word will now see and understand.²⁵³ The death and exaltation of the Davidic Messiah of Isaiah 53 make this possible. Paul uses the cultic and judgmental action of the Davidic Messiah in Romans 15:16–21 for his apostolic mission. His mission fulfills the pattern of the Gentiles' salvation through the Davidic Messiah that appears in 52:15.

In addition, continuity between the faith of Abraham and believers is emphasized in 4:24 (τοῖς πιστεύουσιν ἐπὶ τὸν ἐγείραντα Ἰησοῦν τὸν κύριον ἡμῶν ἐκ νεκρῶν).²⁵⁴ Like the believing of Abraham, which is in the resurrecting power of God (17, 19), Christians trust in the risen Christ. This trust is a common creed in early Christianity (Acts 3:15; 4:10; 13:30; Rom 7:4; 8:11; 10:9; 1 Cor 15:4–7, 11, 12, 20; Gal 1:1; Eph 1:20; Col 2:12; 1 Thess 1:10; 1 Pet 1:21).²⁵⁵ Seifrid comments,

> In his third and final characterization of God in this passage, Paul equates the faith of Abraham with that of those who "believe in the him who raised from the dead Jesus our Lord" (4:24). In fact, he underscores the identity of their faith and its object ('the justifier of the ungodly' and 'the one who raised Jesus') by means of diction which otherwise is unusual for him: πιστεύουσιν ἐπί. The material link with the previous characterization is likewise obvious. In both cases, faith grasps God as the Creator, who makes the dead alive—a reversal of the rejection of the Creator which Paul describes in Romans 1.²⁵⁶

The faith of believers in the Messiah is the power of salvation for those who believe. This is manifest in the flow of Paul's argument in Romans 4. Therefore, Paul emphasizes the Messiah's death and resurrection for justification of the ungodly, who are following the pattern of Abraham's faith. It surpasses the covenant boundary, and Paul emphasizes the faith of the ungodly in the Messiah of the ungodly.

---

251. Seifrid, "Romans," 691.
252. Seifrid, "Romans," 691.
253. Seifrid, "Romans," 691.
254. Schreiner, *Romans*, 424.
255. Schreiner, *Romans*, 424.
256. Seifrid, "Paul's Use of Righteousness Language," 62.

CONCLUSION

In response to the question of the Messiah's faithfulness, it was contended that the statement of Paul in 1:18–4:25 is mainly focused on God's judgment over sinners. The main flow of Paul's argument is that God's judgment is accomplished through the Davidic Messiah in his death and resurrection. Paul weaves his argument with the thread with the strand that is the Davidic-messianic language. The entire thread of Romans 1:18–4:25 is God's wrath and the resolution for his wrath, which is justification by faith in the Messiah. Paul stresses that the Davidic Messiah is the agent of God's judgment (2:16), the place of God's judgment, ἱλαστήριον, (3:25), and the justifying Messiah (4:25). The Davidic Messiah, the agent of God's judgment, justifies all believers. The Messiah justifies them by his death and resurrection in righteousness. This simultaneously shows the Davidic Messiah's main role as the agent of God's judgment as in the Old Testament and Jewish literature. Paul emphasizes the resolution of God's wrath through the Davidic Messiah's bearing sins and receiving God's judgment. In other words, the Davidic Messiah's atonement is God's solution for God's wrath over sins. Paul concentrates on God's righteousness, rather than on the Messiah's faithfulness in the covenantal relationship. The Davidic Messiah's faithfulness does not fully support his role as the agent of God's judgment. Instead, perceiving faith in the execution of God's judgment is a more suitable understanding of Paul's writing, even though several scholars recently have maintained that the meaning of "faith of Christ" is the "faithfulness of the Messiah." In light of Paul's recognition of the Davidic Messiah's role, and Jesus as the agent of God's judgment, excluding the Messiah's faithfulness better fits Paul's Davidic Messiah description in his letter to the believers in Rome.

Chapter 6

Summary and Conclusion

SUMMARY

Chapter 1 introduced the main idea and provided a history of research within which to place the question of the Davidic Messiah and his covenantal faithfulness. Many modern scholars describe the faith of Christ as Christ's covenantal faithfulness. The analysis of the Davidic Messiah in Jewish tradition, though, is to unearth the ubiquitous ideas about the Davidic Messiah in the Old Testament and Second Temple writings. It is undeniable that in the concept of the eschatological Davidic Messiah developed in the Old Testament, especially in the post-exilic period, his main role is to carry out God's judgment. In general, second Temple Jewish literature maintains this same emphasis. The consistent features, which are manifest in his executing God's judgment, are closely related to equity and righteousness, rather than the Davidic Messiah's covenantal faithfulness.

Chapter 2 investigated a continual expectation for the Davidic Messiah in the Old Testament. Genesis 49 and Numbers 24 are the basis for the expectation of the Davidic Messiah in the Old Testament. The expectation of the Davidic Messiah, which is based on Genesis 49 and Numbers 24, continues throughout the Old Testament. The Davidic Messiah, within the prophets, includes the expectation of the Davidic Messiah, whose main role will be that of the agent of God's judgment. He will administer righteousness and justice as David and Solomon did (2 Sam 8:15 and 1 Chr 18:14). God's judgment through the Davidic Messiah shows retributive and impartial righteousness. In addition, the Suffering Servant in Isaiah 53 can be characterized as the Davidic Messiah, who bears God's judgment in the heavenly courtroom (Isa 40–55). This fact corresponds to his role as the agent of God's judgment. The text focuses on executing of God's judgment through his suffering, and exaltation is emphasized, rather than his covenantal faithfulness. Thus, the Old Testament maintains a consistent witness that the main role of the expected Davidic Messiah is the executor of God's judgment.

In chapter 3, our attention turned to the Davidic Messiah in the Second Temple Jewish literature, often described as the executor of God's judgment. Contrary to scholars who maintain that either various messiahs exist in the Jewish writings, or that there is no concept for the Davidic Messiah, the Davidic Messiah, however, is clearly characterized as the figure in Genesis 49 and Numbers 24. The Second Temple Jewish writings present this figure consistently as the Davidic Messiah.

In *Psalms of Solomon*, the Davidic Messiah is expected as the executor of God's righteousness and justice in the seventeenth chapter. The righteousness in executing God's judgment is realized as impartial righteousness for God's just judgment. The Davidic Messiah's judgment of secret things in 1 *Enoch* is similar to Paul's statement in Romans 2:16. The Son of Man—the messianic figure—possesses the characteristics of the Davidic Messiah as the agent of God's judgment, although it is debatable whether Enoch can be identified with the Davidic Messiah. The political circumstances of the date of composing the Qumran writings should be considered, and the date of writing could influence the Davidic Messiah features. The Davidic Messiah's main role is that of the agent of God's judgment, though. While he has the characteristics of the victorious warrior in the eschatological war, he can be designated as the executor of God's judgment. The term "righteous one" is primarily employed when writers concentrate on the execution of God's judgment through the Davidic Messiah. When he is described as the suffering messianic figure of Isaiah as interpreted in Qumran writings, his role is the resolution of God's judgment, rather than faithfulness to God's promises. In Jewish literature, the "faithfulness" language of the faithful Messiah in suffering is sparse in describing God's judgment through the Davidic Messiah.

Chapter 4 centered on Romans 1:3–4; the consistent wording of the gospel characterized by the Davidic Messiah in the Old Testament and Jewish literature appears in the opening of Romans. Messianic allusions are closely related to the Davidic Messiah's features as the agent of God's judgment, rather than to features of the Messiah's faithfulness. The Davidic Messiah, who is described with judgmental language in 15:12, can be particularly paralleled with the gospel statement in 1:3–4.

Then, what is stressed in Paul's letter to the Romans: the Messiah as the agent of God's judgment, or the Messiah as the faithful One? Paul consistently argues God's judgment through the Davidic Messiah in his gospel. He asserts God's judgment in the next chapter of Romans, in which judgment through the Davidic Messiah is stated (Rom 2:16).

Chapter 5 provided examinations of the Davidic Messiah in Romans 1:18–4:25. The Messiah Jesus, in Paul's preaching of his gospel, is the agent of God's judgment. The Davidic Messiah was expected in the Old Testament and Jewish writings. The language of these expectations is implemented in Romans to state the theme of God's judgment in 1:18–4:25. The Messiah Jesus is the agent of God's judgment. This is the basis of Paul's contention regarding God's wrath and his justification of sinners. God's wrath is paralleled with retributive righteousness in 1:17–18. The execution of God's judgment is impartial, and it is identified with God's judgment through the Davidic Messiah in the Old Testament and Second Temple Jewish writings.

The Messiah Jesus accomplishes God's impartial judgment as described in 3:21–26. In his judgment of all sinners, God put him forth as ἱλαστήριον. The Davidic Messiah is bearing sins, receiving God's punishment, and justifying sinners as the suffering Messiah in Isaiah 53. The language of this judgment emphasizes the impartial or just nature of the judgment to resolve God's wrath over sinners. It cannot be identified with the faithfulness language, although it can be supposed that God or the Messiah is the faithful one in the covenantal relationship.

The Davidic Messiah in Romans 4:24–25 alludes to the suffering Messiah in Isaiah 53. The Psalm 110 language is presupposed in the enthronement and exaltation of the Davidic Messiah in Romans 8. He is the priestly Messiah as in Psalm 110 and 11Q13, who makes atonement for his people and justifies the many as in Isaiah 53. Belief is the believers' faith in Isaiah about the suffering Messiah, with the role of a sacrificial offering in Isaiah. It is likewise the trusting of Abraham, which is believing in the resurrecting God.

CONCLUSION

This book began with my question concerning Christ's faithfulness in executing God's judgment. After researching the Davidic Messiah in Jewish tradition, I conclude that Christ's faithfulness is an unfamiliar idea in Romans 1:18–4:25. Affirming that the Davidic Messiah informs Paul's Christology does not require the belief that the Old Testament and Second Temple writings do not inform Christ's faithfulness in Romans. The Davidic Messiah is the agent of God's judgment in Romans; Paul's description of him parallels the concept of the agent of God's judgment in Jewish tradition—both Old Testament and Second Temple Jewish literature. However, his covenantal faithfulness for the faith of Christ is irrelevant in his role, God's judgment. Several scholars emphasize the Messiah's faithfulness in the covenantal relationship based on Jewish tradition. This theme is sparse in the Old Testament and Jewish tradition. Rather, equity and justice are stressed in the Davidic Messiah's execution of God's judgment. Also, when the royal and priestly language related to the agent of God's judgment is utilized in Romans 3:25 and 4:25, the Messiah is to be understood as the object of God's wrath in Romans 1:18–3:20. Paul's attention in Romans 1:18–4:25 is on God's wrath over sin and on the fulfillment of God's judgment that is executed on the Messiah, Jesus, instead of on sinners. In Paul's discourse, the Messiah's faithfulness is unfamiliar because God judges sinners through the Davidic Messiah in Paul's gospel (Rom 2:16).

The agent of God's judgment, the Davidic Messiah, receives God's judgment. He is the resolution of God's wrath. It demonstrates that God's judgment should be recognized as just and impartial judgment. In this way, God's judgment is executed in Paul's understanding of the Davidic Messiah, who assumes the role of both priestly and royal Messiah. I fully concur with Bavinck's reference to Christ:

> But the miracle of the gospel consists in that God manifests his righteousness apart from the law in a way that enables him to remain righteous and in virtue of (not in spite of) that righteousness justifies those who believe in Jesus and who in themselves, judged according to the law, are ungodly (4:5). And that has now been made possible by God's putting Christ forward as an expiation, by faith, in his blood.[1]

In this emphasis, Christ's faithfulness is unfamiliar in God's judgment through the Davidic Messiah in Romans 1:18–4:25 because Paul's understanding with respect to the role of the Davidic Messiah is as the agent of

---

1. Bavinck, *Reformed Dogmatics*, 3:370.

God's judgment. Several scholars, especially in the New Perspective, stress God's faithfulness in covenantal relationship with his people, namely, that is Paul's main narrative in Romans. In God's faithfulness, the faithfulness of the Messiah, Jesus, is additionally emphasized, rather than faith in the Messiah. This book shows that Christ's faithfulness is an unfamiliar idea within his role in Romans. When he is presented as the agent of God's judgment (Rom 2:16), faith in the Messiah is a more prominent idea than is faithfulness.

Bibliography

Abegg, Martin G., Jr., and Crag A. Evans. "Messianic Passages in the Dead Sea Scrolls." In *Qumran-Messianism: Studies on the Messianic Expectations in the Dead Sea Scrolls*, edited by James H. Charlesworth, Hermann Lichtenberger, and Gerbern S. Oegema, 191–203. Tübingen: Mohr, 1998.

Ábel, František. *The Psalms of Solomon and the Messianic Ethics of Paul*. Wissenschaftliche Untersuchungen zum Neuen Testament 416. Tübingen: Mohr Siebeck, 2016.

Alexander, T. Desmond. "Messianic Ideology in the Book of Genesis." In *The Lord's Anointed: Interpretation of Old Testament Messianic Texts*, edited by Gordon J. Wenham, Richard S. Hess, and Philips. E. Satterwaite, 19–40. Grand Rapids: Baker, 1995.

———. "Royal Expectation in Genesis to Kings: Their Importance." *Tyndale Bulletin* 49.2 (1998) 191–212.

Allen, David L. "Substitutionary Atonement in Isaiah 53." In *The Gospel according to Isaiah 53: Encountering the Suffering Servant in Jewish and Christian Theology*, edited by Darrell L. Bock and Mitch Glaser, 171–90. Grand Rapids: Kregel Academic, 2012.

Allen, Leslie C. *Ezekiel 20–48*. Word Biblical Commentary 29. Dallas: Word Books, 1990.

———. "Old Testament Background of (pro)horizein in the New Testament." *New Testament Studies* 17.1 (October 1979) 104–8.

Allison, Dale C., Jr. *The New Moses: A Matthean Typology*. Minneapolis: Fortress Press, 1993.

Anderson, A. A. *2 Samuel*. Word Biblical Commentary 11. Dallas: Word Books, 1989.

Armerding, Carl E. "Were David's Sons Really Priests?" In *Current Issues in Biblical and Patristic Interpretation: Studies in Honor of Merrill C. Tenney Presented by His Former Students*, edited by Gerald Hawthorne, 75–86. Grand Rapids: Eerdmans, 1975.

Atkinson, Kenneth. *I Cried to the Lord: A Study of the Psalms of Solomon's Historical Background and Social Setting*. Leiden: Brill, 2004.

Auld, A. Graeme. *I & II Samuel*. The Old Testament Library. Louisville: Westminster John Knox Press, 2011.

Averbeck, Richard E. "Sacrifices and Offerings." In *Dictionary of the Old Testament: Pentateuch*, edited by T. Desmond Alexander and David W. Baker, 706–32. Downers Grove, IL: InterVarsity Press, 2003.

Bailey, Daniel P. "Jesus as the Mercy Seat: The Semantics and Theology of Paul's Use of Hilasterion in Romans 3:25." Ph.D. diss., Cambridge University, 1999.

———. "Jesus as the Mercy Seat: The Semantics and Theology of Paul's Use of Hilasterion in Romans 3:25." *Tyndale Bulletin* 51.1 (2000) 155–58.

Baltzer, Klaus. *Deutero-Isaiah: A Commentary on Isaiah 40–55*. Translated by Margaret Kohl. Hermeneia. Minneapolis: Fortress Press, 2001.

Barclay, John M. G. *Paul and the Gift*. Grand Rapids: Eerdmans, 2015.

Barrett, C. K. *The Epistle to the Romans*. Black's New Testament Commentaries. New York: Harper & Row, 1957.

Barthelemy, D. *Etudes d'Histoire du Texte de l'Ancien Testament*. Göttingen: Vandenhoeck & Ruprecht, 1978.

———. "Le grand rouleau d'Isaïe trouvé près de la Mer Morte." *Revue Biblique* 57.4 (October 1950) 530–49.

Bassler, Jouette M. *Divine Impartiality: Paul and a Theological Axiom*. Society of Biblical Literature Dissertation Series 59. Chico, CA: Scholars Press, 1982.

Bates, Matthew W. "A Christology of Incarnation and Enthronement: Romans 1:3–4 as Unified, Nonadoptionist, and Nonconciliatory." *The Catholic Biblical Quarterly* 77.1 (2015) 107–27.

Bauckham, Richard. *Jesus and the God of Israel: God Crucified and Other Studies on the New Testament's Christology of Divine Identity*. Grand Rapids: Eerdmans, 2008.

Baumgarten, Joseph M. "Messianic Forgiveness of Sin in CD XIV, 19 (4Q266 10 I, 12–13)." In *The Provo International Conference on the Dead Sea Scrolls: Technological Innovations, New Texts, and Reformulated Issues*, edited by Donald W. Parry and Eugene C. Ulrich, 537–44. Leiden: Brill, 1999.

Bavinck, Herman. *Reformed Dogmatics*. Edited by John Bolt. Translated by John Vriend. Grand Rapids: Baker Academic, 2003–2008.

Beale, G. K. *A New Testament Biblical Theology: The Unfolding of the Old Testament in the New*. Grand Rapids: Baker Academic, 2011.

Becker, Joachim. *Messianic Expectation in the Old Testament*. Philadelphia: Fortress Press, 1980.

Becker, Jürgen. *Auferstehung der Toten im Urchristentum*. Stuttgart: KBW Verlag, 1976.

Bell, Richard H. *No One Seeks for God: An Exegetical and Theological Study of Romans 1.18–3.20*. Wissenschaftliche Untersuchungen zum Neuen Testament 106. Tübingen: Mohr Siebeck, 1998.

———. "Sacrifice and Christology in Paul." *Journal of Theological Studies* 53.1 (2002) 1–27.

Berkley, Timothy W. *From a Broken Covenant to Circumcision of the Heart: Pauline Intertextual Exegesis in Romans 2:17–29*. Atlanta: Society of Biblical Literature, 2000.

Betz, Otto. *What Do We Know about Jesus?* Philadelphia: Westminster Press, 1968.

Bird, Michael F. "'Raised for Our Justification': A Fresh Look at Romans 4:25." *Colloquium* 35.1 (May 2003) 39–46.

Black, Matthew. *The Book of Enoch or 1 Enoch: A New English Edition*. Studia in Veteris Testamenti pseudepigrapha 7. Leiden: Brill, 1985.

———. *Romans*. New Century Bible Commentary. Grand Rapids: Eerdmans, 1989.

———. "The Messianism of the Parables of Enoch: Their Date and Contribution to Christological Origins." In *The Messiah: Developments in Earliest Judaism and Christianity*, edited by James H. Charlesworth, 145–68. Minneapolis: Fortress Press, 1992.

Blenkinsopp, Joseph. *David Remembered: Kingship and National Identity in Ancient Israel*. Grand Rapids: Eerdmans, 2013.

———. *Isaiah 1–39: A New Translation with Introduction and Commentary*. Anchor Bible 19. New York: Doubleday, 2000.

———. *Isaiah 40–55: A New Translation with Introduction and Commentary*. Anchor Bible 19A. New York: Doubleday, 2002.

Block, Daniel I. "Bringing Back David." In *The Lord's Anointed: Interpretation of Old Testament Messianic Texts*, edited by Gordon J. Wenham, Richard S. Hess, and Philip E. Satterthwaite, 167–88. Grand Rapids: Baker Books, 1995.

———. "My Servant David: Ancient Israel's Vision of the Messiah." In *Israel's Messiah in the Bible and the Dead Sea Scrolls*, edited by Richard S. Hess and M. Daniel Carroll R., 17–56. Grand Rapids: Baker Books, 2003.

Boccaccini, Gabriele, ed. *Enoch and the Messiah Son of Man: Revisiting the Book of Parables*. Grand Rapids: Eerdmans, 2007.

Bock. Darrell L., and Mitch Glaser, eds. *The Gospel according to Isaiah 53: Encountering the Suffering Servant in Jewish and Christian Theology*. Grand Rapids: Kregel Academic, 2012.

Bockmuehl, Markus N. A. *Revelation and Mystery in Ancient Judaism and Pauline Christianity*. Wissenschaftliche Untersuchungen zum Neuen Testament 2.36. Tübingen: Mohr Siebeck, 1990.

Boda, Mark J. *The Book of Zechariah*. The New International Commentary on the Old Testament. Grand Rapids: Eerdmans, 2016.

———. "Figuring the Future: The Prophets and Messiah." In *The Messiah in the Old Testament and New Testament*, edited by Stanley Porter, 35–74. Grand Rapids: Eerdmans, 2007.

Boers, Hendrikus. *The Justification of the Gentiles: Paul's Letters to the Galatians and Romans*. Peabody, MA: Hendrickson, 1994.

Bornkamm, Günther. *Early Christian Experience*. New York: Harper & Row, 1969.

———. "Paul's Christology." *Pittsburgh Perspective* 4.2 (June 1963) 11–24.

Bousset, Wilhelm. *Kyrios Christos: A History of the Belief in Christ from the Beginnings of Christianity to Irenaeus*. Translated by John E. Steely. Nashville: Abingdon Press, 1970.

Bovati, Pietro. *Re-establishing Justice: Legal Terms, Concepts, and Procedures in the Hebrew Bible*. Journal for the Study of the Old Testament: Supplement Series 105. Sheffield: Sheffield Academic, 1994.

Brooke, George J. "4QTestament of Levid and the Messianic Servant High Priest." In *From Jesus to John: Essays on Jesus and New Testament Christology in Honour of Marinus de Jonge*, edited by Martinus C. de Boer, 83–100. Sheffield: Sheffield Academic, 1993.

———. *Exegesis at Qumran: 4QFlorilegium in Its Jewish Context*. Journal for the Study of the Old Testament: Supplement Series 29. Sheffield: Sheffield Academic, 1985.

Brown, Raymond E. "Messianism of Qumrân." *The Catholic Biblical Quarterly* 19.1 (January 1957) 53–82.
———. *The Semitic Background of the Term "Mystery" in the New Testament.* Philadelphia: Fortress Press, 1968.
Brueggemann, Walter. *1 & 2 Kings.* Macon, GA: Smyth & Helwys, 2000.
———. "David and His Theologian." *The Catholic Biblical Quarterly* 30.2 (April 1968); 156–81.
———. "From Dust to Kingship." *Zeitschrift für die alttestamentliche Wissenschaft* 84.1 (1972) 1–18.
———. *Isaiah 1–39.* Louisville: Westminster John Knox, 1998.
Bruce, F. F. *The Letter of Paul to the Romans: An Introduction and Commentary.* The Tyndale New Testament Commentaries. Grand Rapids: Eerdmans, 1985.
Bultmann, Rudolf. *Theology of the New Testament.* Translated by K. Grobel. New York: Scribner, 1951–1955.
———. "δικαιοσύνη θεοῦ." *Journal of Biblical Literature* 83 (1964) 12–16.
Byrne, Brendan. *Romans.* Sacra Pagina. Collegeville, MN: Liturgical Press, 1996.
Calhoun, Robert M. *Paul's Definitions of the Gospel in Romans 1.* Wissenschaftliche Untersuchungen zum Neuen Testament 2.316. Tübingen: Mohr Siebeck, 2011.
Campbell, Douglas A. *The Deliverance of God: An Apocalyptic Rereading of Justification in Paul.* Grand Rapids: Eerdmans, 2009.
———. "False Presuppositions in the Πίστις Χριστοῦ: A Response to Brian Dodd." *Journal of Biblical Literature* 116.4 (1997) 713–19.
———. *The Rhetoric of Righteousness in Romans 3.21–26.* Journal for the Study of the New Testament Supplement Series 65. Sheffield: Sheffield Academic, 1992.
———. "Romans 1:17–A Crux Interpretation for Pistis Christou Debate." *Journal of Biblical Literature* 113.2 (1994) 265–85.
Capes, David B. *Old Testament Yahweh Texts in Paul's Christology.* Wissenschaftliche Untersuchungen zum Neuen Testament 2. Tübingen: Mohr Siebeck, 1992.
Casey, Maurice. *From Jewish Prophet to Gentile God: The Origins and Development of New Testament Christology.* Louisville: Westminster John Knox Press, 1991.
Charlesworth, James H. "From Jewish Messianology to Christian Christology." In *Judaisms and Their Messiahs at the Turn of the Christian Era,* edited by Jacob Neusner, William Scott Green, and Ernest Frerichs, 225–64. Cambridge: Cambridge University Press, 1987.
———. "From Messianology to Christology: Problems and Prospects." In *The Messiah: Developments in Earliest Judaism and Christianity,* edited by James H. Charlesworth, 3–35. Minneapolis: Fortress Press, 1992.
———. "Messianology in the Biblical Pseudepigrapha." In *Qumran-Messianism: Studies on the Messianic Expectations in the Dead Sea Scrolls,* edited by James H. Charlesworth, Hermann Lichtenberger, and Gerbern S. Oegema, 21–52. Tübingen: Mohr, 1998
Charlesworth, James H., ed. *The Old Testament Pseudepigrapha.* Vol. 2. Garden City, NY: Doubleday, 1983–85.
Charlesworth, James H., Hermann Lichtenberger, and Gerbern S. Oegema, eds. *Qumran-Messianism: Studies on the Messianic Expectations in the Dead Sea Scrolls.* Tübingen: Mohr, 1998.

Chester, Andrew. "The Christ of Paul." In *Redemption and Resistance: The Messianic Hopes of Jews and Christians in Antiquity*, edited by Markus Bockmuehl and James Carleton Pager, 109–21. London: T&T Clark, 2007.
———. *Future Hope and Present Reality*. Wissenschaftliche Untersuchungen zum Neuen Testament 293. Tübingen: Mohr Siebeck, 2012.
———. *Messiah and Exaltation: Jewish Messianic and Visionary Traditions and New Testament Christology*. Wissenschaftliche Untersuchungen zum Neuen Testament 207. Tübingen: Mohr Siebeck, 2007.
Chester, Stephen J. *Reading Paul with the Reformer: Reconciling Old and New Perspectives*. Grand Rapids: Eerdmans, 2017.
Chialà, Sabino. "The Son of Man: The Evolution of an Expression." In *Enoch and the Messiah Son of Man: Revisiting the Book of Parables*, edited by Gabriele Boccaccini, 153–78. Grand Rapids: Eerdmans, 2007.
Childs, Brevard S. *Isaiah: A Commentary*. The Old Testament Library. Louisville: Westminster John Knox Press, 2001.
Chisholm, Robert. "Forgiveness and Salvation in Isaiah 53." In *The Gospel according to Isaiah 53: Encountering the Suffering Servant in Jewish and Christian Theology*, edited by Darrell L. Bock and Mitch Glaser, 191–212. Grand Rapids: Kregel Academic, 2012.
Christiansen, Ellen J. *The Covenant in Judaism and Paul: A Study in Ritual Boundaries at Identity Markers*. Arbeiten zur Geschichte des antiken Judentums und des Urchristentums 27. Leiden: Brill, 1995.
Clifford, Richard J. *Fair Spoken and Persuading: An Interpretation of Second Isaiah*. New York: Paulist Press, 1984.
Clines, David J. A. *I, He, We and They: A Literary Approach to Isaiah 53*. Sheffield: Sheffield Academic, 1976.
Coats, George W. *The Moses Tradition*. Journal for the Study of the Old Testament Supplement Series 161. Sheffield: Sheffield Academic, 1993.
Collins, Adela Yarbro, and John J. Collins. *King and Messiah as the Son of God: Divine, Human, and Angelic Messianic Figures in Biblical and Related Literature*. Grand Rapids: Eerdmans, 2008.
Collins, John J. *Apocalypticism in the Dead Sea Scrolls*. New York: Routledge, 1997.
———. *A Commentary on the Book of Daniel*. Hermeneia. Minneapolis: Fortress Press, 1993.
———. *King and Messiah as Son of God: Divine, Human, and Angelic Messianic Figures in Biblical and Related Literature*. Grand Rapids: Eerdmans, 2008.
———. "Messianism and Exegetical Tradition: The Evidence of the LXX Pentateuch." In *The Septuagint and Messianism*, edited by M. A. Knibb, 129–49. Leuven: Leuven University Press, 2006.
———. "Messianism in the Maccabean Period." In *Judaisms and Their Messiahs at the Turn of the Christian Era*, edited by Jacob Neusner, William Scott Green, and Ernest Freichs, 97–109. Cambridge: Cambridge University, 1987.
———. "The Nature of Messianism in the Light of the Dead Sea Scrolls." In *The Dead Sea Scrolls in Their Historical Context*, edited by Timothy H. Lim, 199–217. Edinburgh: T&T Clark, 2000.
———. "Pre-Christian Jewish Messianism: An Overview." In *The Messiah: Developments in Earliest Judaism and Christianity*, edited by James H. Charlesworth, 1–20. Minneapolis: Fortress Press, 1992.

———. *The Scepter and the Star: Messianism in Light of the Dead Sea Scrolls*. Grand Rapids: Eerdmans, 2010.

———. "The Son of God text from Qumran." In *From Jesus to John: Essays on Jesus and New Testament Christology in Honour of Marinus de Jonge*, edited by Martinus C. de Boer, 65–82. Sheffield: JSOT Press, 1993.

———. "The Suffering Servant at Qumran." *BR* 9.6 (December 1993) 25–27.

Collins, John J., and George W. E. Nickelsburg, eds. *Ideal Figures in Ancient Judaism: Profiles and Paradigms*. Chico, CA: Scholars Press, 1980.

Condra, Ed. *Salvation for the Righteous Revealed: Jesus amid Covenantal and Messianic Expectations in Second Temple Judaism*. Arbeiten zur Geschichte des antiken Judentums und des Urchristentums 51. Leiden; Boston: Brill, 2002.

Cooke, Gerald B. "The Israelite King as Son of God." *Zeitschrift für die alttestamentliche Wissenschaft* 73.2 (1961) 202–25.

Craigie, Peter C., Page H. Kelley, and Joel F. Drinkard. *Jeremiah 1–25*. Word Biblical Commentary 26. Dallas: Word Books, 1991.

Craigie, Peter. C., and Marvin E. Tate. *Psalms 1–50*. 2nd ed. Word Biblical Commentary 19. Waco, TX: Word Books, 1983.

Cranfield, C. E. B. *A Critical and Exegetical Commentary on the Epistle to the Romans*. The International Critical Commentary. Edinburgh: T&T Clark, 1975–1979.

Cremer, Hermann. *Biblisch-theologisches Wörterbuch der neutestamentlichen Gräcität*. Gotha: Perthes, 1872.

———. *Die paulinische Rechtfertigungslehre im Zusammenhange ihrer geschichtlichen Voraussetzungen*. Gütersloh: Bertelsmann, 1900.

Cross, Frank M. "Notes on the Doctrine of the Two Messiahs at Qumran and the Extra-Canonical Daniel Apocalypse (4Q246)." In *Current Research and Technological Developments on the Dead Sea Scrolls: Conference on the Texts from the Judean Desert, Jerusalem, 30 April 1995*, edited by Donald W. Parry and Stephen D. Ricks, 1–13. Leiden: Brill, 1996.

Cullmann, Oscar. *The Christology of the New Testament*. Translated by Shirley C. Guthrie and Charles A. M. Hall. Philadelphia: Westminster Press, 1959.

Cummins, Stephen A. "Divine Life and Corporate Christology: God, Messiah Jesus, and the Covenant Community in Paul." In *The Messiah in the Old Testament and New Testament*, edited by Stanley E. Porter, 190–209. Grand Rapids: Eerdmans, 2007.

Dahl, Nils A. *The Crucified Messiah, and Other Essays*. Minneapolis: Augsburg, 1974.

———. *Jesus the Christ: The Historical Origins of Christological Doctrine*. Edited by Donald Juel. Minneapolis: Fortress Press, 1991.

———. *Studies in Paul: Theology for the Early Christian Mission*. Minneapolis: Augsburg Publishing House, 1977.

Das, A. Andrew. *Paul and the Stories of Israel: Grand Thematic Narratives in Galatians*. Minneapolis: Fortress Press, 2016.

———. *Paul, the Law, and the Covenant*. Peabody, MA: Hendrickson, 2001.

Davenport, Gene L. "The 'Anointed of the Lord' in Psalms and Solomon 17." In *Ideal Figures in Ancient Judaism: Profiles and Paradigms*, edited by John J. Collins and George W. E. Nickelsburg, 67–92. Chico, CA: Scholars Press, 1980.

Davies, Glenn N. *Faith and Obedience in Romans: A Study in Romans 1–4*. Sheffield: JSOT Press, 1980.

Davies, W. D. *Paul and Rabbinic Judaism: Some Rabbinic Elements in Pauline Theology*. Philadelphia: Fortress Press, 1948.

Day, John. "The Canaanite Inheritance of the Israelite Monarchy." In *King and Messiah in Israel and the Ancient Near East: Proceedings of the Oxford Old Testament Seminar*, edited by John Day, 72–90. Journal for the Study of the Old Testament Supplement Series 270. Sheffield: Sheffield Academic, 1998.

———. *The Psalms*. Sheffield: JSOT Press, 1990.

DeClaissé, Nancy L., Rolf A. Jacobson, and Beth LaNeel Tanner. *The Book of Psalms*. New International Greek Testament Commentary. Grand Rapids: Eerdmans, 2014.

Deissmann, A. *Bible Studies*. Translated by A. Grieve. Edinburgh: T&T Clark, 1901.

de Jonge, Marinus. "Christian Influence in the Testaments of the Twelve Patriarchs." *Novum Testamentum* 4.3 (July 1960) 182–235.

———. "The Expectation of the Future in the Psalms of Solomon." *Neotestamentica* 23.1 (1989) 93–117.

———. "Jesus' Death for Others and the Death of the Maccabean martyrs." In *Text and Testimony: Essays on New Testament and Apocryphal Literature in Honour of A. F. J. Klijn*, edited by T. Baarda et al., 142–151. Kampen, Netherlands: J. H. Kok, 1988.

———. "Two Messiahs in the Testaments of the Twelve Patriarchs." In *Tradition and Re-interpretation in Jewish and Early Christian Literature: Essays in Honour of Jürgen C. H. Lebram*, edited by J. W. Van Henten et al., 150–62. Leiden: Brill, 1986.

———. "The Use of the Word 'Anointed' in the Time of Jesus." *Novum Testamentum* 8 (1966) 132–48.

de Jonge, Marinus, and Adam S. van der Woude. "11QMelchizedek and the New Testament." *New Testament Studies* 12.4 (July 1966) 301–26.

Dell, Katharine J. "The King in the Wisdom Literature." In *King and Messiah in Israel and the Ancient Near East: Proceedings of the Oxford Old Testament Seminar*, edited by John Day, 163–86. Journal for the Study of the Old Testament Supplement Series 270. Sheffield: Sheffield Academic, 1998.

De Villiers, Pieter G. R. "The Messiah and Messiahs in Jewish Apocalyptic." *Neotestamentica* 12 (1978) 75–100.

de Vries, Simon J. *1 Kings*. Word Biblical Commentary 12. Nashville: Thomas Nelson Publishers, 2003.

Dodd, C. H. *The Bible and the Greeks*. London: Hodder & Stoughton, 1935.

———. *The Epistle of Paul to the Romans*. New York: Harper & Row, 1932.

Donaldson, Terence L. *Paul and the Gentiles: Remapping the Apostle's Convictional World*. Minneapolis: Fortress, 1997.

Duling, Dennis C. "Promises to David and Their Entrance into Christianity: Nailing Down a Likely Hypothesis." *New Testament Studies* 20.1 (October 1973) 55–77.

Dunn, James D. G. "Christology as an Aspect of Theology." In *The Christ and the Spirit: Collected Essays: Christology*, 1:377–87. Edinburgh: T&T Clark, 1998.

———. *Christology in the Making: A New Testament Inquiry into the Origins of the Doctrine of the Incarnation*. Grand Rapids: Eerdmans, 1996.

———. *Did the First Christians Worship Jesus? The New Testament Evidence*. Louisville: Westminster John Knox, 2010.

———. "How Controversial Was Paul's Christology?" In *The Christ and the Spirit: Collected Essays: Christology*, 1:212–28. Edinburgh: T&T Clark, 1998.

———. "Jesus—Flesh and Spirit: An Exposition of Romans 1:3-4." *The Journal of Theological Studies* 24.1 (April 1973) 40-68.

———. "Jesus the Judge: Further Thoughts of Paul's Christology and Soteriology." In *The New Perspective on Paul: Collected Essays*, 389-406. Wissenschaftliche Untersuchungen zum Neuen Testament 185. Tübingen: Mohr Siebeck, 2005.

———. *The New Perspective on Paul: Collected Essays*. Wissenschaftliche Untersuchungen zum Neuen Testament 185. Tübingen: Mohr Siebeck, 2007.

———. *Romans 1-8*. Word Biblical Commentary 36A. Dallas: Word Books, 1988.

———. *Romans 9-16*. Word Biblical Commentary 36B. Dallas: Word Books, 1988.

———. *The Theology of Paul the Apostle*. Grand Rapids: Eerdmans, 1998.

———. "Works of the Law and the Curse of the Law (Galatians 3.10-14)." *New Testament Studies* 31.4 (October 1985) 523-42.

Du Toit, Andreas B. "Romans 1, 3-4 and the Gospel Tradition: A Re-assessment of the Phrase kata pneuma hagiōsynēs." In *The Four Gospels 1992: Festschrift Frans Neirynck*, edited by F. Van Segbroeck, 249-56. Leuven: Leuven University Press, 1992.

Eaton. J. H. *Kingship and the Psalms*. London: SCM, 1976.

Ehrman, Bart D. *How Jesus Became God: The Exaltation of a Jewish Preacher from Galilee*. New York: HarperOne, 2014.

Eichrodt, Walther. *Ezekiel: A Commentary*. Translated by Cosslett Quin. The Old Testament Library. Philadelphia: Westminster Press, 1970.

———. *Theology of the Old Testament*. Translated by J. A. Baker. Philadelphia: Westminster, 1961-67.

Eissfeldt, Otto. "The Promise of Grace to David in Isaiah 55:1-5." In *Israel's Prophetic Heritage: Essays in Honor of James Muilenburg*, edited by B. W. Anderson and W. Harrelson, 196-207. London: SCM 1962.

Elliot, Neil. *The Rhetoric of Romans: Argumentative Constraint and Strategy, and Paul's Dialogue with Judaism*. Journal for the Study of the New Testament Supplement Series 45. Sheffield: Sheffield Academic, 1990.

Engberg-Pedersen, Troels. *Paul and the Stoics*. Edinburgh: T&T Clark, 2000.

Eskola, Timo. *Messiah and the Throne: Jewish Merkabah Mysticism and Early Christian Exaltation Discourse*. Wissenschaftliche Untersuchungen zum Neuen Testament 142. Tübingen: Mohr Siebeck, 2001.

———. *Theodicy and Predestination in Pauline Soteriology*. Wissenschaftliche Untersuchungen zum Neuen Testament 2.100. Tübingen: Mohr Siebeck, 1998.

Evans, Craig A. *Jesus and His Contemporaries: Comparative Studies*. Arbeiten zur Geschichte des antiken Judentums und des Urchristentums 25. Leiden: Brill, 1995.

———. "The Messiah in the Dead Sea Scrolls." In *Israel's Messiah in the Bible and the Dead Sea Scrolls*, edited by Richard S. Hess and M. Daniel Carroll R., 85-102. Grand Rapids: Baker Books, 2003.

———. "'The Two Sons of Oil': Early Evidence of Messianic Interpretation of Zechariah 4:14 in 4Q254 4 2." In *The Provo International Conference on the Dead Sea Scrolls: Technological Innovations, New Texts, and Reformulated Issues*, edited by Donald W. Parry and Eugene C. Ulrich, 566-75. Leiden: Brill, 1999.

Fee, Gordon D. *Pauline Christology: An Exegetical-theological Study*. Peabody, MA: Hendrickson, 2007.

Fitzmyer, Joseph A. *According to Paul: Studies in the Theology of the Apostle*. New York: Paulist, 1993.

———. "The Christology of the Epistle to the Romans." In *The Future of Christology: Essays in Honor of Leander E Keck*, edited by Abraham J. Malherbe and Wayne A. Meeks, 81–90. Minneapolis: Fortress, 1993.

———. *The One Who is to Come*. Grand Rapids: Eerdmans, 2007.

———. *Romans: A New Translation with Introduction and Commentary*. Anchor Bible 33. New York: Doubleday, 1993.

———. *Scripture and Christology: A Statement of the Biblical Commission with a Commentary*. New York: Paulist, 1986.

Fitzmyer, Joseph A., Jerome D. Quinn, and John H. P. Reumann. *"Righteousness" in the New Testament: "Justification" in the United States Lutheran-Roman Catholic Dialogue*. Philadelphia: Fortress, 1982.

Fredriksen, Paula. "From Jesus to Christ: The Contribution of Paul." In *Jews and Christians Speak of Jesus*, edited by Arthur E. Zannoni, 77–92. Minneapolis: Fortress, 1994.

———. *Jesus of Nazareth: King of the Jews*. New York: Vintage, 1999.

Frost, Stanley B. *Old Testament Apocalyptic*. London: Epworth Press, 1952.

Fuller, Michael E. "The Davidic Messiah in Early Jewish Literature." In *The Spirit and the Mind: Essays in Informed Pentecostalism*, edited by T. L. Cross and E. B. Powery, 65–86. Lanham, MD: University Press of America, 2000.

Fuller, Reginald H. *The Foundations of New Testament Christology*. London: Lutterworth, 1965.

Gager, John. *The Origins of Anti-Semitism: Attitudes Towards Judaism in Pagan and Christian Antiquity*. New York: Oxford University Press, 1983.

———. *Reinventing Paul*. New York: Oxford University Press, 2000.

Galington, Don B. *Faith, Obedience, and Perseverance: Aspects of Paul's Letter to the Romans*. Wissenschaftliche Untersuchungen zum Neuen Testament 79. Tübingen: J. C. B. Mohr, 1994.

———. "Israel's Triumphant King: Romans 1:5 and the Scriptures of Israel." In *Jesus and Paul: Global Perspectives in Honor of James D.G. Dunn for His 70th Birthday*, edited by B. J. Oropeza, C. K. Robertson, and Douglas C. Mohrmann, 173–83. London: T&T Clark, 2009.

Gaston, Lloyd. "Paul and the Torah." In *Antisemitism and the Foundations of Christianity*, edited by Alan Davies, 48–71. New York: Paulist Press, 1979.

———. *Paul and the Torah*. Vancouver: University of British Columbia Press, 1987.

Gathercole, Simon J. "Justified by Faith, Justified by His Blood: The Evidence of Romans 3:21–4:25." In *Justification and Variegated Nomism*, edited by D. A. Carson, Peter T. O'Brien, and Mark A. Seifrid, 2:147–84. Wissenschaftliche Untersuchungen zum Neuen Testament 2.140. Grand Rapids: Baker, 2004.

Gillingham, Susan. E. "The Messiah in the Psalms: A Question of Reception History and the Psalter." In *King and Messiah in Israel and the Ancient Near East: Proceedings of the Oxford Old Testament Seminar*, edited by John Day, 209–37. Journal for the Study of the Old Testament Supplement Series 270. Sheffield: Sheffield Academic, 1998.

Goldingay, John. *A Critical and Exegetical Commentary on Isaiah 40–55*. The International Critical Commentary. London: T&T Clark, 2006.

Goldstein, Jonathan A. "How the Authors of 1 and 2 Maccabees Treated the 'Messianic' Promises." In *Judaisms and Their Messiahs at the Turn of the Christian Era*, edited by Jacob Neusner, William Scott Green, and Ernest Freichs, 69-96. Cambridge: Cambridge University, 1987.

Gray, John. *The Biblical Doctrine of the Reign of God*. Edinburgh: T&T Clark, 1979.

———. *The Legacy of Canaan: The Ras Shamra Texts and Their Relevance to the Old Testament*. Leiden: Brill, 1965.

Grelot, Pierre. "Sur Isaïe LXI: La première consécration d'un grand-prêtre." *Revue Biblique* 97.3 (July 1990) 414-31.

Haacker, Klaus. *Der Brief des Paulus an die Römer*. Theologischer Handkommentar zum Neuen Testament 6. Leipzig: Evangelische Verlagsanstalt, 1999.

Hafemann, Scott J. *Paul, Moses, and the History of Israel: The Letter/Spirit Contrast and the Argument from Scripture in 2 Corinthians 3*. Wissenschaftliche Untersuchungen zum Neuen Testament 81. Tübingen: J. C. B. Mohr, 1995.

Hägglund, Fredrik. *Isaiah 53 in the Light of Homecoming after Exile*. Tübingen, Mohr Siebeck, 2008.

Hahn, Ferdinand. *The Titles of Jesus in Christology: Their History in Early Christianity*. London: Lutterworth Press, 1969.

Hahn, Robert R. "Christos kyrios in PsSol 17:32: 'The Lord's Anointed' Reconsidered." *New Testament Studies* 31.4 (October 1985) 620-27.

Halpern, Baruch. *The Constitution of the Monarchy in Israel*. Chico, CA: Scholars Press, 1981.

Hamilton, Mark W. *The Body Royal: The Social Poetics of Kingship in Ancient Israel*. Biblical Interpretation Series 78. Leiden: Brill, 2005.

Hansen, G. Walter. *Abraham in Galatians: Epistolary and Rhetorical Contexts*. Journal for the Study of the New Testament: Supplement Series 29. Sheffield: Sheffield Academic, 1989.

Hanson, Paul D. "Messiahs and Messianic Figures in Proto-Apocalypticism." In *The Messiah: Developments in Earliest Judaism and Christianity*, edited by James H. Charlesworth, 67-75. Minneapolis: Fortress, 1992.

———. "The World of the Servant of the Lord in Isaiah 40-55." In *Jesus and the Suffering Servant: Isaiah 53 and Christian Origins*, edited by William H. Bellinger Jr. and William R. Farmer, 9-22. Harrisburg, PA: Trinity Press, 1998.

Haran, Menahem. *Temples and Temple Service in Ancient Israel: An Inquiry into the Character of Cult Phenomena and the Historical Setting of the Priestly School*. Oxford: Clarendon, 1979.

Harvey, Anthony B. *Jesus and the Constraints of History*. London: Duckworth, 1982.

Hawthorne, Gerald, ed. *Current Issues in Biblical and Patristic Interpretation: Studies in Honor of Merrill C. Tenney Presented by His Former Students*. Grand Rapids: Eerdmans, 1975.

Hay, David M. *Glory at the Right Hand: Psalm 110 in Early Christianity*. Society of Biblical Literature Monograph Series 18. Nashville: Abingdon, 1973.

Hays, Richard B. "Christ Prays the Psalms: Paul's Use of an Early Christian Exegetical Convention." In *The Future of Christology: Essays in Honor of Leander E. Keck*, edited by Abraham J. Malherbe and Wayne A. Meeks, 122-36. Minneapolis: Fortress, 1993.

———. *Echoes of Scripture in the Letters of Paul*. New Haven, CT: Yale University Press, 1989.

———. *The Faith of Jesus Christ: The Narrative Substructure of Galatians 3:1-4:11*. Grand Rapids: Eerdmans, 2002.

———. "'Have We Found Abraham to Be Our Forefather according to the Flesh?' A Reconsideration of Rom 4:1." *Novum Testamentum* 27.1 (January 1985) 76–98.
———. "Πίστις and Pauline Christology: What Is at Stake?" In *The Faith of Jesus Christ*, 272–97. Grand Rapids: Eerdmans, 2002.
Heliso, Desta. *Pistis and the Righteous One: A Study of Romans 1:17 against the Background of Scripture and Second Temple Jewish Literature*. Wissenschaftliche Untersuchungen zum Neuen Testament 2.235. Tübingen: Mohr Siebeck, 2007.
Hengel, Martin. *Between Jesus and Paul: Studies in the Earliest History of Christianity*. Translated by John Bowden. London: SCM, 1983.
———. *Judaism and Hellenism: Studies in Their Encounter in Palestine during the Early Hellenistic Period*. Translated by John Bowden. London: SCM, 1991.
———. *The Pre-Christian Paul*. Translated by John Bowden. Philadelphia: Trinity Press International, 1991.
———. "Sit at My Right Hand!" In *Studies in Early Christology*, 119–226. Edinburgh: T&T Clark, 1995.
———. *The Son of God: The Origin of Christology and the History of Jewish-Hellenistic Religion*. Translated by John Bowden. Philadelphia: Fortress, 1976.
———. *Studies in Early Christology*. Edinburgh: T&T Clark, 1995.
Hengel, Martin, Anna Maria Schwemer, and Ernst Axel Knauf. *Paulus zwischen Damaskus und Antiochien: die unbekannten Jahre des Apostels*. Tübingen: Mohr Siebeck, 1998.
Hengel, Martin, and D. Bailey. "The Effective History of Isaiah 53 in the Pre-Christian Period." In *The Suffering Servant: Isaiah 53 in Jewish and Christian Sources*, translated by Daniel P. Bailey, edited by Bernd Janowski and Peter Stuhlmacher, 75–146. Grand Rapids: Eerdmans, 2004.
Hengstenberg, Ernst W. *Christology of the Old Testament and a Commentary on the Messianic Predictions*. Grand Rapids: Kregel Publications, 1970.
Hermisson, Hans-Jürgen. "The Fourth Servant Song in the Context of Second Isaiah." In *The Suffering Servant: Isaiah 53 in Jewish and Christian Sources*, translated by Daniel P. Bailey, edited by Bernd Janowski and Peter Stuhlmacher, 16–47. Grand Rapids: Eerdmans, 2004.
Hertzberg, Hans W. *I & II Samuel*. Translated by J. S. Bowden. The Old Testament Library. Philadelphia: Westminster Press, 1964.
Heskett, Randall. *Messianism within the Scriptural Scrolls of Isaiah*. Library of Hebrew Bible/Old Testament Studies 456. London: T&T Clark, 2007.
Hess, Richard S. "The Image of the Messiah in the Old Testament." In *Images of Christ: Ancient and Modern*, edited by Stanley E. Porter, Michael A. Hayes, and David Tombs, 22–33. Sheffield: Sheffield Academic, 1997.
———. "Messiahs Here and There." In *Israel's Messiah in the Bible and the Dead Sea Scrolls*, edited by Richard S. Hess and M. Daniel Carroll R., 103–8. Grand Rapids: Baker Books, 2003.
Higgins, A. J. B. "Priestly Messiah." *New Testament Studies* 13.3 (April 1967) 221–39.
Hill, Wesley. *Paul and the Trinity: Persons, Relations, and the Pauline Letters*. Grand Rapids: Eerdmans, 2015.
Ho, Ahuva. *Ṣedeq and Ṣedaqah in the Hebrew Bible*. New York: Peter Lang, 1991.
Hofius, Otfried. *Paulusstudien*. Wissenschaftliche Untersuchungen zum Neuen Testament 51. Tübingen: J. C. B. Mohr, 1989.

Horbury, William. *Herodian Judaism and New Testament Study*. Wissenschaftliche Untersuchungen zum Neuen Testament 193. Tübingen: Mohr Siebeck, 2006.

———. "Jewish and Christian Monotheism in the Herodian Age." In *Early Jewish and Christian Monotheism*, edited by Loren T. Stuckenbruck and Wendy E. S. North, 16–44. London: T&T Clark, 2004.

———. *Jewish Messianism and the Cult of Christ*. London: SCM, 1998.

———. *Messianism among Jews and Christians: Twelve Biblical and Historical Studies*. London: T&T Clark, 2003.

———. "Messianism in the Old Testament Apocrypha and Pseudepigrapha." In *King and Messiah in Israel and the Ancient Near East: Proceedings of the Oxford Old Testament Seminar*, edited by John Day, 402–33. Journal for the Study of the Old Testament Supplement Series 270. Sheffield: Sheffield Academic, 1998.

———. "Monarchy and Messianism in the Greek Pentateuch." In *The Septuagint and Messianism*, edited by Michael A. Knibb, 79–128. Bibliotheca Ephemeridum Theologicarum Lovaniensium 195. Leuven: Leuven University; Paris; Dudley: Peeters, 2006.

Horsley, Richard A. "Palestinian Jewish Groups and Their Messiahs in Late Second Temple Times." In *Messianism through History*, edited by Wim Beuken, Seán Freyne, and Antonius Weller, 14–29. London: SCM, 1993.

Houston, Walter. *Contending for Justice: Ideologies and Theologies of Social Justice in the Old Testament*. Library of Hebrew Bible/Old Testament Studies 428. London: T&T Clark, 2006.

Hugenberger, Gordon. "The Servant of the Lord in the 'Servant Songs' of Isaiah: A Second Moses Figure." In *The Lord's Anointed: Interpretation of Old Testament Messianic Texts*, edited by Gordon J. Wenham, Richard S. Hess, and Philip E. Satterthwaite, 105–40. Grand Rapids: Baker, 1995.

Hultgren, Arland J. *Paul's Letter to the Romans*. Grand Rapids: Eerdmans, 2011.

Hunter, A. M. *Paul and His Predecessors*. London: SCM, 1961.

Hurtado, Larry W. "Jesus' Divine Sonship in Paul's Epistle to the Romans." In *Romans and the People of God: Essays in Honor of Gordon D. Fee on the Occasion of His 65th Birthday*, edited by Sven K. Soderlund and N. T. Wright, 217–33. Grand Rapids: Eerdmans, 1999.

———. *Lord Jesus Christ: Devotion to Jesus in Earliest Christianity*. Grand Rapids: Eerdmans, 2003.

———. *One God, One Lord: Early Christian Devotion and Ancient Jewish Monotheism*. Edinburgh: T&T Clark, 1998.

Irons, Chales L. *The Righteousness of God: A Lexical Examination of the Covenant-Faithfulness Interpretation*. Wissenschaftliche Untersuchungen zum Neuen Testament 2.386. Tübingen: Mohr Siebeck, 2015.

Janowski, Bernd. *Sühne als Heilsgeschehen: Studien zur Sühnetheologie der Priesterschrift und zur Wurzel KPR im Alten Orient und im Alten Testament*. Neukirchen-Vluyn: Neukirchener, 1982.

Jeremías, Joachim. *New Testament Theology*. Translated by John Bowden. New York: Scriber, 1971.

Jewett, Robert. "The Redaction and Use of an Early Christian Confession in Romans 1:3–4." In *The Living Text: Essays in Honor of Ernest W. Saunders*, edited by Dennis E. Groh and Robert Jewett, 99–122. Lanham, MD: University Press of America, 1985.

———. Romans. Hermeneia. Minneapolis: Fortress, 2007.
Jipp, Joshua W. "Ancient, Modern, and Future Interpretations of Romans 1:3-4: Reception History and Biblical Interpretation." *Journal of Theological Interpretation* 3 (Fall 2009) 241-59.
———. *Christ Is King: Paul's Royal Ideology*. Minneapolis: Fortress, 2015.
Johnson, Elliott E. "Hermeneutical Principles and the Interpretation of Psalm 110." *Bibliotheca Sacra* 149.596 (1992) 428-37.
Johnson, Luke T. "Rom 3:21-26 and the Faith of Jesus." *The Catholic Biblical Quarterly* 44.1 (January 1982) 77-90.
Joyce, Paul. "King and Messiah in Ezekiel." In *King and Messiah in Israel and the Ancient Near East: Proceedings of the Oxford Old Testament Seminar*, edited by John Day, 323-37. Journal for the Study of the Old Testament Supplement Series 270. Sheffield: Sheffield Academic, 1998.
Juel, Donald H. *Messianic Exegesis: Christological Interpretation of the Old Testament in Early Christianity*. Philadelphia: Fortress, 1988.
Kaiser, Otto. *Isaiah 1-12*. Translated by John Bowden. The Old Testament Library. Philadelphia: Westminster, 1972.
Kaiser, Walter C., Jr. *The Messiah in the Old Testament*. Grand Rapids: Zondervan, 1995.
Käsemann, Ernst. *Commentary on Romans*. Translated by Geoffrey W. Bromiley. Grand Rapids: Eerdmans, 1980.
———. "'The Righteousness of God' in Paul." In *New Testament Questions of Today*, 168-82. Philadelphia: Fortress, 1969.
———. *New Testament Questions of Today*. Translated by W. J. Montague. Philadelphia, Fortress, 1969.
Keck, Leander E. "Christology, Soteriology, and the Praise of God (Romans 15:7-13)." In *The Conversation Continues: Studies in Paul & John in Honor of J. Louis Martyn*, edited by Robert T. Fortna and Beverly R. Gaventa, 85-97. Nashville: Abingdon, 1990.
———. "'Jesus' in Romans." *Journal of Biblical Literature* 108.3 (1989) 443-60.
Keesmaat, Sylvia C. *Paul and His Story: (Re)Interpreting the Exodus Tradition*. Journal for the Study of the New Testament Supplement Series 181. Sheffield: Sheffield Academic Press, 1999.
Kim, Seyoon. "Jesus the Son of God as the Gospel (1 Thess 1:9-10 and Rom 1:3-4)." In *Earliest Christian History: History, Literature, and Theology: Essays from the Tyndale Fellowship in Honor of Martin Hengel*, edited by Michael F. Bird, Martin Hengel, and Jason Maston, 117-141. Wissenschaftliche Untersuchungen zum Neuen Testament 2.320. Tübingen: Mohr Siebeck, 2012.
———. *The Origin of Paul's Gospel*. Wissenschaftliche Untersuchungen zum Neuen Testament 4. Tübingen: J. C. B. Mohr, 1981.
Klauck, Hans-Josef. *4 Makkabäerbuch: Jüdische Schriften aus hellenistisch-römischer Zeit*. Gütersloh: Gütersloher Verlagshaus Gerd Mohn, 1989.
Klausner, Joseph. *The Messianic Idea in Israel: From Its Beginning to the Completion of the Mishnah*. Translated by W. F. Stinespring. New York: Macmillan, 1955.
Knibb, Michael A. "Eschatology and Messianism in the Dead Sea Scrolls." In *The Dead Sea Scrolls After Fifty Years: A Comprehensive Assessment*, edited by Peter W. Flint and James C. VanderKam, 379-402. Leiden: Brill, 1998.
———. "The Septuagint and Messianism: Problems and Issues." In *The Septuagint and Messianism*, edited by M. A. Knibb, 3-19. Leuven: Leuven University Press, 2006.

Knight, George A. *Servant Theology: A Commentary on the Book of Isaiah 40–55*. Grand Rapids: Eerdmans, 1984.

Knoppers, Gary N. "David's Relation to Moses: The Contexts, Content and Conditions of the Davidic Promises." In *King and Messiah in Israel and the Ancient Near East: Proceedings of the Oxford Old Testament Seminar*, edited by John Day, 91–118. Journal for the Study of the Old Testament Supplement Series 270. Sheffield: Sheffield Academic, 1998.

Kobelski, Paul J. *Melchizedek and Melchireša*. Washington, DC: Catholic Biblical Association of America, 1981.

Konradt, Matthias. *Gericht und Gemeinde: Eine Studie zur Bedeutung und Funktion von Gerichtsaussagen im Rahmen der paulinischen Ekklesiologie und Ethik im 1 Thess und 1 Kor*. Berlin: Walter de Gruyter, 2003.

Koole, Jan L. *Isaiah III*. Translated by Anthony P. Runia. Leuven: Peeters, 1998.

Kraft, Robert A. "Setting the Stage and Framing Some Central Questions." *Journal for the Study of Judaism in the Persian, Hellenistic and Roman Period* 32 (2001) 371–95.

Kramer, Werner. *Christ, Lord, Son of God*. Translated by Brian Hardy. London: SCM, 1966.

Kraus, Hans-Joachim. *Psalms 60–150*. Translated by Hilton C. Oswald. Minneapolis: Augsburg, 1989.

Kraus, Wolfgang. *Der Tod Jesu als Heiligtumsweihe: eine Untersuchung zum Umfeld der Sühnevorstellung in Römer 3,25–26a*. Wissenschaftliche Monographien zum Alten und Neuen Testament 66. Neukirchen-Vluyn: Neukirchener Verlag, 1991.

Kvanvig, Helge S. "The Son of Man in the Parables of Enoch." In *Enoch and the Messiah Son of Man: Revisiting the Book of Parables*, edited by Gabriele Boccaccini, 179–215. Grand Rapids: Eerdmans, 2007.

Laato, Antti. *A Star is Rising: The Historical Development of the Old Testament Royal Ideology and the Rise of the Jewish Messianic Expectations*. Atlanta: Scholars Press, 1997.

Leclerc, Thomas L. *Yahweh is Exalted in Justice: Solidarity and Conflict in Isaiah*. Minneapolis: Fortress, 2001.

Lee, Aquila H. I. *From Messiah to Preexistent Son: Jesus' Self-consciousness and Early Christian Exegesis of Messianic Psalms*. Wissenschaftliche Untersuchungen zum Neuen Testament 2. 192. Tübingen: Mohr Siebeck, 2005.

Levine, Baruch A. *Numbers 21–36*. Anchor Bible 4A. New York: Doubleday, 2000.

Lichtenberger, Hermann. "Messianic Expectations and Messianic Figures." In *Qumran-Messianism: Studies on the Messianic Expectations in the Dead Sea Scrolls*, edited by James H. Charlesworth, Hermann Lichtenberger, and Gerbern S. Oegema, 9–20. Tübingen: Mohr, 1998.

Lincoln, Andrew. "A Life of Jesus as Testimony: The Divine Courtroom and the Gospel of John." In *Divine Courtroom in Comparative Perspective*, edited by Ari Mermelstein and Shalom E. Holtz, 145–66. Leiden: Brill, 2015.

Lindblom, Johannes. *The Servant Songs in Deutero-Isaiah: A New Attempt to Solve an Old Problem*. Lund: Gleerup, 1951.

Loader, William R. G. "Christ at the Right Hand: Ps 110:1 in the New Testament." *New Testament Studies* 24.2 (1978) 199–217.

Longenecker, Richard N. *The Christology of Early Jewish Christianity*. London: SCM, 1970.

———. *Contours of Christology in the New Testament*. Grand Rapids: Eerdmans, 2005.

———. *The Epistle to the Romans: A Commentary on the Greek Text*. New International Greek Testament Commentary. Grand Rapids: Eerdmans, 2016.

Longman, Tremper, III. "The Messiah: Explorations in the Law and Writings." In *The Messiah in the Old Testament and New Testament*, edited by Stanley Porter, 13–34. Grand Rapids: Eerdmans, 2007.

Lucass, Shirley. *The Concept of the Messiah in the Scriptures of Judaism and Christianity*. The Library of Second Temple Studies 78. London: T&T Clark, 2011.

Lundbom, Jack R. *Jeremiah*. Anchor Bible 21A. New York: Doubleday, 1999.

Lust, J. *Messianism and the Septuagint: Collected Essays*. Leuven: Leuven University Press, 2004.

Mack, Burton L. "Wisdom Makes a Difference." In *Judaisms and Their Messiahs at the Turn of the Christian Era*, edited by Jacob Neusner, William Scott Green, and Ernest Freichs, 15–48. Cambridge: Cambridge University, 1987.

MacLeod, David J. "Eternal Son, Davidic Son, Messianic Son: An Exposition of Romans 1:1–7." *Bibliotheca Sacra* 162.645 (January/March 2005) 76–94.

MacRae, George. "Messiah and Gospel." In *Judaisms and Their Messiahs at the Turn of the Christian Era*, edited by Jacob Neusner, William Scott Green, and Ernest Freichs, 169–86. Cambridge: Cambridge University, 1987.

Malchow, Bruce V. *Social Justice in the Hebrew Bible*. Collegeville, MN: Liturgical Press, 1996.

Marcus, Joel. *The Way of the Lord: Christological Exegesis of the Old Testament in the Gospel of Mark*. Louisville: Westminster, 1992.

Marshall, I. Howard. *The Origins of New Testament Christology*. Downers Grove, IL: InterVarsity Press, 1976.

Martínez, Florentino G. *The Dead Sea Scrolls Translated: The Qumran Texts in English*. Leiden: Brill, 1996.

———. "Two Messianic Figures in the Qumran Texts." In *Current Research and Technological Developments on the Dead Sea Scrolls: Conference on the Texts from the Judean Desert, Jerusalem, 30 April 1995*, edited by Donald W. Parry and Stephen D. Ricks, 14–40. Leiden: Brill, 1996.

Martínez, Florentino G., and Eibert J. C. Tigchelaar, eds. *The Dead Sea Scrolls Study Edition*. Leiden: Brill, 2000.

Martyn, J. Louis. *Galatians: A New Translation with Introduction and Commentary*. Anchor Bible 33A. New York: Doubleday, 1997.

Mason, Rex. "The Messiah in the Postexilic Old Testament Literature." In *King and Messiah in Israel and the Ancient Near East: Proceedings of the Oxford Old Testament Seminar*, edited by John Day, 338–64. Journal for the Study of the Old Testament Supplement Series 270. Sheffield: Sheffield Academic, 1998.

McConville, J. G. "Messianic Interpretation of the Old Testament in Modern Context." In *The Lord's Anointed: Interpretation of Old Testament Messianic Texts*, edited by Gordon J. Wenham, Richard S. Hess, and Philip E. Satterthwaite, 1–18. Grand Rapids: Baker, 1995.

McFadden, Kevin W. *Judgment According to Works in Romans*. Minneapolis: Fortress, 2013.

Melugin, Roy F. "On Reading Isaiah 53 as Christian Scripture." In *Jesus and the Suffering Servant: Isaiah 53 and Christian Origins*, edited by William H. Bellinger Jr. and William R. Farmer, 55–69. Harrisburg, PA: Trinity Press, 1998.

Merrill, Eugene H. "The Book of Ruth: Narration and Shared Themes." *Bibliotheca Sacra* 142.566 (April/June 1985) 130–41.

———. "Royal Priesthood: An Old Testament Messianic Motif." *Bibliotheca Sacra* 150.597 (January/March 1993) 50–61.

Miller, Merrill P. "Function of Isa 61:1–2 in 11QMelchizedek." *Journal of Biblical Literature* 88.4 (December 1969) 467–69.

Miller, Patrick D. "Moses My Servant: The Deuteronomic Portrait of Moses." *Interpretation* 41.3 (July 1987) 244–55.

Mitchell, David. *The Message of the Psalter: An Eschatological Programme in the Book of Psalms*. Journal for the Study of the Old Testament Supplement Series 252. Sheffield: Sheffield Academic, 1997.

Moo, Douglas J. *The Epistle to the Romans*. New International Commentary on the New Testament. Grand Rapids: Eerdmans, 1996.

Morris, Leon. *The Apostolic Preaching of the Cross*. Grand Rapids: Eerdmans, 1965.

———. *The Epistle to the Romans*. Grand Rapids: Eerdmans, 1988.

Motyer, J. A. *The Prophecy of Isaiah: An Introduction & Commentary*. Downers Grove, IL: InterVarsity Press, 1993.

Mounce, Robert H. *Romans*. The New American Commentary 27. Nashville: Broadman & Holman, 1995.

Mowinckel, Sigmund. *He That Cometh: The Messiah Concept in the Old Testament and Later Judaism*. Translated by G. W. Anderson. New York: Abingdon, 1954.

Muller, Christian. *Gottes Gerechtigkeit und Gottes Volk: Eine Untersuchung zu Römer 9–11*. Forschungen zur Religion und Literatur des Alten und Neuen Testaments 86. Göttingen: Vandenhoeck & Ruprecht, 1964.

Newman, Carey C. *Paul's Glory-Christology: Tradition and Rhetoric*. Leiden: Brill, 1992.

Nickelsburg, George W. E. *Ancient Judaism and Christian Origins: Diversity, Continuity, and Transformation*. Minneapolis: Fortress, 2003.

———. *Resurrection, Immortality, and Eternal Life in Intertestamental Judaism*. Cambridge, MA: Harvard University Press, 1972.

———. "Salvation without and with a Messiah: Developing Beliefs in Writings Ascribed to Enoch." In *Judaisms and Their Messiahs at the Turn of the Christian Era*, edited by Jacob Neusner, William Scott Green, and Ernest Frerichs, 49–68. Cambridge: Cambridge University Press, 1987.

North, Christopher R. *The Second Isaiah: Introduction, Translation and Commentary to Chapter XL–LV*. Oxford: Clarendon Press 1964.

———. *The Suffering Servant in Deutero-Isaiah*. New York: Oxford University Press, 1949.

Noth, Martin. *Numbers: A Commentary*. Translated by James D. Martin. The Old Testament Library. Philadelphia: Westminster Press, 1968.

Novakovic, Lidija. "4Q521: The Works of the Messiah or the Signs of the Messianic Time?" In *Qumran Studies: New Approaches, New Questions*, edited by Michael Thomas Davis and Brent A. Strawn, 208–31. Cambridge; Grand Rapids: Eerdmans, 2007.

Novenson, Matthew. *Christ among the Messiahs: Christ Language in Paul and Messiah Language in Ancient Judaism*. New York: Oxford University, 2012.

O'Brien, Peter T. "Justification in Paul and Some Crucial Issues of the Last Two Decades." In *Right with God: Justification in the Bible and the World*, edited by D. A. Carson, 69–95. Grand Rapids: Eerdmans, 1992.

Oegema, Gerbern S. *The Anointed and His People: Messianic Expectations from the Maccabees to the Bar Kochba*. Sheffield: Sheffield Academic, 1998.

———. "Messianic Expectations in the Qumran Writings: Theses on Their Development." In *Qumran-Messianism: Studies on the Messianic Expectations in the Dead Sea Scrolls*, edited by James H. Charlesworth, Hermann Lichtenberger, and Gerbern S. Oegema, 52-82. Tübingen: Mohr Siebeck, 1998.

Oswalt, John N. *The Book of Isaiah: Chapters 40-66*. The New International Commentary on the Old Testament. Grand Rapids: Eerdmans, 1998.

Parry, Donald W., and Eugene C. Ulrich, eds. *The Provo International Conference on the Dead Sea Scrolls: Technological Innovations, New Texts, and Reformulated Issues*. Leiden: Brill, 1999.

Petersen, David L. *Haggai and Zechariah 1-8*. The Old Testament Library. Philadelphia; Westminster Press, 1984.

Phillips, Anthony. "The Servant: Symbol of Divine Powerlessness." *The Expository Time* 90.12 (September 1979) 370-74.

Piper, John. "The Demonstration of the Righteousness of God in Romans 3:25, 26." *Journal of the Study of the New Testament* 7 (1980) 2-32.

Pomykala, Kenneth. E. *The Davidic Dynasty Tradition in Early Judaism. Its History and Significance for Messianism*. Atlanta: Scholars Press, 1995.

Porter, Stanley E. "Allusion and Echoes," In *As It Is Written: Studying Paul's Use of Scripture*, edited by Stanley E. Porter and Christopher D. Stanley, 29-40. Atlanta: Society of Biblical Literature, 2008.

Porter, Stanley E., ed. *The Messiah in the Old and New Testaments*. Grand Rapids: Eerdmans, 2007.

Poythress, Vern. S. "Is Romans 1:3-4 a Pauline Confession after All." *The Expository Times* 87.6 (March 1976) 180-83.

Provan, Iain W. "The Messiah in the Books of Kings." In *The Lord's Anointed: Interpretation of Old Testament Messianic Texts*, edited by Gordon J. Wenham, Richard S. Hess, and Philip E. Satterthwaite, 67-86. Grand Rapids: Baker, 1995.

Puech, Émile. "Fragments d'un apocryphe de Lévi et le personnage eschatologique. 4QTestLévic-d(?) et 4QAJa." In *The Madrid Qumran Congress: Proceedings of the International Congress on the Dead Sea Scrolls. Madrid, 18-21 March 1991*, edited by Julio Trebolle Barrera and Luis Vegas Montaner, 449-501. Leiden: Brill, 1992.

———. *La croyance des esséniens en la vie future: immortalité, résurrection, vie éternelle?* Paris: J. Gabalda, 1993.

Reiser, Marius. *Jesus and Judgment: The Eschatological Proclamation in Its Jewish Context*. Minneapolis: Fortress, 1997.

Reventlow, Henning G. "Basic Issues in the Interpretation of Isaiah 53." In *Jesus and the Suffering Servant: Isaiah 53 and Christian Origins*, edited by William H. Bellinger Jr. and William R. Farmer, 23-38. Harrisburg, PA: Trinity Press, 1998.

Ridderbos, Herman N. *Paul: An Outline of His Theology*. Translated by J. R. DeWitt. Grand Rapids: Eerdmans, 1975.

Roberts, J. J. M. *First Isaiah: A Commentary*. Hermeneia. Minneapolis: Fortress, 2015.

———. "The Old Testament's Contribution to Messianic Expectations." In *The Messiah: Developments in Earliest Judaism and Christianity*, edited by James H. Charlesworth, 39-51. Minneapolis: Fortress, 1992.

Ropes, James H. "'Righteousness' and 'the Righteousness of God' in the Old Testament and in St. Paul." *Journal of Biblical Literature* 22.2 (1903) 211-27.

Rose, Wolter. *Zemah and Zerubbabel: Messianic Expectations in the Early Postexilic Period*. Journal for the Study of the Old Testament: Supplement Series 304. Sheffield: Sheffield Academic, 2000.

Roth, Wolfgang M. W. "The Anonymity of the Suffering Servant." *Journal of Biblical Literature* 83 (June 1964) 171–79.

Rowland, Christopher. *Christian Origins: An Account of the Setting and Character of the Most Important Messianic Sect of Judaism*. London: SPCK, 1985.

——— . *The Open Heaven: A Study of Apocalyptic in Judaism and Early Christianity*. New York: Crossroad, 1982.

Sanders, E. P. *Judaism: Practice and Belief*. Philadelphia: Trinity Press International, 1992.

——— . *Paul and Palestinian Judaism: A Comparison of Patterns of Religion*. Philadelphia: Fortress, 1977.

Sapp, David. "The LXX, 1QIsa, and MT Versions of Isaiah 53 and the Christian Doctrine of Atonement." In *Jesus and the Suffering Servant: Isaiah 53 and Christian Origins*, edited by William H. Bellinger Jr. and William R. Farmer, 170–92. Harrisburg, PA: Trinity Press International, 1998.

Satterthwaite, Philip E. "David in the Books of Samuel: A Messianic Expectation?" In *The Lord's Anointed: Interpretation of Old Testament Messianic Texts*, edited by Gordon J. Wenham, Richard S. Hess, and Philip E. Satterthwaite, 41–66. Grand Rapids: Baker, 1995.

Schaper, Joachim. *Eschatology in the Greek Psalter*. Wissenschaftliche Untersuchungen zum Neuen Testament 76. Tübingen: Mohr Siebeck, 1995.

Schlatter, Adolf von, and Siegfried S. Schatzmann. *Romans: The Righteousness of God*. Peabody, MA: Hendrickson, 1995.

Schliesser, Benjamin. *Abraham's Faith in Romans 4: Paul's Concept of Faith in Light of the History of Reception of Genesis 15:6*. Wissenschaftliche Untersuchungen zum Neuen Testament 2.224. Tübingen: Mohr Siebeck, 2007.

Schmid, H. H. "Creation, Righteousness, and Salvation: 'Creation Theology' as the Broad Horizon of Biblical Theology." In *Creation in the Old Testament*, edited by Bernhard W. Anderson, 102–17. Philadelphia: Fortress, 1984.

Schniedewind, William M. "Structural Aspects of Qumran Messianism in the Damascus Document." In *The Provo International Conference on the Dead Sea Scrolls: Technological Innovations, New Texts, and Reformulated Issues*, edited by Donald W. Parry and Eugene C. Ulrich, 523–36. Leiden: Brill, 1999.

Scholem, Gershom. *The Messianic Idea in Judaism and Other Essays on Jewish Spirituality*. New York: Schocken, 1971.

Schreiber, Stefan. *Gesalbter und König: Titel und Konzeptionen der königlichen Gesalbtenerwartung in frühjüdischen und urchristlichen Schriften*. New York; Berlin: De Gruyter, 2000.

Schreiner, Thomas R. *The Law and Its Fulfillment: A Pauline Theology of Law*. Grand Rapids: Baker Books, 1993.

——— . *Paul, Apostle of God's Glory in Christ: A Pauline Theology*. Downers Grove, IL: InterVarsity Press, 1991.

——— . *Romans*. Baker Exegetical Commentary on the New Testament. Grand Rapids: Baker Academic, 1998.

Schröter, Jens. *From Jesus to the New Testament: Early Christian Theology and the Origin of the New Testament Canon*. Translated by Wayne Coppins. Waco, TX: Baylor University Press, 2013.

Schultz, Richard. "The King in the book of Isaiah." In *The Lord's Anointed: Interpretation of Old Testament Messianic Texts*, edited by Gordon J. Wenham, Richard S. Hess, and Philip E. Satterthwaite, 141–66. Grand Rapids: Baker, 1995.

Schweitzer, Albert. *The Mysticism of Paul the Apostle*. Translated by William Montgomery. New York: Holt, 1931.

Schweizer, Eduard. *Neotestamentica*. Zurich: Zwingli, 1963.

Scott, James M. *Adoption as Sons of God: An Exegetical Investigation into the Background of yiothesia in the Pauline Corpus*. Wissenschaftliche Untersuchungen zum Neuen Testament 48. Tübingen: Mohr Siebeck, 1992.

Seifrid, Mark. *Christ, Our Righteousness: Paul's Theology of Justification*. Downers Grove, IL: InterVarsity Press, 2000.

———. *Justification by Faith: The Origin and Development of a Central Pauline Theme*. Leiden: Brill, 1992.

———. "Paul's Use of Righteousness Language." In *Justification and Variegated Nomism*, edited by D. A. Carson, Peter T. O'Brien, and Mark A. Seifrid, 2:39–76. Wissenschaftliche Untersuchungen zum Neuen Testament 2.140. Grand Rapids: Baker, 2004.

———. "Righteousness, Justice, and Justification." In *New Dictionary of Biblical Theology*, edited by T. D. Alexander and Brian S. Rosner, 740–45. Downers Grove, IL: InterVarsity Press, 2000.

———. "Righteousness Language in the Hebrew Scripture and Early Judaism." In *Justification and Variegated Nomism*, edited by D. A. Carson, Peter T. O'Brien, and Mark A. Seifrid,1: 415–42. Wissenschaftliche Untersuchungen zum Neuen Testament 2.140. Grand Rapids: Baker, 2001.

———. "Romans." In *Commentary on the New Testament Use of the Old Testament*, edited by G. K. Beale and D. A. Carson, 607–94. Grand Rapids: Baker, 2007.

———. "Unrighteousness by Faith: Apostolic Proclamation in Romans 1:18–3:20." In *Justification and Variegated Nomism*, edited by D. A. Carson, Peter T. O'Brien, and Mark A. Seifrid, 2:105–46. Wissenschaftliche Untersuchungen zum Neuen Testament 2.140. Grand Rapids: Baker, 2004.

Selman, Martin J. "Messianic Mysteries." In *The Lord's Anointed: Interpretation of Old Testament Messianic Texts*, edited by Gordon J. Wenham, Richard S. Hess, and Philip E. Satterthwaite, 281–302. Grand Rapids: Baker, 1995.

Shum, Shiu-Lun. *Paul's Use of Isaiah in Romans: A Comparative Study of Paul's Letter to the Romans and the Sibylline and Qumran Sectarian Texts*. Wissenschaftliche Untersuchungen zum Neuen Testament 2.156. Tübingen: Mohr Siebeck, 2002.

Silva, Moisés. *Philippians*. Baker Exegetical Commentary on the New Testament. Grand Rapids: Baker Academic, 2005.

Smith, Gary V. *Isaiah 1–39*. New American Commentary 15. Nashville: Broadman & Holman, 2007.

Song, Changwon. *Reading Romans as a Diatribe*. New York: Peter Lang, 2004.

Spieckermann, Hermann. "The Conception and Prehistory of the Idea of Vicarious Suffering in the Old Testament." In *The Suffering Servant: Isaiah 53 in Jewish and Christian Sources*, translated by Daniel P. Bailey, edited by Bernd Janowski and Peter Stuhlmacher, 1–15. Grand Rapids: Eerdmans, 2004.

Starcky, Jean. "Les quatre étapes du messianisme à Qumran." *Revue Biblique* 70.4 (October 1963) 481–505.
Stegeman, Harmut. "Some Remarks to 1QSa, to 1QSb, and to Qumran Messianism." *Revue de Qumran* 17.1/4 (December 1996) 479–505.
Stendahl, Krister. *Paul among Jews and Gentiles, and Other Essays*. Philadelphia: Fortress, 1976.
Stowers, Stanley K. *The Diatribe and Paul's Letter to the Romans*. Chico, CA: Scholars Press, 1981.
———. *A Reading of Romans: Justice, Jews, and Gentiles*. New Haven, CT: Yale University Press, 1994.
Stromberg, Jake. "The 'Root of Jesse' in Isaiah 11:10: Postexilic Judah or Postexilic Davidic King?" *Journal of Biblical Literature* 127.4 (2008) 655–69.
Stuckenbruck, Loren T. "'Angels' and 'God': Exploring the Limits of Early Jewish Monotheism." In *Early Jewish and Christian Monotheism*, edited by Loren T. Stuckenbruck and Wendy E. S. North, 45–70. London: T&T Clark International, 2004.
———. *Angel Veneration and Christology: A Study in Early Judaism and in the Christology of the Apocalypse of John*. Wissenschaftliche Untersuchungen zum Neuen Testament 2.70. Tübingen: J. C. B. Mohr, 1995.
———. "Messianic Ideas in the Apocalyptic and Related Literature of Early Judaism." In *The Messiah in the Old and New Testaments*, edited by Stanley E. Porter, 90–113. Grand Rapids: Eerdmans, 2007.
Stuhlmacher, Peter. "'Christus Jesus ist hier, der gestorben ist, ja vielmehr, der auch auferweckt ist, der zur Rechten Gottes ist und uns vertritt.'" In *Auferstehung—Resurrection: The Fourth Durham-Tübingen Research Symposium Resurrection, Transfiguration and Exaltation in Old Testament, Ancient Judaism and Early Christianity*, edited by Friedrich Avemarie, 351–61. Tübingen: Mohr Siebeck, 2001.
———. *Gerechtigkeit Gottes bei Paulus*. Forschungen zur Religion und Literatur des Alten und Neuen Testaments 87. Göttingen: Vandenhoeck & Ruprecht, 1965.
———. *Das paulinische Evangelium*. Forschungen zur Religion und Literatur des Alten und Neuen Testaments 95. Göttingen: Vandenhoeck & Ruprecht, 1968.
———. "Isaiah 53 in the Gospels and Acts." In *The Suffering Servant: Isaiah 53 in Jewish and Christian Sources*, edited by Bernd Janowski and Peter Stuhlmacher, translated by Daniel P. Bailey, 147–62. Grand Rapids: Eerdmans, 2004.
———. *Paul's Letter to the Romans: A Commentary*. Translated by Scott Hafemann. Louisville: Westminster John Knox, 1994.
———. "Recent Exegesis on Romans 3:24–26." In *Reconciliation, Law, and Righteousness: Essay in Biblical Theology*, translated by E. Kalin, 94–109. Philadelphia: Fortress, 1986.
———. *Reconciliation, Law and Righteousness: Essays in Biblical Theology*. Translated by Everett R. Kalin. Minneapolis: Fortress, 1986.
———. *Revisiting Paul's Doctrine of Justification: A Challenge to the New Perspective*. Downers Grove, IL: InterVarsity Press, 2001.
———. "Theologische Probleme des Römerbriefpräskripts." *Evangelische Theologie* 27.7 (July 1967) 374–89.
Sweeney, Marvin A. *I & II Kings*. The Old Testament Library. Louisville: Westminster John Knox, 2007.

Tate, Marvin E. *Psalms 51–100*. Word Biblical Commentary 20. Dallas: Word Books, 1990.
Tatum, Gregory. "Law and Covenant in Paul and the Faithfulness of God." In *God and the Faithfulness of Paul*, edited by Christopher Heilig, J. Thomas Hewitt, and Michael F. Bird, 311–28. Minneapolis: Fortress, 2017.
Theisohn, Johannes. *Der auserwählte Richter*. Göttingen: Vandenhoeck & Ruprecht, 1975.
Theobald, Michael. "'Dem Juden zuerst und auch dem Heiden': die Paulinische Auslegung der Glaubensformel Rom 1:3 f." In *Kontinuitaet und Einheit; für Franz Mussner*, edited by Paul-Gerhard Müller and Werner Stenger, 376–43. Freiburg: Herder, 1981.
Thompson, J. A. *The Book of Jeremiah*. The New International Commentary on the Old Testament. Grand Rapids: Eerdmans, 1980.
Tilling, Chris. *Paul's Divine Christology*. Wissenschaftliche Untersuchungen zum Neuen Testament 323. Tübingen: Mohr Siebeck, 2012.
Tobin, Thomas H. *Paul's Rhetoric in Its Contexts: The Argument of Romans*. Peabody, MA: Hendrickson, 2004.
Tov, Emanuel., Robert A. Kraft, and P. J. Parsons, eds. *The Greek Minor Prophets Scroll from Naḥal Ḥever: 8ḤevXIIgr*. Discoveries in the Judaean Desert 8. Oxford: Clarendon Press, 1990.
Travis, Stephen H. "Christ as Bearer of Divine Judgment in Paul's Thought about the Atonement." In *Jesus of Nazareth: Lord and Christ: Essays on the Historical Jesus and New Testament Christology*, edited by Joel B. Green and Max Turner, 332–45. Grand Rapids: Eerdmans, 1994.
Tsumura, David T. *The First Book of Samuel*. The New International Commentary on the Old Testament. Grand Rapids: Eerdmans, 2007.
Ulrichs, Karl F. *Christusglaube: Studien zum Syntagma pistis Christou und zum paulinischen Verständnis von Glaube und Rechtfertigung*. Wissenschaftliche Untersuchungen zum Neuen Testament 2.227. Tübingen: Mohr Siebeck, 2007.
VanderKam, James C. "Messianism in the Scrolls." In *The Community of the Renewed Covenant: The Notre Dame Symposium on the Dead Sea Scrolls*, edited by Eugene Charles Ulrich and James C. VanderKam, 211–34. Notre Dame, IN: University of Notre Dame Press, 1994.
―――. "Righteous One, Messiah, Chosen One, and Son of Man in 1 Enoch 37–71." In *The Messiah: Developments in Earliest Judaism and Christianity*, edited by James H. Charlesworth, 169–91. Minneapolis: Fortress, 1992.
VanderKam, James C., and Peter W. Flint, ed. *The Meaning of the Dead Sea Scrolls: Their Significance for Understanding the Bible, Judaism, Jesus and Christianity*. London: T&T Clark International, 2002.
van der Woude, Adam S. "Melchisedek als himmlische Erlöser-gestalt in den neugefundenen eschatologischen Midraschim aus Qumran Höhle XI." *Old Testament Studies* 14 (1965) 354–73.
Vermès, Géza. *The Complete Dead Sea Scrolls*. London: Allen Lane, 1997.
Vickers, Brian. *Jesus' Blood and Righteousness: Paul's Theology of Imputation*. Wheaton, IL: Crossway, 2006.
von Rad, Gerhard. *Old Testament Theology*. Translated by D. M. G. Stalker. New York: Harper, 1962–65.
―――. *Wisdom in Israel*. Translated by James D. Marton. Nashville: Abingdon, 1972.

Waltke, Bruce K. *A Commentary on Micah*. Grand Rapids: Eerdmans, 2007.
Watts, John D. W. *Isaiah 1–33*. Rev. ed. Word Biblical Commentary 24. Nashville: Thomas Nelson, 2005.
———. *Isaiah 34–66*. Rev. ed. Word Biblical Commentary 25. Nashville: Thomas Nelson, 2005.
Weima, Jeffrey A. D. "The Reason for Romans: The Evidence of Its Epistolary Framework (1:1–15; 15:14–16:27)." *Review & Expositor* 100.1 (Winter 2003) 17–33.
Weinfeld, Moshe. "Expectations of the Davidic Kingdom in Biblical and Post-biblical Literature." In *Eschatology in the Bible and in Jewish and Christian Tradition*, edited by H. Reventlow, 218–32. Journal for the Study of the Old Testament Supplement Series 243. Sheffield: Sheffield Academic, 1997.
———. *Social Justice in Ancient Israel and in the Ancient Near East*. Minneapolis: Fortress, 1995.
Wenger, Paul D. *An Examination of Kingship and Messianic Expectation in Isaiah 1–35*. Lewiston, NY: Edwin Mellen Press, 1993.
Wengst, Klaus. *Christologische Formeln und Lieder des Urchristentums*. Studien zum Neuen Testament 7. Gutersloh: Gerd Mohn, 1972.
Wenham, Gordon J., "Were David's Sons Priests?" *Zeitschrift für die alttestamentliche Wissenschaft* 87.1 (1975), 79–82.
Wenham, Gordon J., Richard S. Hess, and Philips. E. Satterwaite, eds. *The Lord's Anointed: Interpretation of Old Testament Messianic Texts*. Grand Rapids: Baker, 1995.
Westerholm, Stephen. *Perspectives on Old and New on Paul: The "Lutheran" Paul and His Critics*. Grand Rapids: Eerdmans, 2004.
———. *Preface to the Study of Paul*. Grand Rapids: Eerdmans, 1997.
Westermann, Claus. *Isaiah 40–66: A Commentary*. Translated by David M. G. Stalker. The Old Testament Library. Philadelphia: Westminster Press, 1969.
Whitelam, Keith W. *The Just King*. Sheffield: University of Sheffield Press, 1979.
Whitsett, Christopher G. "Son of God, Seed of David: Paul's Messianic Exegesis in Romans 1:3–4." *Journal of Biblical Literature* 119 (Winter 2000) 661–81.
Whybray, Roger N. *Thanksgiving for a Liberated Prophet: An Interpretation of Isaiah Chapter 53*. Journal for the Study of the Old Testament Supplement Series 4. Sheffield: Sheffield Academic, 1978.
Wifall, Walter R. "The Breath of His Nostrils." *The Catholic Biblical Quarterly* 36.2 (April 1974) 237–40.
———. "David-Prototype of Israel's Future?" *Biblical Theology Bulletin* 4.1 (February 1974) 94–107.
Wilckens, Ulrich. *Der Brief an die Römer*. Evangelisch-katholischer Kommentar zum Neuen Testament. Bd. 6. Neukirchen-Vluyn: Neukirchener Verlag, 1987.
Williams, Jarvis J. *Christ Died for Our Sins: Representation and Substitution in Romans and Their Martyrological Background*. Eugene, OR: Pickwick, 2015.
———. *For Whom Did Christ Die? The Extent of the Atonement in Paul's Theology*. Milton Keynes, UK: Paternoster, 2012.
———. *Maccabean Martyr Traditions in Paul's Theology of Atonement: Did Martyr Theology Shape Paul's Conception of Jesus's Death?* Eugene, OR: Wipf & Stock, 2010.
———. *One New Man: The Cross and Racial Reconciliation in Pauline Theology*. Nashville: B & H Academics, 2010.

Williams, S. K. "The 'Righteousness of God' in Romans." *Journal of Biblical Literature* 99.2 (1980) 241–90.
Williamson, Hugh G. M. "The Messianic Texts in Isaiah 1–39." In *King and Messiah in Israel and the Ancient Near East: Proceedings of the Oxford Old Testament Seminar*, edited by John Day, 238–70. Journal for the Study of the Old Testament Supplement Series 270. Sheffield: Sheffield Academic, 1998.
Wilson, Gerald. *The Editing of the Hebrew Psalter*. Society of Biblical Literature Dissertation Series 76. Chico, CA: Scholars, 1985.
———. "The Use of Royal Psalm at the Seams of the Hebrew Psalter." *Journal for the Study of the Old Testament* 11.35 (June 1986) 85–94.
Witherington, Ben, III. *The Christology of Jesus*. Minneapolis: Fortress, 1990.
Wright, Christopher J. H. *Old Testament Ethics for the People of God*. Downers Grove, IL: InterVarsity, 2004.
Wright, N. T. *The Climax of the Covenant: Christ and the Law in Pauline Theology*. Edinburgh: T&T Clark, 1991.
———. *The New Testament and the People of God*. Minneapolis: Fortress, 1992.
———. *Paul: In Fresh Perspective*. Minneapolis: Fortress, 2009.
———. *Paul and the Faithfulness of God*. Minneapolis: Fortress, 2013.
———. *Romans*. In *The New Interpreter's Bible*, edited by Leander E. Keck, 1:395–770. Nashville: Abingdon, 2002.
Xeravits, Géza G. "The Use of Royal Psalm at the Seams of the Hebrew Psalter." *Journal for the Study of the Old Testament* 11.1 (June 1986) 85–94.
———. *King, Priest, Prophet: Positive Eschatological Protagonists of the Qumran Library*. Leiden: Brill, 2003.
Yinger, Kent L. *Paul, Judaism, and Judgment According to Deeds*. Society for New Testament Studies Monograph Series 105. Cambridge: Cambridge University Press, 1999.
Young, Stephen L. "Romans 1.1–5 and Paul's Christological Use of Hab. 2.4 in Rom. 1.17: An Underutilized Consideration in the Debate." *Journal for the Study of the New Testament* 34.3 (2012) 277–85.
Zeller, Dieter. "Zur Transformation des Christós bei Paulus." In *Der Messias*, edited by Luis A. Schökel, 155–67. Neukirchen-Vluyn: Neukirchener Verlag, 1993.
Zetterholm, Magnus. "Paul and the Missing Messiah." In *The Messiah in Early Judaism and Christianity*, edited by Magnus Zetterholm, 33–56. Minneapolis: Fortress, 2007.
Ziesler, John A. *The Meaning of Righteousness in Paul: A Linguistic and Theological Inquiry*. London: Cambridge University Press, 1972.
———. *Paul's Letter to Romans*. London: SMC, 1989.
Zimmerli, Walther. *Ezekiel 1: A Commentary on the Book of the Prophet Ezekiel, Chapters 1–24*. Translated by Ronald E. Clements. Hermeneia. Philadelphia: Fortress, 1979.
———. *Ezekiel 2: A Commentary on the Book of the Prophet Ezekiel, Chapters 25–48*. Translated by James D. Martin. Hermeneia. Philadelphia: Fortress, 1983.
Zimmermann, Johannes. *Messianische Texte aus Qumran: königliche, priesterliche und prophetische Messiasvorstellungen in den Schriftfunden von Qumran*. Tübingen: Mohr Siebeck, 1998.

www.ingramcontent.com/pod-product-compliance
Lightning Source LLC
Chambersburg PA
CBHW070252230426
43664CB00014B/2505